TOM WEIR'S SCOTLAND

BY THE SAME AUTHOR

Highland Days	Cassel	(1948)
The Ultimate Mountains	Cassel	(1953)
Camps and Climbs in Arctic Norway	Cassel	(1954)
East of Katmandu	Oliver & Boyd	(1955)
The Scottish Lochs Vol 1.	Constable	(1970)
The Scottish Lochs Vol 2.	Constable	(1972)
Western Highlands	Batsford	(1973)
Batsford Colour Book of the Highlands	Batsford	(1975)
The Scottish Islands	David & Charles	(1976)
The Scottish Lochs (Abridged into one volume)	Constable	(1980)

PART AUTHORSHIP

Wild Life in Britain	Automobile Association	(1976)
Wildlife in Scotland	Macmillan	(1979)
In the Country	Macmillan	(1980)

Tom Weir's
SCOTLAND

GORDON WRIGHT PUBLISHING
55 MARCHMONT ROAD, EDINBURGH, EH9 1HT
SCOTLAND

ISBN 903065 31 2

Photography by Tom Weir

Second Impression · 1980
Third Impression · 1981

Printed and bound by
CLARK CONSTABLE LIMITED
EDINBURGH

INTRODUCTION

For as long as I can remember I have had a passion for wild places and wildlife. Where it came from I have no idea, for as a boy, I did not know anyone who shared my excitement when on a clear day I could see unknown peaks of the Highlands from my home in the highest part of industrial Glasgow. Against the clear blue sky to the north, Ben Lomond sparkling white, filled me with longing to climb it. Sometimes, west beyond the city, the jagged crests of the Arran hills would appear tantalisingly.

I knew so little about that unknown world out there. I had to make-do with the banks of the Forth and Clyde canal at Lambhill or follow it out to the Steps of Kelvin, Cadder woods, green places rich in birds, where I saw my first redpolls, corn buntings and greater spotted woodpeckers. I had been "doon the water" on seaside holidays, but they didn't prepare me for the Scottish Highlands when a school pal invited me to the family croft just north of Spean Bridge below the north-east face of Ben Nevis.

Close to the Mucomer Falls the salmon were leaping, while above me were summer snow-patches which had never been known to melt, so high was the big Ben. Back home I read every book about the Highlands on the shelves of Springburn Public Library, and the ones that excited me most were those by Seton Gordon. Now there was a man who seemed to be really living, wandering the Highlands and Islands, talking to people, studying golden eagles, exploring the remotest corners of the Cairngorms, writing about his travels and illustrating them with his own photographs.

Of course he was a big shot, high in the social scale, whereas I was a working class lad, who was shortly to become a message boy in a grocer's shop. Was it possible that such a life could be mine in a Britain that was entering the great depression when even university graduates were driving tram-cars and doing labouring jobs. In fact when I got a behind-the-counter job in the Co-op my mother described it as "a job for life" which was a death knell ringing in my mind as "born a man and died a grocer".

But it was these bad times which sparked off the outdoor revolution in which I was caught up. Thousands of Glaswegians were off on the bike every weekend, and I was one of them, lighting fires and drumming up on Loch Lomondside or somewhere in the Trossachs. Disaster struck when I was knocked down by a drunken motor cyclist in the street where I lived, my bike thrown for six and I woke up in the Royal Infirmary with a broken collar bone.

Cycling was "out" for the moment, so I took to the hills, using buses and trains, paying half-fare because I was small for my age. The opening chapter of this book tells how I met up with the lad who was to become my greatest friend, Matt Forrester, who exactly matched me in enthusiasm for mountains and wild life. These were not only the great days of discovery when everything was new, but they sparked off the desire in me to work towards the goal of becoming a writer and photographer.

It was a slow hard haul, with despondency overtaking me at times as editors rejected my articles and short stories. But enthusiasm for the mountains and wild places was stronger than ever. The frustration of the grocer's job was becoming intolerable. I felt I was wasting my life and turned my thoughts to becoming a shepherd, a forester, or a deer stalker. But times were hard, and men I met on the hills doing these desireable jobs felt no security and advised me against making a change.

Then in 1939 a break-through. Editors were publishing enough of my work for me to risk leaving the job and embarking on a free-lance career before I was ready for it. Without a job, disappointments at rejections of articles and photographs hurt much more, nor was the life much freer than the shop. In fact it seemed a refined form of solitary confinement. I got over this by taking a summer job in the Isle of Arran, harvesting the crops by day and writing in the evenings in what little spare time I had.

It was in a field in Arran I heard the news that war had been declared, which meant for me postponement of my own affairs for five and a half years while I soldiered in the Royal Artillery, where incidentally I was trained as a battery surveyor and was recruited into the Ordnance Survey in 1946 after a splendid demob leave climbing in the Highlands and typing a book I had written when I was in the army.

I enjoyed the Ordnance Survey, but knew I would be leaving it whenever I had earned enough to finance a climbing trip to the Himalaya, after which I intended to live on the camel's hump until cash came flowing in from my writing and photography. So was born the Scottish Himalayan Expedition in 1950 and a new life for me, exploring different parts of the world from arctic Norway to the High Atlas of Morocco, and from Greenland to the wild peaks of Kurdistan.

Without these travels I do not think I would have been able to get Scotland in proper perspective. This book is about the way I see it, and is a carefully chosen selection of my published work, much of it from the *Scots Magazine* to which I have been contributing for a quarter of a century. The seasonal pieces were published over a two-year period in the *Glasgow Herald* and reflect my stravaigings throughout that period.

Travel I have discovered is not just about landscape or wildlife or people. It is a voyage into oneself. So this is a very personal book which I hope you enjoy.

Tom Weir
Gartocharn 1980.

CONTENTS

"SOME STRAVAIGINGS"

That is the title of Matt's diary which I have just been reading. Actually, it is more than that, for it contains quotations, poems and photographs from various sources, including some of his own. The book has all the ardour and idealism of youth, and its pages shine with love of the Highlands and everything about them—especially the wild life and the mountain tops. The experiences were snatched from a life in Glasgow which gave the writer only Saturday night and Sundays for week-ends, and a fortnight's holiday a year.

I'd like to tell you something of this man, my closest friend, who knew how to use his time so well.

I was travelling half-fare on the train to Tyndrum when we met. Small for my seventeen years, I wore a schoolboy uniform to fool the ticket collectors. The big, ginger-haired lad in the corner with the outsize pack told me he was out for the May holiday week-end, and I was envious because I was out only for the day. It was a Sunday excursion, and I was going to snatch Ben Lui before the train went back.

At this time I had no regular climbing companion, though I was on the hills every week-end. Here was another boy like myself—except he had been more places. Moreover, he was keen on the rocks. By the time we got to Tyndrum I was no longer out for the day but ready to accept his invitation to share his tent. "I've bags of grub and a couple of blankets, we could do the four peaks of Lui and have a day on Ben More and Stobinian tomorrow if you could get a message to your mother that you won't be home."

She got the message, and I took my blessing when I got back, but that sunny week-end, the glitter of blue skies and snow was unforgettable as we kicked steps up the Central Gully, traversed Oss and Dubhchraige, met an orphan lamb which ran up to adopt us as mother, saw ptarmigan and wheatears, identified summits for future exploration, and camped beside a burn where oyster catchers and sandpipers were nesting. In the morning we tramped to Crianlarich, did another three Munros, then I went home to the reckoning.

That was the beginning. Both of us worked Saturday afternoons, I in the Co-op as a grocery apprentice, Matt in a butcher's shop. So the earliest we could get away was 8.30 in the evening, which meant arriving in Aberfoyle or Callander or Balmaha or Blair Atholl very late after a tiring day in the shop. We pooled our money and bought an 80-foot

11

Alpine Club rope to climb rocks wherever we found them.

Matt was the man with the imagination. I was the one with ambition. Given half a chance I would have spent all my time on hard climbs. Matt was more liberal-minded. He loved big journeys. "How about this?" he would say, producing a couple of maps. "We could get to Blair Atholl at midnight, walk up the Tilt, doss out for a few hours, then cross all the tops from the Tarff to the mouth of the Feshie."

We did it, too—at an Easter week-end—though a better variation was at the May holiday when we slept out on top of Ben Bhrotain and traversed everything from Monadh Mor to Braeriach, drumming-up high on the Larig before dashing down to catch the train in Aviemore. On these big journeys we travelled light, no spare clothes except socks; no tent, no tins, only tea and sugar and lots of butcher meat, steak, chops and special beef sausages (prepared by the master!). Twice we crossed Sutherland into Ross by different routes, exploring Glen Golly and the Dionard to Cape Wrath, and from Ben More Assynt to Coigach.

Matt had begun his outdoor life as a fisherman—a passion which evolved from catching "baggies" in the Molendinar, which he used to follow down from Hoganfield Loch. And it was here, when this clear burn had sheep and horses grazing on its wooded banks that he learned his birds. We were poor in the thirties, but Glasgow was rich in green space, before it was swallowed up in housing schemes. In these days there was plenty to explore on your doorstep, and when motor cars were scarce, cycling was a pleasure.

The outdoor men of that time tended to gravitate to the Craigallian fire, a howff near Milngavie, in a hollow by the loch encircled by pinewoods and backed by the steep front of the Campsies. Here, only ten miles from Glasgow, was a crossroads of adventurers. Here is a fragment from Matt:

"Coming along the track of a winter's evening, the glow of light and the merry shouts of laughter brought joy to the heart. One could always be assured of company there, good company, and pleasant tales of the countryside".

Alas, the popularity of something which had become known as "hiking" put an end to Craigallian. The fire was banned because of litter-louts and despoilers. Notice boards went up, and traditional routes to the Campsies were closed. But the true outdoor men knew the ways around these obstacles. They met in caves and "dosses"—and this is where Matt learned much of his climbing lore. Yet he was pretty much a "loner" until we met. So was I.

We never had a relationship of absolute togetherness, however, for Matt loved his own company more than I did mine. He liked to spend some holidays by himself, so when he said, "I think I'll go to Glen Lyon at Easter," I knew he didn't want me. And often enough we opted to spend our annual fortnight separately.

These breaks did not destroy our rapport. They deepened our friendship, and when we met again we would begin planning something exciting, such as an ascent of the Crowberry Ridge, which, in these days, had a fabled reputation as one of the hardest climbs in Britain. Our ascent was made possible by the inauguration of the first bus service through Glen Coe on the newly-built road.

It was the September week-end, and the ridge seemed a very serious undertaking as we drew close to the square-cut crag rising massively to the narrow top of Buachaille Etive Mor. It deflated some of my pent-up ambition, and I knew in my heart I was depending on Matt to see us up. And I can still see him out on Abraham's Shelf, nailed boots scraping as he worried over the hard move. I remember his "Pheeeee" as he got round the holdless corner to better holds. He was not a neat climber, but there were few things he couldn't get up, including the famous Jenny's Lum Arete on the Campsies, which had only been done once until his ascent.

In 1939 Matt and I talked about being abstainers from the folly of going to war, but in the end let ourselves be "called-up," I to the Ayrshire Yeomanry, Matt to the Scots Guards. His was a hard war, but he enjoyed the training in Moidart and Galloway, practising cliff landings from the sea and night marching over huge chunks of hill territory.

Then came North Africa and the battle for the desert. Letters he sent me at this time were full of bird migration notes and interesting species seen, though he was in the thick of battle, moving from foxhole to foxhole. He was wounded in this campaign, but recovered in time to go in with his landing party to Anzio, where his battalion died almost to a man, holding a forward position for the relief that never came.

The journey across the Brenner in overcrowded cattle trucks to prison camp was so desperate that ever afterwards he suffered from cramp if his knees remained bent too long in one position, as in a bus or in the cinema.

Now demobbed, we continued our mountain trips, but the emphasis was now mainly on ornithology. We had a marvellous week in the Cairngorms in early June, sleeping out in a cave in Glen Slugain in the afternoons, and climbing at night to avoid the heat of the sun, which softened the considerable snow cover and made it heavy for walking.

The Cairngorms can be called an Arctic island in Britain, in vegetation, wild life and scenery. Atlantic islands gave us the same pleasure—and good climbing, too—as we explored the coast and hills of Eigg, Rhum, Tiree, Canna, Iona, Harris, Gigha, Colonsay, Coll and many another. Islay was a special favourite with Matt, for its astonishing variety of birds, and his energy on it and other islands was a never-failing source of wonder to me. Leaving me asleep, he would have something of interest to recount as he made my breakfast, for he believed in early rising and late bedding when he was on holiday. It was due to him I made

13

a film of Hebridean birds in exactly one week.

While I was in the hide filming a sequence of little tern, ring plover, or oyster catcher, he was finding twite, dunlin or red-necked phalarope. His patience was endless, for the watching and tracking of birds was a joy to him. And on a trip he got happier and happier every day he was out, singing Scots airs or Gaelic songs and he was always ready to recite a piece of poetry appropriate to the occasion.

It was Matt who started me off writing and printing my own photographs. He enthused me with his own passion for literature by showing me passages from his favourite books, for we used to meet every Friday night in Townhead Library to plan the week-end. It was only after a time he showed me some of the things he had written himself, some of it published work.

I had always been a diary-keeper. Matt encouraged me to join an "Art of Writing" class at Glasgow University, where I had many a red face as my poor efforts were analysed by Edward Scoular, the W.E.A. lecturer. Curiously enough, as I started to break into print myself, Matt stopped writing for publication, though he never lost the scribbling habit.

In my first nineteen years as a professional writer Matt was a tower of strength as a sort of instant encyclopaedia, for dates, historical events, or bits of personal information gained from practical experience on the ground. Matt had the grasp of history which I lacked, and I profited much from his informed mind. By merely lifting the phone, I could get an opinion I valued. Nor did I fear anyone's censure more than his.

I remember, on our very last outing to Loch Tay. We talked about the early days and compared them with what we get from our lives now. "No matter what erudition you bring, you can never recapture the thrill of these first days," said Matt. "It comes only once, and the mere act of repetition tarnishes it. I remember the first time I went to Mull. I thought it was a marvellous place, but when I went back there I couldn't find it. It's something in yourself, not just the countryside or the weather." I knew what he meant—the joy of being alive that makes a young colt gambol and fox cubs play—that, plus the thing of the mind we call idealism.

Home by Glen Lyon in a snow flurry, I remember how relaxed Matt looked in the house that night. The next time I saw him was in hospital, and a month later he was dead. Matt, the invincible enthusiast, wasted away in seven weeks of a tumour. And in the midst of his illness he made the hardest climb of his life—up the three flights of tenement stairs to his home in Dennistoun.

As it happened, I arrived in at the house an hour or two after he was dropped by taxi at the close on the Saturday. He was so exhausted he couldn't speak beyond a whisper. "It'll take months and months before I'm fit for anything." He was taken back to the Royal Infirmary on the Monday, and died fourteen days later after great suffering.

14

I went to see him in the ward. The sight of three lesser black backed gulls at his window had cheered him up. They were his first and last migrants. He told me about them with excitement.

Luckily I had taken some photographs to show him that day or my pretence at cheerfulness would have broken down as his eyes lit up when I talked about spring and the life which had flowed back to his favourite marshes, with the trilling of redshank, oyster catchers and curlews filling the air, the snipe drumming and the black-headed gulls screaming. It was to take these eyes off me I gave him the photographs. It was the last time I saw him.

I am not an emotional man, but the beauty of these Easter days between his death and his funeral stung with a pain and a sweetness which I have never experienced before. Death and life, in the wonderful renewal of the countryside.

The morning of the day he was cremated was so beautiful, sunny and warm after night frost, and I took my thoughts for a walk down by the lochside. I doubt if I have ever felt the songs of birds with such intensity, especially three tree creepers in different locations, singing their marvellously sweet four-second song—yet I had only heard it once or twice in my lifetime.

Above the torrent of skylark, blackbird and thrush song you could hear the marsh and water birds, the whistling of wigeon and teal, the quark of mallard, the whinnying of curlews and the melancholy wheezings of reed buntings. Wherever you walked there were birds, rooks, herons, grey lag geese, swans, long-tailed tits, a buzzard and thousands of shouting gulls.

Matt was fifty-eight when he died. He was part-owner of a butcher's shop in Lenzie where he had worked for over thirty years. He lived with his brother and sister in Glasgow, in a house which was my second home when his mother was alive. And I got the rough edge of her tongue too, at times, especially when we came in late on a Sunday night to eat a dinner that had been kept hot for us long past our time.

"You saw the best side of Matt," said his sister. "He would talk to you because you are interested in birds and hills. But he could sit in the house and not open his mouth for hours.

Yet he was highly thought of in the shop. Look how many of his customers came to his funeral. He had a word for everybody and he was a great favourite with the children. He had a good life, we know that . . . I still can't believe it. . . "

Matt didn't like anything to do with houses. He liked to be out and free. He had a good life because he shaped it that way. Because he had little free time, he valued it all the more, and crammed an amazing amount into it. He liked to go to bed early and read, because he had to be up before 6 a.m. And as his passion for hills diminished, his life-long interest in wildlife grew in range.

Matt's mind continued to quest to the very end. The body gave way, but he used it to the full so long as he was able. Of him you could say that he used every day as if it were his last. Which is a pretty good epitaph.

15

SAVING OUR SCENERY

Ask me to define forty of the regions of Scotland I regard as being the most beautiful and you set me a problem. How do I define them?

For me there is a trap. It is that I am caught in my own emotional involvement with so many places where I have had great adventures.

In my teenage days the only criteria were that the region had to be wild and empty of people. It was the wilderness I craved and sought. I didn't analyse the attractions of the Cuillin or the thrusting peaks of Torridon and the wilderness stretching from Loch Maree to Little Loch Broom. Nor did I compare the scenery of the western shore of Loch Lomond with that of the east. I knew I liked the steep, steep side of Ben Lomond because there were no roads. You had to work for the magic of Craigroyston, following footpaths north of Rowardennan through bird-loud oakwoods, to the real mountain land.

My pal Matt and I were Munro-baggers and rock-climbers, who lived for the week-ends and holidays when we would take on some new region, so we explored everything within public transport range of Glasgow, and were experts on train and bus time-tables. The Clyde was well served with boats in those days, and Scotland seemed to us inexhaustibly wild in this period of the early 30's when the present Glencoe road was just being built.

My choice of Scotland's most scenic places would therefore be confused a bit by memories of times very different from today, before the building of the North of Scotland Hydro-Electric pylon lines and concrete dams and the spread of vast forestry operations in once-remote glens. Idyllic places where I camped in Glen Affric and Glen Cannich are now below water. Caravans and tents are lined in rows at Ardmair, north of Ullapool, which once we had to ourselves.

It was a golden age because travellers were few and you were made very welcome at any croft-house. Just occasionally you were snarled at by deer-stalkers frightened of losing their jobs, although land-owners around Glasgow were much more jealous of their property.

After the war, in more prosperous times for working-class folk, I acquired a car like many another. What scope! Loch Lomond and the Trossachs were no more than an evening outing from Glasgow. We could have a day on the Bass Rock or a climb in Glencoe. Skye was only a week-end away, and we tried to do the whole Cuillin Ridge on one occasion between Saturday afternoon and Monday morning. New car ferries enabled us to island-hop from Skye and drive the length of the once remote Outer Hebrides.

With the removal of remoteness, though, something of the romance of these wilder places disappeared. It was not that the scenery had changed —it was our attitude that had changed. Glencoe, Glen Nevis, Torridon, Glen Affric, The Cuillin, the north side of the Cairngorms, Loch Lomond, the Trossachs, Kintail, even lonely Ardnamurchan had become too popular. Caravans, campers, erosion of places we loved drove us from them. The magic was still there, but we had to work harder for it—use our knowledge and experience. As tents became more palatial and bigger, ours got smaller and lighter to enable us to get away from the car-bound.

I am not making a plea for a return to the old times when the most scenic places belonged to only an adventurous few. I am trying to show how one's memory bedevils judgement of beauty. Emotion mixes us up, and when this happens we call it subjective judgement. Yet we cannot define scenery unless it moves us in some way or another. In immaturity, all I needed was for it to be wild, remote and preferably rocky, a launching pad for adventure. Today I love variety in the landscape, and I seek different things from Scotland than I did in the past.

These abstract thoughts I have put down result from some fascinating hours studying a book with maps called *Scotland's Scenic Heritage*, published by the Countryside Commission for Scotland, and identifying forty areas of outstanding merit from the Solway to Shetland. They amount to 3,868 square miles, just over one-eighth of the entire land and inland water surface of Scotland.

How do they go about choosing them? They summarise by saying:

" . . . we have sought to identify scenery which best combines these features which are most frequently regarded as beautiful. On the whole, this means that richly diverse landscapes which combine prominent landforms, coastline, sea and freshwater lochs, rivers and woodlands and moorlands with some admixture of cultivated land are generally the most prized."

Their method was to begin with the five special areas selected by the Scottish National Parks Survey Committee in 1945 proposed as future "Parks," moving on from there to other quality areas suggested to them from a close study of maps and other publications. Their investigation was a follow-up to an important document called *A Park System for Scotland*, published in 1974 as part of their remit to:

" . . . develop and improve facilities for the enjoyment of the Scottish countryside and for the conservation and enhancement of the natural beauty and amenity of that countryside."

Both of these publications, *Scotland's Scenic Heritage* and *A Park System,* take me back a wheen o' years when I was a member of Study Group 9 and used to attend exhausting all day meetings in St Andrews House to discuss the future of the Scottish countryside. Nor was it an abstract exercise. In a study of over fifty papers we scrutinised the planning and development situation in Scotland, and came to the conclusion that for *The Countryside in 1970* there needed to be set up a body with power to acquire land and water in Scotland, and have the finance to make grants of money and get things done.

For want of a better name we advocated the setting up of a "Countryside Commission," whose aim would be the best multi-purpose use of land, with objectives of conservation and appropriate development, with a big emphasis on recreation. We saw in our minds an organisation which would undertake research and survey, backed by a highly expert staff and a large financial budget, able to make grants to local authorities and give advice to the Secretary of State for Scotland on all matters pertaining to the countryside.

Alas, the Countryside Commission, set up in 1968, was not the agency we had in mind, since it is an advisory body with no executive power. We hoped they would be able to buy land for the nation and manage it in a multi-purpose way. Alas, proposed National Park areas are still being bought up by Arabs or European investors—the latest sale is the area between Loch Maree and Little Loch Broom, regarded as the last great mountain wilderness in the Highlands, but no one can stop the new owners driving roads into it or putting up buildings.

What then is the purpose, you might ask, of producing a book about Scotland's scenic heritage, costing £3 to buy, and the result of four years of intensive work if it is simply another "Report" by a Government agency without power to back it? Thumbing through the document, I thought of the five areas which might have been acquired for the nation and bought when land was cheap to be set up as National Parks. These were:

Loch Lomond/Trossachs,
Glen Affric/Glen Cannich/Strathfarrar,
Ben Nevis/Glencoe/Blackmount,
The Cairngorms,
Loch Torridon/Loch Maree.

All of these areas would be more eroded than they are today but for the fact that they were earmarked for special protection by reason of their National Park status. Nothing could be done by the local planning authority inside their boundaries without reference to the Secretary of State for Scotland.

Of course, things were done which should not have been done. Fly over the Cairngorms now and you look down on the white scars of bull-dozed roads creeping from the glens right up to the tops of the hills. Dr Adam Watson estimates that there could be a thousand miles of them, built for deer-stalking and grouse moor interests.

Of the three great glens which feed into the Strathglass and the Beauly

18

river, the Countryside Commission book says:

> "Glen Strathfarrar, Glen Canich and Glen Affric. All three are in the form of a long, deep trough, studded with lochs, declining eastward from high mountains and becoming avenues of wooded verdure while still flanked by lofty skylines. In scenic terms, all three have been adversely affected by hydro-electric schemes, Glen Cannich and Glen Strathfarrar more so than Glen Affric, with the exception of the lower-middle portion of Glen Strathfarrar"

Certainly we have to use the catchment of high hills for hydro-electricity schemes, even in National Park Areas. The question is, which ones do you safeguard at any price so long as there are alternatives? Take the proposed Craigroyston Pumped Storage Scheme, which, if it comes, will mean massive roadbuilding and excavations on the priceless eastern shore of Loch Lomond for a period of ten years or so, resulting in a dam 1600 feet up Ben Lomond and pylon lines crossing the shoulder of the mountain.

Here is the view of a top planner:

> "Loch Lomond must be a test case in our whole approach to scenic heritage, because it is as near to perfection as this world can attain, yet it stands close to one of the biggest urban industrial areas in the world, from which escape to virtual wilderness and to outstanding beauty is as necessary as food. Loch Lomond is here and now, and could be ruined in the next twenty years by being increasingly regarded as an area of exploitation for one resource or another, whether for pumped storage, water supply, extraction of concrete aggregate or tourist gold."

The Countryside Commission have listed forty regions of scenic attraction for a very real reason. They would like to see these outstanding areas given the same protection as the original five proposed National Parks, and subject to control by the Secretary of State for Scotland until long-term planning strategies and development control policies have been drawn up in structure and local plans.

That extension of protection is wholly good, but from it follows the question—what about the National Parks? When are we going to have them? In fact, we have a dozen registered Country Parks, grant-aided by the Countryside Commission who also pay 75% of the cost of the Ranger Service provided.

Clyde-Muirshiel Park has been going since 1967, but will take time yet before it becomes something midway between a Country Park and the large tract of wild country we think about as a National Park. There is only one other Regional Park at the moment, the Pentland Hills, with a small countryside centre at Hillend, and a Ranger Service. There is no doubt at all that these parks fulfil a great need, situated as they are within short reach of our two principal cities.

Add to them the properties of the Forestry Commission, Queen Elizabeth Park, Glen Trool, Glen More, Argyll and part of Kielder. Think of the variety of National Nature Reserves stretching from the Solway to St Kilda, over forty of them covering every kind of habitat in Scotland, free to all except for a minor restriction here and there. Then the National Trust for Scotland, in Kintail, Torridon, Glencoe, Inverewe and many other places, and you'll see we have come a long way since National Parks were first talked about in Scotland.

We are in a piece-meal situation now. With all these disparate bodies, including the RSPB and the Scottish Wildlife Trust with its Reserves, we have no legislative control of wilderness. We lost our great opportunity in the 1940's when the Ramsay Committee defined the five important areas, when the land was cheap and could be had for as little as 7s 6d an acre. We could have exercised control as well as integrated development of Loch Lomond and the Cairngorms which have become greyer areas because of the lack of it.

The Countryside Commission for Scotland is all too well aware of it. The Chairman, Dr Jean Balfour, said to me recently:

"Our countryside is our greatest asset, to be used as well as cherished. This responsibility is a NATIONAL one, and not just for local authorities and voluntary bodies alone, if the well-being of our land is to be retained for future generations."

Notice that she stressed the "national" level, because that is where the reins have got to be held. The Commission can give advice and grants and help to pay the wages of sixty-two full-time rangers and forty part-timers under the Countryside (Scotland) Act 1967. They have aided the setting up of Country Parks and Regional Parks. We shall see more and more of them in the future. The Strathclyde Park near Hamilton is being intensively used, yet this area was mainly derelict before.

The Commission has not lost sight of National Parks in the future, though they prefer to call them Special Parks.

In a paper called *The Economic Impact of National Parks on the United States Economy,* Professor E.W. Swanson declared a profit figure of forty times the outlay, and supported it with facts and figures.

He wrote:

"There is nothing on this earth today which will yield such a high, non-gambling reward as proper management of scenically grand and wildlife-rich landscape."

A Park System for Scotland and *Scotland's Scenic Heritage* are therefore very much more important documents than they seem. We should cash in—fast. We have riches beyond measure if we will use them!

20

SETON GORDON: MAN OF NATURE

You never know who you'll meet on the Skye ferry. In this case it was Sam Meekin and his wife Rea from Glasgow, old-age pensioners and keen cyclists who told me they were heading north for Uig, to cross to North Uist and cycle through the Outer Hebrides. I shook my head. "I've done it once and been blown to a standstill. The only good thing about cycling out there is when you stop."

They thought I was joking. "I'm a bit worried about the wind myself." I explained, "I'm meeting up with two pals at Uig who'll be rounding Ardnamurchan Point about now in a 36 ft. ketch, and the theory is that I'm joining them tomorrow night for a sailing trip to remote islands. I think I'd rather be with you in Uist than out there on that sea if the weather keeps rough."

I had opted out of the long approach sail in a small boat to Skye since I intended to spend it more profitably by driving north to spend the day with that doyen of naturalists, Seton Gordon, at his home in Upper Duntuilm, close to the spot where Flora Macdonald lies buried. For me it was a voyage into another historical period with a tall kilted figure whose liveliness made it difficult for me to grasp that he had just celebrated his 90th birthday on 11 April, just a month before my visit.

"Show him the photographs," smiled Betty, his wife. "That's my son—he builds houses in Canada and came over from Vancouver for the birthday party. That's my daughter who lives at Dunsyre. I have a daughter in Australia, but it was too far for her to come. With the grand-children, it was quite a family gathering." Then, as we sat down to talk, he said, "The last time we met was in Edinburgh. You gave a lecture, and I played *Farewell to St. Kilda* on the pipes. We were fund-raising for the National Trust." At which I could only reply, "And twenty years later you are still hanging on to your own teeth and looking remarkably unchanged. Are you still playing the pipes?"

"I still have a blow," he chuckled. "They are in Portree getting a new bag put on. Angus MacPherson of Invershin, who died in April this year, would have been ninety-nine in July if he had lived. He played until he was ninety-seven, which is the record I have to beat. He was the last of the old type of pipers who put the soul of the tune above all. Fingerwork is not enough. To go by the book is to have technique without expression. Piping is in a state of flux. People are all fingers. You have to put away the book to realise the music and the beauty of the tune.

21

"Without the pleasure of piping and judging at competitions my life would just not have been the same. I remember long ago when the Corrour Bothy had a lock and I had a key. It was December, and I went up with a companion to climb Cairn Toul. It was deep snow, and a severe blizzard turned us back. On the way down we found ptarmigan sheltering at the bottom of every footprint. They were more numerous then than they are now.

"Back in the bothy we drew lots to see who would go to the spring for water, which was a fair distance. My companion had to face the blizzard. He didn't come back, and I could not see a thing from the door, so I played the pipes and the sound enabled him to work his way back. In twenty yards be had lost sight of the bothy."

Brought up in Aboyne, and author of his first book, *Birds of the Loch and Mountain,* at the age of eighteen, there seems to have been no time when Seton Gordon was not interested in writing and nature. "I remember as a small boy, before the turn of the century, a pike used to live in a backwater near the bridge at Aboyne. I was determined to catch it, and with a small fish on a cast, hooked it. My governess held me round the middle and went backwards with me as I drew it in. Lord Huntly happened along just as I got it ashore, and couldn't believe such a small boy had caught a seven-pound fish."

I asked about his writing. The only thing his memory was weak on was the exact number of books he has written. "Twenty-nine, I think. For me, writing has always been 99 per cent pleasure, I think I got it from my mother, who was sometimes called 'the Queen's poetess.' As an author and nature photographer I was able to support myself, helped out by lecturing."

Luck played its part, too. "I remember coming from Oxford to Aviemore, hiring transport to Loch Einich and walking to Corrour carrying kit, and listening to the snow bunting singing. My memory of collecting bog fir for the Corrour fire, and exploring the corries collecting alpine plants to help in a forthcoming examination, is as clear as if it happened yesterday."

Back at Oxford the luck came when the question on his examination paper read, "Write all you know about alpine botany." His detailed answer gave him the distinction of being the first student at Oxford to get an honours degree in botany through writing of the alpine flora of the Cairngorms. "My idea was to get a job with the Board of Agriculture. I took a diploma in forestry, and an honours degree in natural science, but didn't get the job.

"I went to Russia in 1912 with Prince Felix Youssoupoff. He was with me at Oxford; he owned thirty-two properties and wanted me to be one of his foresters. He was the Prince who killed Rasputin and married the Czar's niece, and if I had taken the job I might have died in the Revolution."

Instead, the outbreak of war in 1914 found him planning to join in the action by driving an ambulance. Then out of the blue came the offer of a job organising a secret coastguard service under the guise of being a travelling birdwatcher. Based on Mull, and with his own fishing boat, *Lustre Gem*, a whole new world opened up as he got to know the Inner Hebrides while watching out for enemy submarines. "It seemed all wrong that I had this marvellous chance to go where I pleased, landing on uninhabited islands and enjoying wild life, while friends were being killed in France."

Married in 1915 to Audrey, who was to be a tower of strength to him for forty-four years, he had no doubt that his two years at Ardura from 1914 to 1916 were the happiest of his life. "I don't think anybody ever got to know Mull so well. And even although I'm a bad sailor, I enjoyed the freedom of that boat to go anywhere."

Then came a move to Aultbea as Naval Centre Officer, and here he met 80-year-old Osgood Mackenzie and helped him write one of the classic books of this century, *A Hundred Years in the Highlands*. "Osgood was so thrilled, like a boy, with the book, that he began writing another. He died as he was writing. I can't really say I got to know him, for the gap in our ages was too great. He had no use for English, and his wife left him because he would speak nothing but Gaelic."

At this point Mrs Gordon came in to ask us through to lunch, and now I had a real chance to speak to her, for she had tactfully stayed out of the way to let us get on with our talk. "Betty was a great friend of ours before my wife died in 1959," Seton Gordon had confided.

It was a happy meal, with whisky to go with our soup and chicken, and I heard about a walk they had done in 1960, lasting from 7 a.m. until 4 a.m., twenty-one hours, and causing a police search-party to be raised.

Mrs Gordon took up the tale. "We set off from Lui Beg. I am used to the Kintail hills, and have been deer-stalking on them for twenty-two years, but it was my first time in the absolutely vast country of Braeriach, so rough with stones. The real surprise to me was to find the whole summit pink with flowers of *Silene acaulis,* growing from gravel. We saw ptarmigan with young, and a red deer hind with a spotted calf. . . "

Recollection stirred Seton Gordon, "I'll never forget the richness of colouring as the sun went down, intensifying the blaze of red from the flowers, I've never seen anything like it. Ben Nevis was clear. So were Cruachan and the Glencoe peaks."

As he talked, I made a small calculation in my mind, that he would be seventy-four when he saw that sight on the remotest top in the Cairngorms. Also, that fifty years earlier he had written the *Cairngorm Hills of Scotland,* which was one of the first mountain books I read as a teenager, gripped by climbing and wildlife. It profoundly influenced my own desire to see these things and write about them when I grew up.

The memory of that visit to Braeriach sparked off another. "I remember going every day to the Wells of Dee to get the incubation period of the dotterel at 4,000 feet. In twenty-six days the dotterel got to know me, and as I watched on one occasion a daddy-long-legs landed on my arm. The dotterel ran to my sleeve, swallowed it, and instead of flying away, gazed into my face steadily, then went back to the eggs. I felt I had been recognised as a friend.

"But if my collie got up from where it was lying the dotterel would do the broken-wing trick. I recall one day of showers when the eggs were chipping and a storm of hail was battering the hill, when the bird came running to the nest at top speed and looked up as it covered the eggs as if to say, 'Just got back in time.' It hatched them all safely."

With such a love of the high Cairngorms and the ancient Caledonian pines of its glens, I asked him how he came to choose a headland as bare as Upper Duntuilm in Skye as a permanent home. "We came here in 1931. The house had originally been a manse and has seventy acres of croftland. We liked the place. I could write, and my wife worked the land. We had eight or nine cows, some sheep. We grew oats and potatoes. There were men in those days to cut peats. We planted the shelter belt round the house.

I asked about his working discipline. "Six hours writing a day was my usual, three in the morning, off in the afternoon, then another three hours after tea. The roads were quieter in these days and travelling was easier. A car was essential. I used to go lecturing during February and March, travelling all over Scotland, Ireland and England. At the Royal Institution I was the only nature man to be exclusively honoured.

"I always showed my own slides taken with a half-plate camera. You had to be strong to be a nature photographer in the old days, everything was so big and heavy for the distance you had to carry it. I always finished my lectures so as to be back at Duntuilm for the nesting of the golden eagle. It is four miles to the eyrie from here, I used to leave in the morning for the walk, sit for five or six hours, then home. The eagle didn't mind.

"I saw the mating of the pair once. There was twenty inches of snow on the ground at the time—soft snow. The bird came straight down on the hen, pushing her out of sight as he mated her. Come through to my untidy study and I'll show you some of the things I've collected over the years."

It is not very often I meet my match for untidyness, but this was getting close to it—desk and tables covered in letters and papers, books everywhere, lively bird paintings on the walls and photographs jostling each other for room to show themselves on the ledges. "My typewriter," he smiled. "It's a genuine antique, but still in use. I don't do much real writing now, but I get a lot of correspondence from readers, and I always answer it."

Anecdotes flowed from him as we went around the walls, and here is a point I must make about Seton Gordon. He is a much more humorous

24

man than is apparent in his writings. He is also a very good mimic, and I only wish I could tell some of the stories he asked me to keep secret in case of giving offence. Tact and kindliness are built-in responses. Lairds in the old days, it would seem, were not only jealous of stray tourists, but of other lairds who might dare to walk over their property.

On Deeside the situation was particularly critical, "At the beginning of the century, when Mar Lodge was really private, you could not cross Victoria Bridge to the Lodge without special permission. Now it is a hotel, and a jeep road goes almost to the top of Beinn a' Bhuird.

"I've taken advantage of that road, too. I'll tell you what we did when we were staying with Farquharson of Invercauld. We went to church in the morning at Crathie. Went home for lunch. Then drove to Mar Lodge, got the key of the lock on the gate, and drove off for the top of Beinn a' Bhuird at 2.30 p.m. It's a terrible drive, as I'm sure you know, but it got us up there so quickly there was time to walk over the tops and look at the snowfields. The sun was low, lighting the zig-zag shore of Loch Etchachan when we got back to the Land-Rover. It made the shore look like an aircraft—a kind of portent."

I could see he liked that bad road to the top of Beinn a' Bhuird. The old adventure instinct was still alive. "Yes, I look back with some nostalgia to the days when the roads were full of potholes. You got to know them, and motoring was fun. Driving on good roads at higher speeds is actually more tiring. When I drive from Skye to Invercauld it seems such a long way, especially from Tomintoul to Braemar over the Lecht. I still enjoy driving, but I don't like to go more than forty miles an hour."

We talked about Aviemore, where Seton Gordon and his wife Audrey had lived for sixteen years, doing some of their best golden eagle work, spending no less than 167 hours in one season at a Speyside eyrie. "Our old home is now the Nature Conservancy Office, which shows how things have become organised in the inverval of time since we lived there.

"In the past, if you knew of a golden eagle eyrie in occupation you got on with the pleasure of watching it and seeing it rear its young. Nowadays you have to apply for a permit to watch, let alone take a photograph. I wouldn't want to do it now.

"I think seventy-five per cent of my enjoyment of the Highlands now is made up of memories, of times when you knew everyone, landowners, keepers, countryfolk. Wherever you went you stayed the night with friends—they would have been offended if you had done anything else."

Inevitably, the world becomes a lonelier place when you grow old and outlive your contemporaries. I asked him how he felt about death. "I feel it's something to look forward to, for the people you have known and want to meet again. One believes in a future life because of one's own experience. I am impressed by the goodness of people, and I believe in telepathy. I have felt it very strongly.

"There is less to do here at Duntuilm when you lose the strength to go long cross-country walks. You realise how terribly exposed to weather the headland is. My wife's home is Biddlesdon, in Northamptonshire, and we winter there. She has a little house in Kintail where we stay, but I like to spend the summer here and take a walk every day. It is a wonderful place for sunsets."

Seton Gordon would agree that life has been good to him, blessing him with exceptional health, a good brain and a creative imagination to use it. In terms of stickability and sheer stamina in the field of natural history he has set an Olympic standard. One of the great strengths of his writing is the strongly personal thread that runs through all of it. Few reference books are more valuable to a writer than his *Highways and Byways in the Western Highlands* and *Highways and Byways in the Central Highlands*.

My problem in talking to Seton Gordon that long day as wind and rain beat upon the windows of his home was to keep the conversation oriented towards him and not on me. Then as I got up to go, I told him that I was heading down to Uig to meet up with my sailing friends who should now have pushed their way up from Ardnamurchan.

He was intensely interested in our plans, and I could see the old coastguard officer was envying us the option of the wide seas and the kind of landings on remote skerries he had made himself. But, being a bad sailor like me, he was apprehensive about the weather. We shook hands. It had been a grand day, but it was not quite goodbye to Mr and Mrs Seton Gordon.

We were destined to meet yet again at the end of my sailing trip, when who should be waiting on the quay but the old kiltie himself, balmoral bonnet at a jaunty angle. "You came past Duntuilm in the white boat. I was watching you through the long glass. Where have you been and how did you get on?"

His face wore a happy smile as he cupped his ear and listened to me telling him of threading a way through the cathedral cave on the Shiants and clambering over the boulderfields under the great organ-pipe formations of columnar basalt. I talked of the brilliant orange colour of the lichens and the clouds of puffins hurrying back and fore between the sea and the hanging ribbons of greensward.

Then up to the top of Garbh Eilean, through housing schemes of Guillemots and razorbills, with the reptilean heads of shags poking up from dunneys in the boulders, mouthing threats and guarding eggs or young. Up top we were amongst singing skylarks and looking across the North Minch to the strange monoliths of Sutherland.

In North Uist we had climbed Eaval, only 1,138 ft, but one of the most awkward hills in Scotland to reach because it is almost surrounded by fresh and salt water. To reach it had been a wild sail from Harris, twelve hours in a Force six wind, with no snug anchorage at the end of it in a bay called Bagh a' Bhiorain in Loch Eport.

The light of memory was in his face as I spoke. It was my last conversation with him. The grand old man of Scottish natural history died just short of his ninety-first birthday. But in his very last summer of life he had been up on the Cairngorm plateau with my friend Adam Watson. These two had become aquainted in 1944 when Adam was thirteen and Seton Gordon showed him his first golden eagle eyries. Until then they had known each other only through correspondence. Adam still has an early letter which says "It is a fine thing for you to have a love of the hills, because on the hills you will find yourself near grand and beautiful things, and as you grow older you will love them more and more." The truth of experience from a great man who had discovered it for himself.

THE OCHILS: WITCHES AND WARLOCKS
AND A RUMBLING BRIDGE

"How pleasant the banks of the clear winding Devon"

That's what Robert Burns wrote about this stream coming down from the Ochils. Strange, because Burns was not a notable lover of the natural scene. His interest was in people, and in this case he was using the Devon to compare it with the charms of a local lass he hoped to win—unsuccessfully as it turned out.

The Gaelic gives us a truer description of the Devon. It is the *Dubh Abhainn,* Black River. There is a similar explanation in Down Hill, which should be *Dubh Bheinn.* It's even moved away from Doon to Down. Thus do we become anglicised.

For example, we are in the county of Kinross here. In Gaelic, Ross tells us it is a promintory, and the word Kin tells us that it is a place at the head of the promintory. The foot of the promintory is of course the Kingdom of Fife. We're going to follow "the clear winding Devon" which rises only six miles from where it joins the Forth—as the crow flies—but the Devon takes a full thirty-four miles to cover that horizontal distance. The 'cruick' or bend of the Devon is where it suddenly goes west when you would expect it to flow east. Take the A823 for Rumbling Bridge, lean over and you are in for a surprise. You are poised above the rock slit of a gorge with the river roaring in waterfalls and cataracts 120ft. below. Once you have got over the shock of the verticality, take note of the way the rock walls are potholed on each side and for a long way up the faces. The highest ones are 40 ft. up and they give a clue as to how the gorge was carved.

Potholes are made by the whirling action of stones under a force of water. The stones grind hollows in the rock which are constantly deepened according to the force of the water keeping the activity going. In the case of the Devon, the water was provided by melting ice-age glaciers which once covered the Ochils. This was the reservoir which enabled the Devon to slice its way through the rocks. It is a glacier-melt water channel, and it accounts for the winding nature of the Devon. Originally the Devon did not make the big bend at the Crook of Devon, but wound directly east to where Loch Leven is situated. Today it joins the River Forth at Cambus, not far from Stirling.

There is also clear evidence that when the sea-level was higher than it is now, whales swam where cows now graze in the Carse of Stirling, as the geological record and the discovery of jawbones and other artefacts show.

It was logical that when man arrived and learned in time how to build roads he should throw a bridge across this narrowest part of the Devon. The present Rumbling Bridge was built in 1816, but peer below and you will see the arch of the old stone bridge built for horses and carts in 1713. There is no parapet despite its narrowness and there is an 80ft drop into the river below.

So Rumbling Bridge is really Rumbling Bridges, and well named by the constant vibrations of the river imprisoned and rushing through its narrow bed. What you should do now is go to the hotel just around the corner from the bridge and take the descending path by a series of rock staircases to the "Devil's Mill". In a dramatic place like this it is always fine to meet a man who can give some of the local colour, and we had that man in Willie Shand from the Crook of Devon.

Willie, a man who knows the Scottish hills better than most, came with me along a ledge of stone steps and bade me listen to the special noise of the river. "Can you hear the thump and clatter that's just like millstones grinding corn. It works seven days a week, so it must be the Devil's Mill, mustn't it?" The sound was being made by the spurting waterfalls and the churning movement of stones whirling in potholes—a demonstration of how they are cut.

This impressive gorge area of the Devon extends for the best part of half a mile, yet fish manage to get above it, though salmon are stopped at the Cauldron Linn, if they can get through the pollution of the Forth. I put it to Willie that the Devil had also a very special interest in his village, to which he reacted instantly. "Aye, the Deil was very active in these parts and had a good going coven at the Crook. I'll take you to the very spot where they were executed. It's near to where the railway station used to be, but all you can see is a mound in a field called Lamblairs— and I've no idea what it means."

A short drive and we were there, walking across a ploughed field by permission of the farmer. In front of us was the wee kirk and cottages of the village street with the green Ochils rising behind. "It was in 1662 the victims were brought here to be executed. They were strangled first, then burned at the stake. One warlock and twelve witches. They were given a proper trial presided over by the Justice Depute for Scotland. One was reprieved but was retried on the same evidence within three months and strangled."

We talked about the torture of thumbscrews and breaking irons and the sticking of sharp instruments into every part of the body until the victim would scream out a confession. Names would be demanded of them, names of other witches in the coven. And so the butchery continued.

In the sixteenth century it was accepted that witches should be destroyed. In Germany, over 100,000 catholics and protestants had been

29

executed. It became a crime under Mary Queen of Scots in 1563, but the death penalty was not enforced until "that reforming Soloman" King James VI set the first epidemic going after listening to the confessions of witches plotting with Satan against his life. Under torture, the witches had told of using their powers to try and wreck the ship bringing the King and his bride from Denmark.

The wisest fool in Christendom had started something which was to go on for eighty years during which time three or four thousand poor and ignorant people, mainly women, were strangled and burned at the stake. The blackest spots were the Lothians, Fife, the Clyde Valley and parts of Perthshire. The big epidemics were 1590-97, the 1620's, 1640's and 1660-63. Revulsion against the practice set in after 1700, but as late as 1727 an old woman was strangled at Dornoch for turning her daughter into a pony—judgement by the Sheriff-Depute. Lowlanders held the Highlanders to be uncivilised at this time, yet there is no record of witch-hunting and burning anywhere in the Highlands and Islands.

Willie went on to explain that the present village called Crook of Devon is really Waulkmill of Tullibole and the old village of Crook lies to the north of the old Perth Road. We walked there, and saw the old coach house where the horses were changed and the old field dykes on Fossoway Hill where the villagers had holdings and were allowed to take peat or turf for roofing or 'gooding' manuring.

Willie has reason to have a true sense of belonging as I found out when he whisked me up the peak of Inverdownie standing 2,004ft above Glen Quey Reservoir in Glen Devon. From the top we could look down over Fife and the Lothians, but it was something else Willie wanted to show me—a wee drystane enclosure built into a cliff just under the summit on the Dollar side.

"My father and my uncle built that" he said, "They sledged up all the materials and built a wee wooden hut inside the enclosure and lived there for two summers of wonderful weather in the early eighteen nineties. They were drystane dykers, and all the walls you see running up and across the slopes around us were built or repaired by them. They were two wonderful summers, especially 1892, and they were notable for the severity of the winters following them. My uncle was a small man, but he is still remembered as a strong man, who, for a wager, lifted nine and a half hundredweights off the ground."

I looked at the walls with renewed interest, thinking of the labour of gathering the stones and fitting them together. "Aye, they walked down to Dollar once a week to collect provisions. It would be gey simple fare. They were paid on progress, so there was every incentive to work."

Jogging downhill to the music of shrilling curlews and the whooping cries of peewits, I had the feeling that up here the wall builders would find things very much as they had left them, even if below us there was blasting and building to make a new reservoir and send the waters of the Devon east to Fife, where they used to flow before the age of man.

By following the clear winding Devon, the Dubh Abhainn, we had encompassed a lot of history, ancient and modern.

WINTER DIARY

Arthur's Seat

One of the Scottish stories I like is of the great Alpine guide, Emile Rey, who on seeing Arthur's Seat was asked how long he thought it would take him to climb it.

Emile estimated two and a half hours or thereabouts. He was astonished to find himself on top in twenty-five minutes. I've had many a shock in the opposite direction in the clear air of his own mountains.

I wish Emile could have seen "the Seat" in mid-January, 1977, on the morning when the professor and I stood on the frozen edge of Duddingston Loch, a scampering of coots and mallard slipping about our feet, and beyond them a tight pack of perhaps 2,000 ducks bobbing and diving in the only bit of open water.

It was the professor who mentioned Emile Rey as we turned our backs on the glittering ice of Duddingston to greenery that could have been alpine meadows rising to rocks, real crags, above which was the thrust of a snowy peak. The "Gutted Haddie" looked like an ice-fall, and the peak like a Munro.

This is where the fathers of Scottish mountaineering at the end of last century made their early rock climbs, so to pay them homage we drove round the peak to traverse along below Salisbury Crags.

Harold Raeburn, the most accomplished of the pioneers, wrote: " . . .a half sovereign is smaller than a five shilling piece, and many a Highland Ben of ten times its bulk has less of a real mountain about it than Arthur's Seat." Climbing the rocks is frowned upon nowadays because of the danger to other users, but the professor and I in the past have snatched the Cat Nick on a wet windy day of rain when nobody was about.

Our walk on the slippery ledge of frozen turf was enlivened by little flocks of redwings trying to get a picking in these hard times. A kestrel hovered and meadow pipits "pipped" plaintively, but the snow buntings we hoped for were absent as we forsook the tourist route for the fun of crisp snow and rock leading directly up to the Lion's Head.

"We could do with ice-axes. I never feel too happy without them on ground like this," grinned the bespectacled professor conspiratorially, as we wedged in a rock chimney leading us sportingly to the Ordnance Survey point at 823ft. on the basaltic plug of the last volcanic eruption.

We had been climbing in shelter. Now we were in a wind with an ice-age blast to it, appropriate to the unblemished white of the Pentlands, Lammermoors, Moorfoots, Ochils and the tips of the Fifeshire Lomonds and Largo Law seen over a grey haar covering the Forth.

Sunrise

There are mornings of such splendour that you don't wash and shave as usual, but throw on your clothes and get out as soon as you can, to walk up to the ridge above the house and watch the sunrise above the Kilpatrick hills.

4 January 1978, was such a morning. To the west a sickle of silver moon was just beginning to pale as the southern sky was lit by twin vapour-trails of fire from a climbing aircraft.

Here was artistry, the moving ball-point of the aircraft, and behind it the twin strokes of its jets, tracing its course from take-off to a height of a few thousand feet. There were other aerial movers flying about as I climbed the quarter mile to my viewpoint, skeins of grey lag geese, wedge after wedge of them, moving in different directions.

From up there I commanded the Highlands and Lowlands, a snowy world in both directions, but as yet the only warm colour was to the south where the hidden sun was warming the clouds making them redder minute by minute. Then came what I was waiting for, the first flush of pink on Ben Lomond and a suffusion of rose light over the whole northern sky, as every snow peak encircling Loch Lomond took on the hue of a red hot poker.

Beneath me was Gartocharn village lying under the black bump of Duncryne Hill, the chimney smoke of the houses rising white in thin spirals. There was no wind, and the silence so complete that I could hear the whistling beat of a mute swan's wings as it flew past me 300 yards away.

The sun was up now. The magical colours had already faded. The pink snows had paled to ordinary white, and the main feast of colour was now on the low ground, in sunlit beech hedges, in the intense green of spruces, and in the shining bark of oaks and birches.

Now I took my breakfast, put out a big marrow-bone on the bird table, hoping it wouldn't be hogged by the starlings, and set off along the shore of the loch heading for the marshes.

A sudden change of weather, such as occurred on the night of 2, January when rain gives way to snow, always brings in new birds, but I hardly expected it to start the mistle thrush singing so lustily.

The birds that came in quantity with the cold snap were field fares and redwings, wheezing and chuckling, to add their voices to the flock-calls of siskins which have been delighting me in the alders at the foot of my garden. And down on the marshes I put up such a pack of these tiny dark-headed greenfinches that it could only be called a swarm, hundreds of them in all stages of plumage.

Craigroyston

The four mature cyclists were sprawled comfortably round a big blaze from a crackling log fire on the Craigroyston shore of Loch Lomond, roughly mid-way between Inversnaid and the hiker's bothy of Rowchoish. The time was 3.30p.m. last Sunday when we met up with the pathstormers. "It made a great day," I said by way of a greeting, "much better than the forecast. You're going to be caught out in the dark if you sit there much longer."

They grinned, knowing me well. "We were drumming-up here when you were just a wee boy. Nae problem to us getting to Rowardennan." I nodded to the top of the Cuilness Gorge. "We've been up there, in the corrie, and we'll have to move for our eyes are dimmer than yours."

"Have you been taking a look at the north side before the hydro engineers ruin it?" asked one with a merry twinkle in his eye, knowing that I have been working hard to stiffen opposition to the proposed hydro-electrocution of the most valuable wilderness area in Scotland—valuable because it's a lung of the Glasgow out-door fraternity, unspoiled and as natural today as it was in the time of Rob Roy, I imagine.

"I'm depending on you to put up a fight," I said, as we took the climbing path that traverses the ruins of former MacGregor homesteads, disturbing two of the famous wild goats which live here, well set-up shaggy animals, dark-haired with noble horns. It was dusk by the time we reached Inversnaid Garrison and picked up the car.

We had been away only four hours on what I reckon is the finest short hill walk known to me. Perhaps the easiest way to do it for the first time is to keep low on the shore path from Inversnaid and after two miles strike uphill immediately after crossing the footbridge over the Cuilness Burn. There is a path which climbs steeply through oaks and birches, giving views into the waterfalls of the gorge.

In half an hour you have Loch Long in view, seen over the narrow neck of Tarbet, with the rock prongs of the Cobbler as skyline. On again you round the hill shoulder and suddenly before you is the noblest aspect of Ben Lomond, its north corrie rising in dark cliffs to a narrow point of summit above a foreground hollow much favoured by red deer stags and hinds.

This is the hollow which the North of Scotland Hydro-Board engineers would flood, by pumping water from Loch Lomond 1,600ft. uphill, and storing it behind a high rock-fill dam 2,000ft. long, with pylons leading over the ridge to link up with those of the Cruachan Scheme. Slim figures of deer looked down on us as we passed them last Sunday.

Traversing north from here the most interesting way is to retain height and follow the high edge of the Craigroyston, following a ledge just under the topmost tier of cliff. This of course was our outward way, and on it we had the company of two golden eagles, sailing on stiff wings right above our heads, like black aeroplanes.

I cannot believe we would be so silly as to wreck Craigroyston, when at Inveruglas just across the loch there is Loch Sloy, ideally suited for conversion to pumped storage, according to the North of Scotland Hydro Electric Board.

Why don't they do it then? Their argument that it would cost an extra £50m sounds to me cheap at the price, when over there is road and railway.

Snow Buntings

It's an ill wind that blows snow-buntings to a farmstead in Gartocharn, and there they were, feeding on seeds dropped from hay bales put out for the cattle, brownish and undistinguished as sparrows until they fluttered over the snow on white wings, living up to their old country name of "snow-flakes."

It was the call note, a sharp drawn-out "Pseet" which drew my attention to them on a dour morning dark with the threat of more snow. I love Saxby's writing about the "snow-flake" in Shetland. "I am acquainted with no more pleasing combination of sight and sound than that afforded when a cloud of these birds, backed by a dark grey sky, descend as it were in a shower to the ground, to the music of their own tinkling notes." My little party were hardly a shower, but they gave out the authentic tinkling notes as they darted about before settling.

Saxby had obtained a nest with eggs on Unst in 1861, but the snow-bunting flock he was referring to would be immigrants, from Iceland, Greenland, or Scandinavia, Arctic nesters wintering on sea-shores and high hills, forever on the hunt for grass seeds. Here in Gartocharn we get them only in the hardest weather, and normally I have to go to the Campsies or the Luss hills to find them.

But last year produced an exceptional number of breeding records from the high Grampians, together with unique records of Lapland buntings. Why should this be? I think it was because of a similarity between Scottish hills last spring, and the conditions which normally prevail in the Arctic in June and July.

Actually the biggest flock of snow-buntings I have seen was on Culloden Moor in April on a day when snow showers were sweeping the battlefield, and the flock of hundreds flying and settling truly fitted the Saxby description. And once when I was walking up a path in Torridon I had a merlin go over my head and take a snow-bunting at ground level in front of me.

But that first morning of the snow brought in a few other immigrants to us, flocks of skylarks and meadow pipits, hosts of Scandinavian thrushes, and the fine sight of seventeen partridges rising from a little oasis of green with querulous calls, showing me their lovely soft chestnut and lavender colours as they whirred away on brown wings, rufus tails conspicuous.

The big clump of grey-lag geese were where I expected—like black stones dumped on the snow, heads down, digging out potatoes which had been left ungathered because of poor prices—good for the birds and the jinking white stoat which occupies that territory.

Beinn a' Ghlo

These sudden changes from thick-lying snow to thaw, which have been the despair of the weekend skiers throughout January, posed us with a problem at Blair Atholl—whether to ake skis for a traverse of Beinn a' Ghlo or set off on foot.

Our minds were made up at frozen Loch Moraig when we saw more heather on the mountain than snow, and that the bouldery summit ridge was standing clear in the sun, while below us stretched a sea of cloud filling the trench of Glen Garry.

Down there on the A9 we had felt cold in the chill air. Up here the air was warm. The grouse were crowing and wing-clashing in courtship battles, as stimulated by the temperature inversion as ourselves apparently.

Joyfully, too, the walking was easy, thanks to the ice which had hardened the bogs and brought crispness to the snow-patches.

In three miles of up-hill ridge to 3,000 feet we stood above two worlds. South of us stretched the shimmering cloud-sea, with only the tips of the highest peaks in Perthshire projecting through it.

But northward to the Tilt and the Tarf everything was startlingly clear, billows of heathery hills stretching to Glen Feshie and the cleft of the Lairig Ghru cutting the great white plateau of the high Cairngorms. And like an arrow pointing that way lay our ridge, dotted everywhere with red deer hinds and stags, sunning themselves above drifting swirls of vapour rising from the corries.

We were sorry to disturb their tranquility by dropping in their direction, and felt we didn't deserve to have our heads haloed "in glory," but there we were, each with his shadow projected on a screen of mist, encircled by rainbow, brightening and dimming as the vapour dissolved. The atmospheric effect is sometimes called the "Broken Spectre" and occurs when sun and mist are exactly angled on each side of a body.

Very soon after this we were down in the cold mist, marvelling at the instinct of the deer which had sent them up to enjoy the warm air of the ridge. We were glad to begin climbing up again to the next top at over 3,500 feet, where we could sit on a glittering edge of snow-cornice overhanging pendulous frozen slopes.

In the vast empty landscape of rolling hills and corries and empty glens there was no sound. "I'll tell you what we should do," suggested my companion. "Retrace our way back across the tops, and we might just have a great sunset above the clouds." Which meant that we would have to move fast, also that we would have to come down off the mountain in the dark.

It was a great idea, rich in reward as the snow-patches became salmon pink and the heather glowed as if in bloom as the orange ball of the sun became diffused and shapeless before being lost in the mist, causing the whole cloud-sea to smoulder with its fire.

The moon was silvering as we struck down, noticing the increasing cold as we went. The numerous white hares we had flushed that day would be feeding now.

Meall a' Bhuridh

Meall a' Bhuridh of Glencoe, abbreviated to M and B, is the ski-ing mountain par excellence for the hardened skier who can cope with challenging runs through rocks and steep gullies.

In icy conditions it can be daunting to skiers familiar with the gentler Cairngorms and Glen Shee hills. The very experienced skier who died last Saturday was unlucky.

People in the ski-tow queue that day saw just how dangerously icy conditions were when one of their number slipped and shot into the funnel of a steep gully out of sight. He went the whole way, but was unhurt.

Scottish ski-ing has been rightly described as a sport for spartans, yet my last two ski-ing days on Meall a' Bhuridh during January compare for quality with any I have had abroad in the last thirty years.

The winter sun blazed unobscured from dawn till sunset, and an almost full moon hung above the shoulder of Schiehallion as we whistled down from the very top of the mountain at 3,600ft. to its base on the last run of the day.

The fast upper basin does not get the sun in January, so in the ringing frost of the early morning the arrival out of shadow on the corniced edge of Corrie Ba was thrilling. As you unhooked from the bar you were in a world of sparkling jewels—barnacles of ice encrusting the summit rocks—a frothing foreground for skylines of peaks stretching in every direction. For colour relief there was the Atlantic under the twin spires of Ben Cruachan, with dark headlands of Mull rising from it.

Then the delight of the ski-running on powder so flattering to the technique that you heard yourself and other people singing for joy in the effortless obedience of the racing boards to the rise and fall of the body.

I was among many friends, most of them mountain men who had winter-climbed hard ways in their keenest years, but like me had found less demanding enjoyment in ski-ing as age caught up with them.

Our real pleasure is ski-touring, but we do not scorn mechanisation, especially when there are few people on the mountain.

We certainly had it good that first day, with virtually no queueing, so it was run after run after run, each of about 1,200 ft. in an exciting variety of ways. At the Alpenglow, as the red sun spread its light over the entire mountain-scape from west to east, we stood spellbound on top of the mountain as snow spume from the corrie, torn up vertically, showered like red sparks from a fire.

We waited to see the red ball of the sun finally disappear, then with wild yodels let the skis rip.

The Endrick Marshes

Luck in bird watching is an odd thing. Circumstances which seem bad can turn out to be good; a disturbance can sometimes send the very things you want to see scurrying towards you. So it was on the River Endrick marshes of Loch Lomond last Saturday morning when I went there early, hoping to have the place to myself before the world wakened up.

It was a strange morning, mild and balmy, more like April than the severities of February which had brought us frost, fog, snow and floods in quick succession over the previous few days. As I got to the loch shore I looked out on an atmospheric scene, a soft cotton-wool of trailing clouds making a mosaic of greens and browns, so mirrored in the loch, that it was hard to tell what was reflection and what was real.

Eastward, I could tell that the sun was going to rise into clear sky. Then came the annoying crack of gunshot and I cursed inwardly, while at the same time catching my breath at the explosion of birds taking the air in babblings of geese, whistling of wigeon, and yelpings of teal. I was lucky to be beside a tree for cover as the waves of birds came so low over my head that you could hear the wind rattling through their pinions.

The movement was all the more glorious for the burst of the sun on the whirling birds, brilliantly plumaged against the clouds, green heads of mallard, face-spots of goldeneye, white wing flashes of 500 wigeon were as vivid as in any bird painting.

This marsh is backed by Strathendrick and the north corries of the Campsies, and in the sun-light it became a shimmering foreground of tawny yellow.

The noise died away, and in a moment of stillness I heard the one sound which for me symbolises spring more than any other, the first exhaltation of the skylark, a faint shower of silver notes at first, becoming a cascade as I picked up the fluttering bird dropping ever lower from perhaps 1,000ft.

I was enjoying myself. A kestrel hovered near the river, tail spreading and contracting as it fanned its wings to suspend itself in one spot. Behind me were mewing calls of buzzards, a trio of birds which became five over the wood where I have found an eyrie in the past. Eagle-like in appearance with soaring flight, it was easy to tell that two were females by their larger size. If this game of swooping at each other was true pairing, then one male was going to be unlucky.

Next came a clamouring of whooper swans as five flew low over the marsh, and as I followed them in my glass I glimpsed a cock hen harrier, pale as a seagull but with long straight wings, tipped with black.

Above the Clouds

It is a cold morning of drizzling mist and I am at the wheel of my car above Tyndrum heading for Buachaille Etive Mor for a climb. No view.

Suddenly we emerge from the mist as through a door and we are in a dazzling world of snow-peaks and blue sky. My companion the Doctor whoops for joy. I have other preoccupations for I am on a shallow bend, sliding on a skin of ice, and drifting towards the crash barrier on the far side of the road. It is dangerously close.

I try a little correction. No use. I hit the concrete barrier a glancing broadside. The world takes a whirl and we leap off the road, uphill fortunately, nose pointed upward, so we don't roll over as the bonnet tries to burrow itself into the peaty hillside.

"I never did like bloody motor cars," says the Doctor calmly as he unclips his safety belt. A feeling of exhilaration grips us as we realise we have got away with it unhurt. As we step out, other cars are drawing up. "Did you see that skid?" one driver is saying to the other. Then turning to me, "Glad you're OK, and thanks a million for showing us the ice."

The inmates of the cars were mountaineering friends. Hammers were produced to bend back the bumper and wings to allow the wheels to turn. We rolled the car downhill on to the road, and despite smashed headlamps and the protesting sounds from the engine, decided to continue northwards so as not to waste what was going to be a glorious climbing day.

Ironically we had skidded on the only bit of dangerous road on the drive, as we discovered when we resumed, and went back into clouds drizzling all the way to our mountain. We were in high spirits, for we were sure it wouldn't be long before we would be leaving the cold of the lower ground for the warmer air of the upper mountain. And it was magically so where the heather ended against the thrust of the North Buttress. We sat in the sun, while below us the shadow of our peak was outlined on the gossamer clouds drifting below.

"Hard enough for us today, wouldn't you say," suggested the Doctor, remembering the difficult drive home ahead of us without headlights. The buttress rises 1,000ft. and ends close to the pointed summit of the peak. Holds are good with plenty of variation on the steep face.

To save time we moved unroped, taking care on icy sections, and stopping often to look behind us at the marvellous vistas opening up.

Like a return to the Ice Age the clouds covering Rannoch Moor stretched like glaciers. In the brittle clear air the Cuillin of Skye stood clear. It was hard to tear ourselves away from the summit of the peak.

Islay

Sailing down West Loch Tarbert for Islay looking out for great northern divers and Slavonian grebes, I was enjoying myself.

The divers were there, low as battleships in the water, the grebes holding aloft thin necks like pencil stalks. Plenty of black guillemots too, and in the Sound of Gigha lots of common scoter and a few velvet ones, distinguished by white wing and face patches. You had to be fond of a heave and impervious to cold and rain to stay on deck thereafter.

Morning brought the foretaste of April-in-February that I was looking for, with sunshine on the greenery, skylarks in good voice overhead, and so many different kinds of birds in sight as I walked along the Lochindal shore that I got out my notebook to make a list, remembering that the late Prof. Maury Meiklejohn once got ninety-nine species in a weekend but was stumped for the one that would have given him a round figure.

Round figure sent me thinking of that most extrovert of introverts who for years delighted readers of the *Glasgow Herald* with his weekly articles. He loved the sea inlets, saltmarshes, woods, fields, moors, and hills of Islay above all other haunts, and I remembered how after one February weekend we had together on Islay, he described me in his Saturday article as "The Admirable Crichton" of the outdoor world, which made me chuckle.

He would have enjoyed himself that morning, among the whooper swans and the big pack of scaup seen through a flock of 300 twites and backed by yelping masses of geese. He would have enjoyed too, the sight of a chough coming over the houses of Port Ellen like a starling. But even more he would have been agog watching a pair of these acrobats plummeting out of the sky above a rocky headland, dropping like stones and opening wings with piercing cries to land on the steep slope.

Through the glass I could see the choughs' red legs, glossy black plumage, and slender curved bills as they moved about the steep ledge. Then I saw them begin to edge up stones, using their curved bills to send them rolling downhill, at which they would sieze what happened to be hiding beneath. The bugs had no chance to escape.

That was an unexpected bonus, seeing such rare birds doing something so interesting.

The Gruinard flats were more predictable, but the thrill was no less great, on seeing what looked like a gigantic grey mat stretched across the green become mobile at my appearance on the landscape. The geese were simply walking away at first, then when a yelping chorus started to develop I waited for the great spectacle as thousands of wings beat the air and the yelps became a great wave of single sound, louder than the noise from any children's playground.

In that flock movement above green fields and watery hollows even a Meiklejohn would have been hard put to take in everything that was going on.

To the ornithologist it is all delight to see so many geese. To the Islay farmers it is anathema. But come April they will be off to Greenland.

Derry Cairngorm

Lui Beg Cottage above Braemar was our destination, but it was obvious that we were not going to make it in the car, with visibility restricted to a mad whirl of snow-flakes and with a drift big enough to bury a bus blocking the road.

Annoying, because the house where we were expected was only four miles away, but we had no intention of abandoning the car while the blizzard blew, so we lit the special oil-heater, kept normally for putting below the bonnet of the car, crammed on spare pull-overs, and waited.

We were not downhearted. We had food and had plenty to talk about, so much so that we hardly noticed that the tree-tops had stopped swaying and that stars were appearing. Everything creaked with frost as we unstrapped our skis, packed our rucksacks, placed the heater under the car bonnet, and poled off, gliding easily over the snow where a man on foot would have floundered.

In the starlit world it was exhilarating to be moving towards the big white shrouds looming above the Lairig Ghru.

It was half past two in the morning when we battered the door and let out yodelling cries. "God, hoo did ye manage it?" growled the sleepy Bob as he bundled dry sticks in the fireplace to make a blaze and boil water for tea. "I'm away tae ma bed," he grinned when he saw we were too fresh to lie down just yet.

We could have lain-in at daybreak but for Bob's cry to "Come and get it." And now we could hardly wait to get our skis on and head up through the snow-laden pines to Carn Crom among red deer too hungry to get out of our way.

High on Derry Cairngorm we were in a textured world of snow-sculpture, the only drawback for my friends being the necessity of hastening back to Aberdeen.

"See you next weekend," I said as they left. I did too, after every kind of weather. Torrential rain began falling that night, but before the drifts were melted hard frost had set in and it was snowing again, big flakes feathering down in still air.

41

"Good for working," said Bob. "How about the pair o' us taking the horse and sledge up the Derry and cutting up yon big fallen pine tree? I've been waiting for a time when there was a man tae help me and a good snow-fall. I'll harness the horse if you get the cross-cut fae the stickshed."

It was the thick trunk of the 300-year-old tree that Bob was interested in, and with the saw we cut it into sections each the size and shape of a big bass drum, a heavy lift on to the sledge for two of us, but an easy pull for the horse and sledge.

Nor was I idle on my skis, poling up among the ptarmigan and white hares, helping to feed the deer and joining Bob in a round of his fox traps. The finish of my stay was a tour to the top of Ben Macdhui with my two friends who brought the good weather with them, and memorable indeed was the powder-swoop from that second highest summit in Scotland all the way back to the house.

But these events didn't happen last weekend. The blizzard which stopped us was a more ordinary one, the kind which happens there most years.

Hardy Animals

The first song thrush of 1978 is in the garden, singing lustily from a poplar, and setting off a concert party of voices which have been absent until now.

The chaffinch is stammering out its staccato phrase, getting better and better at it as the morning goes on. The dunnock is managing a rattle of jangled quicksilver, tits are loudly belling, and behind all is the sonorous roo-rooing of a collared dove.

Yet the snow blanket still covers the lawn, and the Highland hills are as Arctic as I ever remember them—a heart-filling sight on a frosty morning like this, towering above a grey mist-sea filling the narrow trough of loch below Ben Lomond. The broad base is a clear mirror of water reflecting islands and peaks.

It is the smooth whiteness of the tops which is so startling, seemingly untouched by thaw, crags still submerged in drift, ridges and gullies moulded with knife-edges of cornices, an invitation to climbers and skiers with a built-in warning to steer clear of steeper slopes if temperatures keep rising. I had been up there last Sunday, visiting my friend Iain whose farm is the highest in a glen with no through way beyond.

Nor was I willing to risk my car beyond a certain point when the surface of his narrow road was wet ice between snow falls trenched by the big wooden plough lying beside his house. "It's been this way for the last three weeks," said Iain, as he coaxed a red Highland heifer into the big cattle shed, and from his Land-Rover brought out her shivering calf, born that morning. "The heifer is a poor mother, but she'll take to it once she's locked up with it."

From where we stood I noticed that the black-face sheep were scraping with their feet high on the hill. "So long as they can do that, they are strong," said Iain. "They're better up there on the exposed ridges than in the hollows, where they can get suffocated if they get covered. I expect I'll have lost a few. We'll find out when the snow melts."

Above us a Highland pony was rolling on its back in the snow, legs kicking in the air, and I took a wee stravaig to the burn in the hope of hearing a water ousel singing, but there was nothing. With snow up to my knees the walking was tiring. Apart from a red deer stag and three hinds the only wild life was a trio of flighting blackcock and four crows, two hoodies, and two carrion.

Grey clouds had been closing in and rain was falling heavily when I got back to the farm, elbowing my way through a herd of hairy Highland cattle waiting at the gate to be fed, dangerous looking but docile animals. Those with calves were in the shed and many were due to calf.

"I hope it will keep raining and shift that snow," said Iain hopefully.

That morning in Gartocharn had been so mild that insects had hatched out and were buzzing about, and the thaw had revealed the first snowdrops.

Ski-ing the Campsies

It's probably true to say that in the last quarter of a century I've never missed out on ski-ing on the Campsies if winter conditions made it worth while. Nineteen sixty-three was a peak year, and I never expected to see these rolling hills so beautifully snow smoothed again. Last Saturday, however, they were even better, because of the feather-lightness of the powder resulting from frost and low temperatures.

Poling across from the Crow Road to the Meikle Bin we made a diamond trail of scintillating crystals.

And not just a world of cold beauty. The spruces which flank the north side of the Bin were green. Every distant peak had texture, north faces in shadow, summit ridges etched with silver, so that Ben More looked like the Swiss Weisshorn.

No life, however, except for a minute mouse-shape with a hump back and a tapering snout, a shrew—that minute insectivore with the aggressive nature and big appetite.

Moving jerkily along like a clockwork toy it had, I hoped, a store of worms hidden somewhere.

For us the true climb began at the hanging cornices above the crinkly ice covering the Bin Burn, a lift to 1,870ft. into a bitter wind. No lingering since we couldn't savour the tremendous view from Argyll to Perthshire with our eyes watering.

In any case we were eager to point our skis down the silk-smooth powder slopes—and bliss it was, feeling the skis glide and swing as if on air. All too soon we were cutting parallel lines on the steep snow walls above the Bin burn.

Too good to call it an afternoon at that, when we could climb neighbouring Lecket Hill by another snow-moulded burn. We were up there, at 1,792ft., in time to enjoy a blood-red sunset over the Kelvin Valley, with below us, the source of the river Carron. Our parked car was two miles due north of us, with an 800ft. descent down a steepish face, thence by the snow-smoothed banks of the Carron.

But we were on the shadowed side of the hill and daylight was ebbing. Judging snow textures and angles was trickier, all the more fun then when ridge led to gully and to lower glades with everything working for us.

Galloway

In the genial heat coming through the windows of the car you would hardly have guessed it was February in Ayrshire, with the sun giving a sheen to the rolling fields. You felt that it was full Spring, though you blessed the winter for the quietness of the coast road which made the driving so enjoyable.

You could look around you and take everything in—Girvan harbour packed with fishing boats in lustrous colours of blues and golds backed by Ailsa Craig thrusting a thousand feet of silhouette. But cast your eyes right, and there was Arran—high island—its snow peaks gleaming above wisps of cloud, intangible and mysterious.

A pity to turn from coast overlooking Ireland and the Mull of Kintyre, but I was heading for high Galloway on the A714 along the windings of the river Cree. Narrow and twisting, this road demands concentration, and I hadn't noticed the river was frozen until I saw a dozen whoopers on the ice, a few of them breasts down to keep their legs warm, the remainder doing balancing acts on one leg, the other leg under the wing to keep it warm.

In a setting of yellow reed beds and foothills dotted with sheep and cattle they inspired a photograph, but when I crept towards them trying to find an opening within range, heads were jerked up and the first warning "whoop" sounded.

They set up a wild bugling as they rose, turned in an arc and went out of shadow into sunlight, dazzling birds in a line against the bracken colours of the middle slopes of the Glen Trool Forest Park.

44

Newton-Stewart is the hub of this country. The guide book which describes it as the "Venice of Scotland" didn't seem so outrageous that day, with the houses on each side of the river reflected in the water—free of ice at this lower level.

The sea was only three miles distant now, where the Cree opens out into the big bite of Wigtown Bay, impressive under towering mountains of cumulus reflecting their white on a mixture of mud and water alive with flighting and feeding duck and waders.

Galloway is unique in having granite hills of Cairngorm-type relatively close to river estuaries like the Cree and the Fleet. So you can easily have a morning above 2,000ft. in the country of red deer and golden eagles, coupled with a late afternoon on the birdy saltmarshes and mudflats.

Morayshire

Because of the sting of the strong wind on the exposed Moray coast we forsook the low ground for the big woods that hem the River Findhorn, knowing we would find shelter and feel the warmth of the sun by the river swirling down from the Monadliaths through secret gorges.

Everything had a shine, the silver bark of the beeches, the hazels spilling yellow pollen from their dangling catkins. But the best of it was above Drynachan where the steep heather banks enclosing the river held snowdrifts in their gullies.

A feeling of constant vitality here, with the noisy cackling of red grouse in courting wing clashes, and mountain hares lolloping on every slope. You could count the white dots of the hares by the dozen, conspicuous on the brown heather.

The golden eagle that suddenly appeared over the ridge like a black aeroplane could have picked one off without trouble. It did not. The hares froze, but grouse scattered in all directions. Cackling resumed when the great bird passed.

There is a wooden box suspended on cables for transporting yourself across this lonely bit of river. I was examining it when I heard a shrill whistle that sent my head round—an otter. And at the same moment as my eye went to the place the maker of the sound leapt from the water like a salmon, hurled itself from the river into the air, to arch its back in space, and drop back in head-first, presenting a comical pot-belly in the dive.

Then from the swirl of the waters popped a black nose and fringe of whiskers with two black beads of eyes regarding me intently. The head came higher, showing me the white throat, then with a flick of hump back and shake of pointed tail, the playful animal went away with a rush for the rapids, leaving me with a feeling of elation. I have had no more than

45

eight encounters with otters in a lifetime devoted to the outdoors.

Woodcock were "roding" and the wind had dropped as I motored back to Forres. The promise of a frosty night was fulfilled, and in the clear air of the morning, snow-peaks of Ross and Sutherland floated like ice-bergs above the calm blue of the Moray Firth. A good day to head for Binsness where the Findhorn enters the sea fringed by the Corsican pines of Culbin, the miracle forest that grows on what used to be called Scotland's Sahara.

The pines are rooted in sand that had to be laid with brushwood before the trees would take hold. Below them is the buried barony of Culbin, whose houses and farms were overwhelmed by blowing sand. I had known it as "desert," and here now I was walking in deep forest, listening to the songs of goldcrest and tree creeper. But the big thrill was to find crested tits and parrot crossbills, which have colonised here, rare bird survivors of our own Caledonian pine woods.

The crested tit is the badge of the Scottish Ornithologists' Club, and there it was, pointed crest barred with black and grey as if escaped from a book-plate. The crossbills were on the pine cones nipping out seeds with their curious plier bills.

Spring Waders, March Hares

Against the cotton-wool roll of clouds clamped over the Campsies, the black volcano of Dumgoyne stood out, sharp as Devil's Point in the Cairngorms.

No hint of snow in the green foreground of fields and hedgerows swelling upward to the villages of Killearn and Balfron. After days of thaw and drizzle the world had suddenly come to life it seemed, skylarks poured down silver songs from above me, and from below came the cheerful whooping of peewits. Long-winged flies danced in the air around my perch on top of Duncryne, enjoying the sun as much as myself unless I am mistaken.

Slow as the thaw was when it began on 21 February, wading birds had moved in from the Clyde to their nesting territories within twenty-four hours, as I saw when I went down to the Endrick marshes and found the first oyster-catchers and redshanks of 1978 flighting over the ice.

Then just one day later in came the first shelduck, half a dozen, two of them drakes, vanguard of our summer breeding colony.

Oyster-catcher numbers had risen to fourteen a day or two later on my next visit, but it was another black and white bird which held my eye then, a goosander drake which took off and joined a whole flotilla of them, no less than fifteen, eight of them females—a species which has not yet bred in our corner of the loch, but I'm sure it will.

Just beyond the marsh is a potato field which has been a great attraction to the geese and whooper swans in the hard weather. Blessings on the farmer for not gathering in his spuds, for it has provided a harvest for not less than fifty-nine of the big arctic swans with the yellow and black bills and loud sonorous calls.

As for the greylag geese, they've been literally shoulder to shoulder in the big field rising in a roar of noise 2,000 and more strong.

Watching them on one of these days of thaw I had the unique experience of being able to compare the loud single note of the snow bunting and the slighter and rather more melancholy note of the reed bunting, which made it my third record of snow buntings in Gartocharn this winter.

And I've seen my first pair of mad March hares, darting about, chasing after each other, stopping to sniff, box, and run on. Winter is still with us on the high tops, however. Very little melting has taken place on the top half of Ben Lomond, as I saw when it stood above the clouds, looking like Mont Blanc.

No wonder white hares have come down among the brown ones recently—unusual and a sign of hard times.

Vernal Equinox

Every naturalist keeps his best spots secret. One of mine is a north-facing outcrop of rock where grow the earliest wild primroses I know. On Monday the first were showing yellow, though yet another skirmish of overnight snow had whitened the hills.

Spring begins officially on 21 March, which is the average date of the vernal equinox when night and day are of equal length. This is the changeover period in the marshes, as the thronging duck and geese which have been with us all winter get restless and thin away as new birds move in.

Instead of the skirling of thousands of geese there is the ear-splitting screaming of black-headed gulls and the loud birling of curlews.

The largest British swans, the whoopers, which feed in the big brown field are no longer sedate. Courtship restlessness infects them. They jerk their heads skyward in an almost continuous twitch, bugling and slow-marching towards each other, big wings spread at their sides like open arms. The excitement spreads from group to group.

These clamorous birds with the slight tinge of yellow on the neck are intensely sociable, and I see a good example of their togetherness when a few hoist themselves into the air, glide down to the nearest water and begin to preen.

Within a few minutes group after feeding group are taking off for a big cleaning-up session, necks coiling like snakes as they stretch up and under to get at every feather. Even the big flat feet get washed, and are poked out one at a time to air.

I'll miss them when they fly away north-west for Iceland and Greenland where I've seen them at their tundra lochans. Swimming near them today is an elegant stranger, ivory neck straight as a pencil stalk, but with an exotic head-style of black devil's horns and what looks like red side whiskers—a great crested grebe, perhaps an oil-spill refugee from the Forth.

Today it is the peewits, hundreds of them in a tight flock, which are providing an air display and divert my attention as they go "whooping" past, air swishing through their lapwings as they cavort in a perfectly co-ordinated movement.

From a height they dash themselves in a suicidal swoop, flatten out, and look black as starlings as they stream away, flashing like helios as they turn and present the white underside to the dark mantle. That this showing off is wildly stimulating to them I have no doubt by the way they shout as they tumble and turn.

CRAIGMADDIE: SECRETS OF THE MUIR

When John MacDougall retired from shepherding the big hills of Glencoe and took over a wee hirsel on Craigmaddie Muir between Milngavie and Blanefield, I was delighted, for it meant he was almost a neighbour and I could stroll over his 600ft. high heathery ground and enjoy his Gaelic turn of phrase as he enthused about sheep and recalled events that seemed to belong to another world.

I remember saying to him on his eighty-third birthday. "John, you must be the oldest working shepherd in Scotland." There was a long pause as he sucked his pipe. Then came a typically droll reply. "I think I'm the oldest in the world." Another pause, then the punch line, "I feel it anyway!"

John was a lonely man when his employer sold the sheep, and when he died, almost ninety, I think he was happy to go. He was the last of my friends of the irreplaceable old school.

The old man was in my mind as I motored past the end of the road with the wee cottage where he finished his life, and instead of driving home I decided to use the last hour of daylight to walk on the moor and listen to the curlews. Ruminatively I made my way over to a pile of three stones called "The Auld Wives' Lifts", scrambled on to the top block, and sat there enjoying the rather sombre atmosphere.

John had never liked this moor, nor these strange stones which have a legend attached to them. The folk-tale is that three witches wagered each other as to who could carry the heaviest stone in their aprons. Two managed to put down their stones side by side, but the third one capped their efforts by placing her larger stone on top of the other two in the form of a roof. A variation of the same tale is that it was a trial of strength to see who could throw a stone the farthest, and the biggest landed on top of the other two.

Hugh MacDonald in his classic *Rambles Around Glasgow* (1854) gives a good summary of the conflicting beliefs held in the nineteenth century about the origin of the stones: "By some this gigantic cromlech is supposed to be a Druidicial altar, whereon, in a dim prehistoric era, the dark rites of pagan worship may have been celebrated." On an old map it was shown as a "Druidicial Cromlech," and the cavity between the stones was thought to be for the reception of human remains after blood sacrifices.

I took all that lot as auld wives' tales, and accepted the geological verdict that the Lifts were a glacial erratic; blocks of stone carried down by a glacier and stranded when the ice melted. That evening I looked at the stones more closely, remembering what a perceptive friend of mine, Peter G. Currie had told me about them.

Peter described his feeling of terror when, as a youth, out on a day visit from Glasgow, he had scrambled onto the stones. To his surprise, he experienced a similar feeling of psychic unease when he went back as a mature man. The whole place affected him with a sense of evil.

I had no such feelings myself as I sat up there until dusk, and I probably would have thought no more about the Lifts had I not stopped at the house of John's former employers. It was a throw-away line by Mrs. Sandeman which made me prick up my ears. "Suddenly there is a great interest in the stones," she said. "Professor Alcock from the Archaeology Department of Glasgow University has been making discoveries which seem to connect them with the Druids. It's something to do with carved Celtic heads. My husband could tell you more."

In fact Mr. Sandeman advised me to phone the Professor, which I did the following afternoon. "So you've known the Lifts for a very long time?" he said in an interested voice. "Tell me what you've noticed as you scrambled about." I had to confess that it amounted to very little, except a crop of initials and dates chiselled into the soft sandstone.

"Now that's very interesting," he said, "and you'll realise why when I tell you my tale. But first, I want you to go back to the stones, and this time, look closely at the north-east corner, then at the south-east corner, and on the rock surface of the capstone between these corners. See what you can find and let me know."

My curiosity thoroughly aroused, I was back at the stones next day with camera and tripod. Nor did I have to look twice at the north-east corner to see the carved face that stared down at me. Startled, I went to the opposite corner, and there was another, a more sinister one in deep shadow. Between them, on the flat surface, were two other heads, and another two round the corner. These last two were at the very place where I had climbed up the previous day, yet I had failed to notice them.

I phoned Professor Alcock next day and told him how amazed I was. He then wrote to me:

"Your reaction of amazement that you'd not seen them before is a common one. I have myself taken a party of students, some of them acute observers, to the Lifts, and have been amused to see them fail to recognise the faces even after they had been repeatedly told they were missing important features on the rocks."

On the phone again, he told me: "I think it's not beyond the bounds of possibility that the capstone was placed on top of the two smaller stones by the Celtic people who carved these heads. The vertical lift is not a big one, and it could have been done with wooden rollers."

I asked him who the people might have been who could have erected and worshipped at this Druid shrine. "I think we could call them Celtic people under Roman influence." he said, "The carvings recall the severed heads of Gaul—one of the leading images of Celtic religion. Notice, too, that the heads are confined to the east and north, while the two most arresting of them look out from the north-eastern and south-eastern edges. That would be a remarkable coincidence if the heads were the work of casual visitors.

What I wanted now was an independent view as to the probable origin and arrangement of the stones. Dr. Ingham and Dr. Rolf of the Geological Department of Glasgow University were in no doubt that they were of glacial origin, but beyond that they were not prepared to speculate.

Professor Alcock had written: "That one of the few (stones) should happen to have been deposited on a pair of supporters may be a remarkable coincidence; that it should have been set virtually level, its irregular undersides fitting the irregularities of the supporters, and its long axis matching the gap between them may be stretching the coincidences to unacceptable lengths."

So a strong case seems to be building up that the heads have been there for a very long time, yet they do not appear to have been studied until 1975. Now we turn to the initials and the dates carved on the stones. The dates go back to 1807 and give us an idea how weathering affects the sharpness of the cuts on the rocks. The heads have an ancient mellowness as if darkened by time. In support of this evidence, an old photograph dating back to the 1880's has turned up showing three of the heads.

As for the weathering of the sandstone, there is yet another source of comparison, for, on the rocks just east of the Lifts, there are cup and ring marks dating back 4,000 years, and they are still wonderfully distinct. These markings are of the Bronze Age, 2,000 years before the Iron Age Celts.

Other discoveries have been made on this remarkable moor. Just east of the Lifts, Professor Alcock has been excavating two chambered tombs, and near them are burial cairns, while among the rocks there is a little millstone quarry with stones in every state of manufacture, from roughly pecked cuts to the finished article, complete with a hole in the centre.

When I used to walk with old John, little did I know that we were in the midst of archaeological treasure, with mysteries all around us waiting to be solved, mysteries like the heads which we failed to see, symbols, perhaps, of decapitation and blood sacrifice on a moor which may have been sacred to this purpose. No trace of human habitation has been found.

THE BIG BEN

I know now, from my own experience, that your memory of youth gets sharper as you get older. Wandering about the Highlands it happens to me more and more, and nowhere more sharply than recently on Ben Nevis. I was passing the point where the half-way house used to be, and in my mind's eye I saw a lad in short trousers and a lithe fair-haired man, their backs bent beneath bulging rucksacks as they prepared to doss down on the floor for the night.

The wee fellow's neck ached under the weight of that sack. He hated it as much as his companion relished doing what few folk would want to do. Ritchie, a champion wrestler, weight-lifter and racing cyclist, prided himself on being a "sourdough." He scorned comfort. An unemployed Clydeside plumber he sought the wilds. He and I had been travelling across country after getting off the train at Taynuilt and crossing on the ferry to Bonawe three days before. Now we were heading for Rannoch Moor, via the top of Ben Nevis and Aonach Mor and Aonach Beag.

It was bliss to get that bag off, get the Primus going for a "drum-up" and curl up on the floor. But continuous sleep was hard to come by for heavy boots kept thumping in—folk on their way to the summit to await the sunrise—unaware that we were on the floor until their eyes became accustomed to the darkness.

As we went up in the mist and drizzle of the morning we met party after party coming down, all of them bedraggled and disappointed at seeing nothing for their effort. Conditions were still the same when we saw the Observatory building looming ahead, less of a ruin than it is today, even to a bit of lead roof remaining. Unpacking the tea-can I went off to find "Wragge's Well" marked on our old map a short distance away. Ritchie gave me a compass bearing and was pleased when I returned with the means of tea-making.

What we didn't know was that the ridge of Carn Dearg has got many climbers into trouble for it is difficult to find. Ritchie set off confidently and still continued on our rough compass bearing when the easy slope became rocks. Soon they were so steep we had to face inward for hand and footholds. Ritchie was enjoying himself, but I was frightened. The drag of the sack was unbalancing me and I could visualise myself falling into the unknown void below. My legs were trembling and once I had to cry for help. Memory is vague now, but I have an image of snow patches and an immense scattering of pink boulders far below and away to our

52

right the narrow ridge we were trying to find. A series of ledgeways led us to it.

Once down on the Aonach Beag col, Ritchie scrapped the idea of humping the bags over the tops in favour of dumping them for a quick race up and down. I really enjoyed myself then, free of ballast. It was fun to be crunching over the ice-hard snow-patches lying in the hollows and then running back down the screes to our bags.

Little could I have guessed after that wet week with Ritchie that it would be the cliffs of Ben Nevis that would draw me back again and again in every season of the year. Or that the least enjoyable part of future days on Britain's highest mountain would be the plod from Glen Nevis and the descent from the summit after a day on the longest rock climbs in Britain.

And now here I was on Ben Nevis again with two young folk who knew as little about the mountain as I did on my first ascent, and this time I was going to the top by the pony track on a promising morning of crisp visibility though a full thousand feet of mist still capped the summit.

Of the half-way hut that was used by the road-men who maintained the track in Observatory days, there is nothing left. When we dossed down in it all these years ago I didn't know that this was one of the places where you paid your one shilling toll fee to be allowed to walk up the track, four shillings if you rode a pony.

To build the track cost £800 in 1883, and until it was opened on that date only a few eccentrics had climbed Ben Nevis. Of these the most extraordinary was Clement Wragge, a gangling red-haired Englishman nick-named "The Inclement Wragge" by the Fort William folk because he climbed the mountain every day regardless of weather. Leaving at five in the morning he aimed to be at the summit at nine and back down in the town at three in the afternoon, having obtained in that time a scientific record of the weather differences between sea-level and 4,406 feet.

It was the astonishing weather variations between sea and summit which decided the Scottish Meteorological Society to build the first mountain-top observatory on Ben Nevis lying in the direct path of Atlantic storms. What Wragge had been doing was a feasibility study over a period of two summers, climbing the Ben from June to October inclusive. The £4,000 required to built the Observatory was raised in Scotland, as was the money for the pony track.

Suddenly everybody wanted to climb Ben Nevis—over 4000 within a year. Many of them would arrive in Fort William by the West Highland Railway which opened in August 1894 bringing the mountain within easy range of the mass of the Scottish population. Trade in the town was brisk. A hotel was built on top to provide bed and breakfast for those wanting to stay for the sunrise, and there was serious talk of extending the railway from the town to the summit.

Talking about these things my young friends and I overtook the first climbers of the morning, a family in yellow oilskins, father and mother with a bright-faced wee girl roped between them. In foreign accent the man asked if I thought the weather would remain fine. "We turned back from here yesterday. We would like to climb up the highest peak in Scotland but perhaps it is too much for this little girl?" She was not quite six.

"She'll do it if you can keep her interested," I told him. "Tell her about the wee house there used to be on the top—the highest in the whole country. Give her something to look forward to."

They were from the flat lands of Holland.

We broke off from the path after crossing the Red Burn to see what we could find in the way of mountain plants among the boulders; fir club and other mosses, alpine ladies mantle, starry saxifrages and the tiny least willow. No snow buntings singing as I had hoped, but I have a feeling they nest here. We were well in the mist at 3,500ft. and at 4,000ft. were on the unbroken snowfield between Carn Dearg and Ben Nevis which Wragge called "The Plateau of Storms".

I used the compass now in this dimensionless world of white mist on snow, to keep on parallel course with the big cliffs which sheer away from the plateau edge for roughly a mile between here and the top of Nevis. Then suddenly came the proof that all was well: the big snow dome of the summit suddenly bulged in front of us, the mist pouring off north-eastwards revealing the black thrust of crags soaring to thick lips of snow cornice.

Our spirits soared as colour flooded around us and below us. There was green-shored Loch Linnhe, a ribbon of soft grey winding to the blue hills of Mull. Corpach on Loch Eil and the Pulp Mill on its peninsula looked like a white toy. Highland topography at a glance. Behind the deep cut of the Great Glen jumbled ridges stretched from Knoydart to Kintail and Glen Affric. There would be even more to see when we reached the top.

Our first delightful surprise on arriving was to find the Dutch family already there. The wee girl said she wasn't even tired and proved it by grabbing my ice-axe and digging furiously into the snow while we talked. They were amused when I told them about the Fort William man who claimed the first wheeled victory on Ben Nevis by pushing a wheelbarrow to the summit, followed in 1911 by a Model T Ford motor car which took three days to reach the Observatory, but a mere 2½ hours to return after a night cooling down.

At the news of the victory of the internal combustion engine over the steeps of the mountain, a public holiday was declared in Fort William and a pipe band played to greet the entry of the motor car into the town. The man with the wheelbarrow was there trundling along in the procession. It was to be another thirteen years before the motor car could equal the wheelbarrow by going up and down in a day. That came in

1928 when a Model A Ford achieved the feat.

We took a walk along the cliffs to identify the peaks stretching from Ben Wyvis to Ben Lawers, Schiehallion, Ben Alder and the high mass of the Cairngorms, the nearest approach to true Arctic terrain we have in Scotland and still very white after an exceptionally long winter and cold spring.

Sheltered by the modern "survival hut" which perches on what used to be the Observatory conning tower, I thought about the disappointment Wragge must have felt when the Observatory was built and he was refused the post of Superintendent which he wanted. But you can't suppress a man's pioneering spirit. He had been in Australia, and he went back there, getting his due as Government meteorologist and setting up mountain-top observatories on Mount Wellington and Mount Kodciusko. The world remembers him as its first long-range weather forecaster. He died in 1922.

The staff of the Observatory was normally four and they seem to have got on comfortably together with little friction. Visiting students came to stay. One was C.T.R. Wilson, a Nobel Prize winner from Glencorse whose work played an important part in the development of nuclear physics. It was the optical phenomena shown when the sun shone on the clouds surrounding the hilltop that turned his thoughts to imitating them in the laboratory which led to forty years of tracking atoms.

Life on the highest mountain had its share of fun. The team enjoyed the snow, tobogganing from the Observatory to the "Plateau of Storms"—a thrilling half-mile course with a 20ft drop and a sensational bit known as McLean's Steep. For skating they made a pond on a big tarpaulin stretched on the flat roof; and for curling matches they would descend 2,000ft. to the half-way lochan. In summer they played quoits and amused themselves hurtling rocks over the cliffs to see them bounce and smash with sulphurous smell.

Later, in 1892, they had to warn tourists not to hurl rocks down the cliff. An incredible thing had happened: a family from the north of England had scaled the 2,000ft. cliffs. In four days the Hopkinson brothers pioneered two of the great classics of Scottish climbing, Tower Ridge and Observatory Ridge. Strangely they wrote not a word in any journal about it.

In March, two years later, a noted Scottish Mountaineering Club alpinist came with a strong party and made the first winter ascent of Tower Ridge which Collie described as being comparable with the Italian ridge of the Matterhorn—powerful praise and not over-stated. These great crags are a volcanic cauldron of lava which did not erupt but subsided inside a mass of softer material, its head changing the nature of the surrounding rocks. It was erosion by moving masses of ice scraping away the softer material which uncovered the inside of the mountain and made its lava the north-eastern outside we see today, a superb architectural form of ridge and spire, buttress and arete, gully and chimney. From below they look even more daunting than from above, so all praise to the Hopkinson brothers in finding two of the best natural lines.

Among the early pioneers was Dr. W. Inglis Clark, Scottish Mountaineering Club President from 1913-19. His name is remembered in the only true alpine cabin in Britain, situated below the Tower Ridge. Dr Clark built it to commemorate his son Charles, who died of wounds in Mesopotamia. It was opened in 1929. This year a large gathering of Scottish Mountaineering Club members plan to celebrate its fifty years of active service.

I've been looking back the record of the official opening of the hut on 1 April five decades ago. The time was 7 p.m. They had just eaten a splendid meal cooked on the club stove. It was snowing hard outside when the door was thrust open and in lurched two climbers. They had fallen from Gardyloo Gully, lost their ice axes, slid 600ft. and were fumbling their way down when they saw the light beside them. Clark wrote: "Thus early our hut had justified itself in time of danger."

Time of danger— In fact mountaineering accidents were very few on Ben Nevis until the sudden popularisation of the sport in the late 50's when the climbing revolution took place and gathering streams converged in all seasons on both sides of the mountain. Death became commonplace, over fifty in two decades, many of the victims totally lacking any idea of what to expect on this most savage of Scottish peaks. There is less excuse for ignorance today than when Ritchie and I went up on our first visit.

How long should you allow yourself to climb Ben Nevis by the pony track? For comfort you want seven hours from Achintee or from the Glen Nevis Youth Hostel. Don't be misled by the fact that runners in the Ben Nevis race, held on the first Saturday in September, will have to beat 1 hour 26 minutes 55 seconds to beat the record from the town park to the summit and back.

Just remember that experienced fell runners regard the Ben Nevis race as the hardest in Britain, not just because it rises so sharply from sea level to summit, but because of the roughness of it, and the severe jolting body and feet have to take on the descent.

August will see hundreds of climbers on any reasonable day setting off up the pony track to the top. If you are one of them, make sure you have some warm clothing and a pair of gloves, even if it is warm and sunny in Fort William. And your footgear should be stout and comfortable, not smooth leather soles, but with nails or cleated rubber to give a grip.

Don't be put off by mere mist for the upper part of the hill is well marked by cairns of stones. You may climb above the clouds or get the same kind of clearing as we did. But don't be too proud to turn back if the conditions become too wet and stormy for comfort. Go back another day. The Big Ben is an experience not to be missed.

56

AVALANCHE

I am writing this with my injured leg propped up on a couch, and every now and then I have to wriggle my posterior to avoid too much pressure on a large and raw scar on that place. This continual wriggling causes pain on my bruised thighs, and if I cough or sneeze, a pain shoots from my lower ribs to my chest. But I shall start from the beginning.

It was a day in February and four of us were keen on a difficult climb. The preceeding week had been glorious with sun and frost, and eagerly we awaited the week-end for an attempt on a classic Scottish mountaineering route—the "upper couloir" of Stob Ghabhar. We knew it would be in superb conditon for an exacting climb on steep frozen snow and ice. The stars on Saturday night as we motored up towards the Black Mount had a frosty sparkle. But overnight there was a dramatic change. Raw winter had returned with a clamping down of visibility and snow falling out of low yellow mists. There was no wind and we saw no reason to call off our climb.

Our intention was to park the car on the south side of the mountain, contour round to the north-east face, climb the couloir, and descend southwards down easy slopes to the car.

The walk up the glen that leads over was uneventful, but in the hour taken to cross the shoulder to the north-east side we could feel a change brewing. The snow fell thicker and the wind became unpleasant. Black crags were hung with icefalls and whitened where snow could lie. We sank deeply at each step.

This was not quite what I had expected. The ice, yes, but not this depth of new snow. Obviously there must have been heavy snow up here for some hours. I was beginning to have misgivings about the couloir. We kept a careful compass check and at last were faced by a steep gully.

The upper couloir of Stob Ghabhar is a narrow 300 ft cleft enclosed by two rock buttresses abutting directly on to the summit. We were 600 feet below it, at the foot of the lower couloir, and it is usual to combine the two couloirs by making one long climb.

We tied on the rope and I led. It was a straightforward steep slope, but at once I noticed that the exceptionally dry and deep surface snow did not seem to be adhering to the mountain. I cut through with my ice-axe to the underlying strata and found a substance hard as ice. The sun and frost of the past week on the thin cover of old snow had made the hillsides so icy that this new snow was merely resting on it. There was danger here, avalanche danger, and I proved it when I slapped the adjacent slope with my ice-axe shaft and caused a large mass to split off.

The couloir was "out" for today, obviously. But unwilling to abandon the mountain we agreed to try a route to the left on what looked to be safer snow. This was indeed safer, and we climbed swiftly in deteriorating conditions of rising wind and blowing snow.

Had we chosen the easiest route to the summit all might have turned out well. Instead of that I broke off at an ice-fall flowing over rocks. "This," I said, "will give a sporting climb and should be every bit as good as the couloir." I got on to it and was soon balanced on a steep wall of ice chipping hand and foot-holds.

This is perhaps the most truly satisfying branch of the climber's craft. Ice climbing calls for delicate balance, judgment in spacing the holds, and ability in shaping them to give secure foot and hand-hold. Now and then I had to hang on and try to glue myself to the mountain as fierce blasts of wind and spume struck.

The ice-fall gave eighty feet of exacting climbing with an exit on to steep and difficult ground. I lost no time in finding a belay and bringing up my second. The others followed.

We were now on a slope of new snow lying ten inches deep on a hard frozen undersurface of ice covering rock. The danger was evident, and I cut every step through to the under-lying strata, and several times had to desist to avoid being swept off by the now ferocious gale with its accompanying blasts of spume.

In three 100ft. rope lengths I found myself above the lowest rocks of the upper couloir and knew I must be close to the summit. But I was faced with a worrying problem. The bank of snow in front of me was so steep that I could almost touch it with my nose, and it looked avalanchy.

I warned my second to find himself a good anchorage by digging the shaft of his axe up to the head in hard frozen snow, and tying himself to it. The others were eighty feet lower down and joined to us by the rope. I prodded the slope with my axe and found it so deep that it was impossible to get through to old underlying snow. This was serious, but such a depth of snow might be reasonably consolidated. I decided to shovel out a groove and tramp it down as I wriggled up.

This is a laborious technique as I knew, but as the summit was so close I began shovelling with the head of my axe. I climbed up a couple of steps and was well pleased with my work. This was going to work out all right after all. As a further test of consolidation I plunged my axe up to its head and gave the shaft a tug. Quite silently and with irresistible force the whole slope heeled over on me, hurtling me downwards.

My second man was torn from his ice axe so firmly planted in the hard snow. The other two members of the party saw a great snow-tide advancing on them and tried to hold. They were lifted bodily and hurled down with us.

I was below the avalanche and my first reaction was that we were going to be smothered by the pressing weight of the snow. At such times a swimming motion is supposed to bring one to the surface, and I began swimming. But I need not have bothered. The next instant I was in the air, turning over and over. Things hit me and jarred my bones, terrific jerks tore at my ribs (the rope joining us). I was a detached spectator who sees himself in a dream hurtling to death and wakes in nightmare.

"No human being could survive this," I remember thinking. And I blamed myself for causing it. Four people were going to die and I was responsible for not turning back when I should. The mind is strangely calm in such moments of crisis. The others told me they, too, were resigned to death.

Then suddenly I felt myself begin to slow up, and at once I started swimming to get to the surface. To be buried and suffocated would be worse than sudden death. I came to rest beside my second and I feared he was dead. His face was covered in blood, but he answered my question and thought he was all right.

My leg was numb from the thigh downwards and I felt it trembling with shock. My gloves had been torn off and my hands were swollen and lifeless with cold. "I had better get something on my hands," I said. I had a spare pair of gloves in my pocket and as I tried to get them blood spurted over my jacket and hands. It was then I realised that my own face was covered in blood.

At that moment there was a shout from above. Neither my second nor myself were yet capable of rising. The other two joined us. The nylon rope had snapped between us like a piece of string, hence the reason why they had stopped at a different point. All were concerned for my eyebrow which was split open and was the source of so much blood, but there was no pain in it.

We reviewed the damage. One man was almost unscathed. The other two were badly bruised and in considerable pain. My second had taken a battering on the face and thighs and his legs hurt. The third had two badly twisted ankles and various bruises, but he thought he could walk. I felt sure that any man left out on the mountain that night would die of exposure in the blizzard which was now raging, and consequently delayed not a moment in starting off on the long traverse back round the mountain.

For three of us each step was an effort of will. Our footsteps of the morning had filled in, and the going was now much harder in the now considerable depth of snow. One man had to lie down and pull himself over such obstacles as he could not climb.

We did not take any chances in the nil visibility. A compass course was maintained on the complicated traverse round the mountain and we struck the hill track that takes such a good line down the broken ground between Beinn Toaig and Stob Ghabhar.

It was nearly 6 p.m. when three of us reached the little school-house of Clash Ghabhar so we had made a speed of about one mile per hour. We were now a couple of miles from the car. The missing man with the twisted ankles was not far behind, we knew. If the two injured members went on for help, the sound man could climb back uphill and help the fourth member.

We were lucky. The keeper at Forest Lodge had a van, and after plying us with tea he ran the vehicle up the rough track to the schoolhouse. His arrival was well timed, for our two companions had just reached the schoolhouse as the van drove up. The injured man could not have gone farther for the snow was balling on his climbing boots, causing his twisted ankles to turn at every step.

Soon we were assembled in the keeper's warm kitchen and assisted into our spare clothes from the car, for we were soaked to the skin. These fine people were kindness itself.

There is always a fortunate side to any unlucky event. We still had a driver for our car and we had friends only twenty miles away. We went there, had baths, a hot dinner, bathed our wounds, and one man went to bed. We motored to Glasgow, arriving in at 2 a.m., and next day had expert attention in the Western Infirmary. No one was called upon to risk his life that terrible night.

Will it stop us climbing? I doubt it. Mountaineering is no more dangerous than many another sport. A combination of events had led us on that day, first the windless morning, then the sound condition of the snow on the earlier part of our climb. Our nearness to the summit and thought of a speedy descent out of the blizzard to the more sheltered south side of the mountain made me reluctant to abandon our climb until I had first tested the safety of the bank that was our undoing.

So much of mountaineering is a matter of judgement. In this case my judgment was wrong, and the descent rather speedier than any of us expected. All of us should be well to climb again in a matter of a few weeks. Fluid and blood on my swollen knee and a fractured patella may retard my own progress a bit longer, but that is just retribution.

*   *   *   *   *   *

I wrote this to beguile the time, not for publication. Since then we have visited the scene of the accident, mainly to look for our ice axes. We found them, and were shocked to see what we had fallen over. The average angle of the slope was around fifty degrees, with one drop of over 100 ft. and sundry smaller drops. One of the ice axes was broken, the one used to belay me on the last part of the climb. It was a new and modern Swiss axe. We had come down a full 600 feet and more.

If this had been an Alpine climb I would not have dreamed of forcing it under such doubtful conditions of snow, and certainly not attempted it under conditions of storm. The moral must be that no matter how keen one is to climb, there is a time for turning back, even if it is just under the summit in a blizzard. Scottish hills in winter must, in fact, be treated as Alpine peaks.

MUNRO AND HIS MOUNTAINS

I have just been into Angus, stravaiging round Kirriemuir, enjoying two worlds, up in the shining snows above Clova and Isla, and down among the green haughs of the South Esk. On the low ground it was spring, with skylarks pouring out torrents of song and peewits tumbling in the fields. But on Mount Keen it was still bitter winter, as I knew, for I had just been up there, bagging my first new "Munro" for a very long time.

It was a dose of tonsilitis and 'flu which sent me up there. While I was swallowing and sneezing, I had opened Volume One of *the Scottish Mountaineering Club Journal* to take my mind off the confines of bed. Soon I was forgetting gargling and pills as a remarkable man stood out from the pages—Sir Hugh Munro, of Lindertis.

I saw him as a lone figure in an Inverness cape with a Balmoral on his head, the snow crunching under his boots in that rolling world of mountains which stretches from Angus to Braemar. I see him stopping on top after top, to get out his aneroid and make an entry in a notebook; or sit on some commanding height to work out the exact details of the topography around him, for he was a great cataloguer of mountain views.

Then, as the pink of sunset gilds the summits, I can see him hitch his pack and set off at some speed for the Milton of Clova or the Spittal of Glen Shee, for Munro was a great cross-country traveller, preferring to traverse his mountains than to retrace his steps to the point of departure.

I like to think how he arrived in Glasgow for the S.M.C. dinner of 1890, held in December. He would be thirty-three years of age then, bearded and wearing the kilt, for he had changed out of his knickerbockers after a morning in the thick mist and deep powder snow of Carn na Caim. Upon this 3,000 ft. summit he had stood at 10 a.m., the early hour of the climb allowing him to catch the 1.15 p.m. train from Dalwhinnie to Glasgow.

He had been climbing at Dalwhinnie for three days before the dinner. This was about the time he wrote in the *Journal*:

> "I should be glad at almost any time during January, February, and March to join small parties of members of the club on expeditions of one or several days' duration. I am willing to go anywhere, but the districts I am most anxious to explore are—the Sutherland Hills, the Ullapool and Loch Maree country, the Cuchuillins, Western Inverness-shire, the Blackmount, Glencoe, Glen Nevis, and Glen Lyon hills. During the months mentioned I can almost always find

time for a trip, but later I am much engaged. I am sometimes free, however, for a few days, and if it fitted my movements I would be glad to join any climbing party on learning of it.

H.T. Munro, Lindertis."

Well, he did explore all these districts, some in company, but mostly alone for he was never put off for lack of a companion. See him on Beinn a' Ghlo on the 22nd January, a day of wind with snow blowing, " . . .in spiral columns several hundred feet high, penetrating everything, filling pockets and drifting between waistcoat and shirt, where it melted and then froze into a solid wedge of ice. In all my winter experience I never suffered so severely from cold."

Yet the cold did not prevent him from recording the details of the views, though the description is mercifully short compared with a tendency towards topographical excess in other accounts. That day he merely says—"Views good—Cairngorms and Ben Alder groups, the Glencoe Hills; Schiehallion (which does not show to advantage from here); Ben Lawers looking well, with Stobinian over his left shoulder; Ben Chonzie; the Fifeshire Lomonds and Sidlaws showing well, with the smoke of Dundee behind. The special feature, however, is the fine view of the higher peaks of Beinn a' Ghlo."

He had started his walk from Blair Atholl, but finished that night two miles above Kirkmichael. "Heavy walking all day in soft snow. At Diranean they had to scrape me down with a knife to get the frozen snow off me before I could enter the house."

The date then was 1891, and just a month later he achieved one of his great desires, a landing in Rhum, where the landowner put the lodges at his disposal. He writes—"In the grey dawn of a drizzling morning—4th February last—I landed in Rhum. The day was not tempting for climbing so I went out to try for woodcock, accompanied by a keeper whose broad Lancashire accent seemed out of place in the Highlands."

Rhum was unknown to mountaineers when Munro got permission to land. The weather was unsettled. Consider his resource therefore, when he climbed into the mist two days later to see what he could achieve on the rocky ridges. He got to the top of Allival at midday, seeing in front of him Askival, clear of cloud and looking impressively difficult with a rock pinnacle blocking the way. He describes himself as being "out for a stroll," but continues—"After casting about a little, I struck an easy way to the col, and a few minutes' ascent by a very narrow ridge brought me face to face with the *Gendarme*, which, as anticipated was quite perpendicular and probably one hundred feet high. The east face, however, though steep—real climbing—presented no particular difficulty. Several attempts to regain the ridge proving abortive, I therefore kept to the face, reaching the summit almost without knowing it at 1.15 p.m.

So far so good. His Munro blood was really up; the day was still young, so now he dropped to the Ashval col for "a nice bit of real rock climbing with some rather awkward smooth slabs of rock." This was done in mist, as was the continuation onwards to Sgurr nan Gillean, 2,503 ft. The only unpleasant problem of the day occurred on the way down when he got into a constricted gully of steep grass and broken rock, "as steep and disagreeable a piece of climbing as I wish to experience alone." But he was back to his usual high spirits in Glendibidil which he thought "vied with Glencoe in rugged grandeur, while its contrasts of glorious views far surpasses it."

I like to think of him leaving Rhum by open boat for Arisaig, its prow pointed towards more snowy mountains in Glen Finnan and Lochaber, where his axe was in constant play as he explored Streaps and its neighbours before walking to Corpach "in wild wind and sheets of rain." He makes the observation—"Members will be taken at this homely and comfortable inn at 8s 6d per day."

From Corpach he climbed to the Carn Mor Dearg arete, enjoying some airy step-cutting and the proximity of the Nevis cliffs. He headed into Glen Nevis next day for a traverse of the An Gearannach ridge, which demanded much care on its very narrow crest. The following morning saw him aboard the *Fusilier* heading home, another mountain journey successfully accomplished. Indeed, he never had an accident.

Nor did he go looking for difficulty. If there was an easy way, then Munro would take it. If not, then as on Rhum, he would not shirk the problem, nor did he refuse invitations from more technically-minded mountaineers. I like his description of climbing a gully on Ben Eunaich in March, when he was "much hampered too, by having an Inverness cape on," a remarkable garment for a place so constricted that he could not wield his axe properly. And the day was so wild that descent from the summit was "as if wrestling with a man. There were moments when I could not make a foot of ground."

It must have been a very bad day indeed to tax a man of Munro's fitness. No journey was too long. To get to Dalmally from Dalwhinnie he walked over the Ben Alder peaks (spending a day climbing) to Loch Rannoch, thence to Glen Lyon and over the hill to the railway at Bridge of Orchy.

Munro refused to believe there was anything dangerous about climbing mountains alone. Even so, he had his moments of worry, as in a February crossing of the Cairngorms via Ben Macdhui, when sudden mist came down, freezing on his clothes, hair and beard. He could have turned and gone back to Aviemore, but it was 4.30 p.m. in the afternoon and he thought he might as well carry on down to Glen Derry.

But he failed to exercise his usual care in computing the compass bearing, and after a thousand feet of frozen mountainside found himself among dangerous cliffs, "the cold so intense that one could scarcely have lived an hour without moving." In something of a panic he clambered back up the slope, hauling himself up on the point of his axe. He tried again, and found himself worse off. Calming his panic, as dusk grew around him in this grim place, he got out the map, worked out his position and this time won clear, to find himself at 5.45 p.m. "on a dark night in early February 3,100 feet above the sea, on the shores of the frozen Loch Etchachan." Nevertheless he was down at Lui Beg by 8.30 p.m., "where I was hospitably entertained by Fraser, the head stalker and his wife."

He has another lively description of a Cairngorm crossing, by the Lairig Ghru on snow hard as a turnpike, when "The sun set in a soft pink haze, graduating through many tints of yellow to an ethereal blue, a sunset of that peculiar type, rare in Scotland, rarer still in England, which always recalls to my memory Egypt and the desert." He was, of course, looking from the summit into Speyside, and the change of scene delighted him.

Munro loved change, and was, in fact, a world traveller, though the only reference I can find to a foreign ascent is of the extinct volcano Irazu, in Costa Rica, made with his wife. Maybe he was too busy on his travels, for he was a King's Messenger, a professional courier who carried foreign despatches for diplomats, though many of his later journeys were done mainly for pleasure.

The climb in Costa Rica was made on Easter Sunday, 1894, just a year after he had unravelled the topography of An Teallach which was very much a mystery mountain at this time. Pennant and McCulloch had described it as "awful" and "terrific."

But the S.M.C. party which included Munro, were stirred in a different way when they saw "the glorious hills themselves, suddenly bursting through the storm clouds, black, snow-slashed, and jagged against the setting sun," a sight encouraging enough for them to hope "that a vague tradition of an unclimbed peak might prove a reality." Certainly they were the first to traverse An Teallach completely, fix the heights of the peaks, and determine its structure by photography.

The information was published in Volume Three of the *Journal* in meticulous detail, with sketches and photographs showing the disposition of the peaks and corries. Munro had a "guidebook" mind but was a dispenser of titbits as well as important information. In Sutherland, for example, he observes—"The charges for forwarding luggage by the Sutherland mails are somewhat high, so pedestrians and cyclists would do well to make up brown paper parcels not exceeding eleven pounds each, and forward them by parcel post."

He explored Sutherland by bicycle, but was a keen user of the West Highland Railway from the time of its opening, pointing out that "by taking the early train, 7.35 a.m. from Glasgow, it is quite possible, without unduly hurrying, to cross Carn Dearg, 3,084 ft; Sgor Gaibhre, 3,128 ft; and Sgor Choinnich, 3,040 ft;* and descending to the foot of Loch Ossian, return over Beinn na Lap, 3,066ft; in time to continue your journey

* These three peaks lie to the north-east of the railway between Rannoch and Corrour. Beinn na Lap is just north of Corrour.

to Fort William by the evening train."

While on the Inverness line he notes that it is possible to dovetail Meall na Cuaich, E.N.E. of Dalwhinnie, 3,120 ft., into a break in the journey from Glasgow or Edinburgh. Of the railway north of Dingwall he had no good word to say.

The motor car in Munro's life does not occur until Volume Twelve, when he writes, "Without doubt, the motor car offers possibilities, and brings within the scope of a day or two's expedition, regions which formerly, even with the help of a bicycle, would have taken thrice as long." The theme of the article is "Tomdoun," and since he drove the 130 miles between Glen Garry and Lindertis in five hours forty minutes the surface must have been reasonable, even if the Loch Laggan stretch was "scandalously bad."

He gives a summary of the road. "Between Spean Bridge and Invergarry (sixteen miles) the road is moderate, except at two places with notice boards 'three water-courses across roadway,' and 'seven ditto ditto.' These places cannot be taken too slowly. Above Invergarry the road is stony, narrow, and twisty, and requires careful driving."

The date was 1912 and Munro was fifty-six. Only seven years of his life were left. He was with his friend Rennie, a companion of An Teallach, whose photography and knowledge of botany delighted him. Together they explored the high peaks of Knoydart, from the top of Sgor na Ciche above Loch Nevis to the peaks of Loch Hourn. As always, Munro notes the wild life in some detail, but reflects "on the whole, I have never seen less animal life on the mountains."

No doubt he would be thinking back to Easter, 1897, when he was glad of the shelter of these lochs after being driven out of Skye by atrocious weather. The occasion was a famous yachting meet. The boat was to be used as a base for climbing on the Cuillin, but foul weather and seasickness drove the twenty members and nine guests eastward to Knoydart. Munro was president of the club then, and the decision to lift the anchor and get out was his.

Walter Barrow gives a good account of the cheerful end to the meet, when sailing back to Oban. "The black peaks of Rhum stood out in rich golden light reflected in the glassy surface of a rolling swell. And on the deck of the yacht, headed by the president in Highland kilt and sporran, we danced a reel and Strathspey to the drone of the Scottish pipes."

I have given you, I hope, something of the spirit and character of the man, as I got to know him from his writings. The time had now come to visit his home, talk with his son, and meet anyone I could find who remembered him. I found the house of "Drumleys" just three miles south of Kirriemuir, and when I rang the bell and the door was opened by a man in a red kilt and tweed jacket I knew I was looking at Sir Torquil Munro, 5th Baronet of Lindertis. "Come in," he said when I told him I wanted to talk to him about his father, to complete a picture I had of him in my mind's eye.

"I don't know that I can tell you very much," he said, "I never really knew him, you know. He was a great traveller, away a lot. He wasn't a very tall man, always wore a beard and dressed in the kilt."

He would not be so unlike his son, I imagined, who is compact, square-shouldered, with a wiry frame, a neatly-built man. Nor do I imagine the Scots voice would be so different, for Sir Torquil was educated at Crieff, Winchester, and Magdalene College, Cambridge, while his father was born in London, studied German at Stuttgart at the age of seventeen, taking a business training at nineteen, and going in 1880 to be Private Secretary to Sir George Colley, Governor of Natal. Out there he had fought in the Basuto War as a cavalryman, returning home with a black boy, a monkey, and a host of curios.

"My father was a widower," Sir Torquil continued. "I was two when my mother died. Although I never really knew him he was very kind. He often came to see me at school in Crieff, and would take me runs in the car. I remember Harold Raeburn staying here, and we went bird nesting. He showed me a long eared owl's nest in a tree out there.

"I was eighteen when my father died in 1919. He died of Spanish flu in France. He ran a canteen for French troops in Tarascon during the war, but he is buried between here and the old family home of Lindertis. He was very fond of the music of Wagner, and he played the flute. He was a great dancer. He had very small feet and neat ankles—I know that because although I have a small foot I couldn't wear his shoes. He never drank tea, just milk, or water, wine at dinner time. He was a water diviner, you know. He had the gift, although he didn't practice it, and I inherited that from him. It's my hobby, and most valuable it has proved to me as a farmer.

"He believed in ghosts. Once when he was staying at an old castle, coming down a narrow stairway for dinner, he met a little old woman coming up, and as it was a narrow stair he stood aside for her to pass. He noticed she was dressed in curious clothes, with an old-fashioned cap and long skirts. He happened to remark at dinner that a servant he had met on the stair wore decidedly odd clothes, when there was a silence from his host who then told him seriously it was the castle ghost he had seen. He also believed in heavenly music. He had heard it several times in the mountains.

"He loved children. This house was always full of them. He loved to give them treats. He was a great story teller, and could always make people laugh. One story that always left him in chuckles was of the man who wrote his will leaving £500 to a nephew and £500 to each of his nieces, but nothing to his wife because she wasn't a relative."

Lindertis is a 3000 acre estate and 260 acre farm, famous today for its pedigree bulls. One was sold for the world-record price of £60,000 in 1963. Seed potatoes are also exported from its fields of light soil. I asked

Sir Torquil if his father had been interested in farming. "He was really a forester," he replied. "He did become interested in farming, and grew a lot of food when the war crisis demanded it. He went heart and soul into farming then, but he was really an estate manager. He managed Lindertis for his uncle, then for his father, before he fell heir to it in 1913."

From where I sat in Sir Hugh's favourite room I looked across a park of green sward to the swell of low hills. Behind me, out of sight, was the old mansion house of Lindertis, where two notable S.M.C. meets had been held in 1915. Sir Torquil invited me to go up there. The mansion, alas, is no more. The house where so many of Munro's mountain journeys started is a ruin, all but the wings, which are inhabited by a farm worker, a retired forester, and the county rabbit trapper. The main building, Sir Torquil told me, was unroofed because of the expense of its upkeep.

Round the farm steadings where the Aberdeen-Angus bulls are housed, I spoke to Mr Nicol, who remembered Sir Hugh, but could not think of him as a mountaineer because he "didna look very strong." But he could tell me: "A' the high hills o' Scotland are ca'd efter him. They ca' them Munros," he said.

And that itself is an irony, because Munro had no use for personal names in mountaineering. He was such a traditionalist that he wrote a criticism of the use of "Angel's peak," for a summit in the Cairngorms because it had been bestowed by a well-known climber. Only two 3,000-footers did not fall below Munro's feet, Carn Cloich-Mhuillin in the Cairngorms, which he was keeping for "the last one," and the Inaccessible Pinnacle in the Cuillin which he had tried just four years before he died.

The cemetery where he lies buried with his wife is not easy to find, sandwiched as it is by a farm hedge on one side and a high garden wall on the other. In that sunny corner I found a small marble cross. Munro's wife was a general's daughter, and she died ten years after their marriage. That decade was Munro's richest as a climber.

The canvas of his life was very much in my mind as I left the grave and took the road which winds from Kirriemuir into Glen Clova. And appropriately it was a day when you could feel the sting of the wind from the gleaming snow wreaths—a day for the hill, and I could almost hear the clip-clop of the horse pulling Sir Hugh's dog-cart as it passed through the little farms, the passenger in the Inverness cape and Balmoral, about to leave one world for another, on another resourceful mountain journey.

Nor could I leave it here. Not until I had been to the head of Glen Isla could I feel my pilgrimage complete, where the Caenlochan glen swings between escarpments and a variety of steep gullies offer challenge, couloirs which were climbed on the January meet at Lindertis so many years ago when Munro kept his guests so busy that none of them saw his house in daylight. They left in the dark and came back in the dark.

Following their route I climbed into the snowy corrie by the stumps of a vanished wood, reaching the summit by a gully fringed by a miniature glacier.

It led into the mist, over a cornice of hard snow to the summit plateau where I was able to discard the compass as the sun broke the mist, a fine moment made charming by a flock of snowbuntings rising from my feet, while on another snow patch some thirty ptarmigan waddled about like domestic hens. Dazzling snow patches among black menacing clouds gave a feeling of immensity to these great hill shapes which stretch without break to Lochnagar.

The hills were, I felt, very much as Munro had described them in one of his earliest articles, "The Braes of Angus," in Volume One of the *Journal*. Listen to this:

> "The enhanced beauty of the mountains in their winter clothing, when the corries are filled with snow, the freedom to roam over the country unchecked by landlords or shooting tenants, the glorious views enjoyed, and, above all, the increased interest of the climb when the rocks are coated with ice, when slopes of hard frozen snow often compel the use of the axe, when every arete has an overhanging cornice of snow, then in short, our Scottish hills present most of the characteristics and many of the difficulties of mountains in the Alps, three or four times their height."

Turning away from the Braes of Angus that night into a blaze of sunset tingeing the snows with fire I felt grateful to that bout of 'flu which sent me north to lay the ghost of an exceptional Scot, whose spirit will be somewhere around each time I tick off another of the few Munros which are outstanding from his list.

And as a postscript to this, I would like to acknowledge my thanks to the wife of the late George Tertius Glover, who presented me with her husband's set of the S.M.C. *Journal* from which I obtained the information for this article.

Glover wrote to me long before I met him. A constant attender of S.M.C. meets from 1899 Glover got to know Munro as a friend. So George Glover, who was my friend, has been a stepping stone to a great figure of the past.

I am glad that I met some of the grand old men before they died, though Munro was not one of them. I was four years old when he passed on.

Sir Hugh Munro was busy re-classifying his table of Scottish mountains and their "Tops" when he died, and the present list, known as Munro's Tables, was prepared from his card index, and newly published Ordnance Survey Maps.

SPRING DIARY

Bowling Green with a Difference

The morning was sunny after overnight frost. Hills were reflected in the blue loch. How best to use such a day?

An idea crystallised as we sped up Loch Lomondside. Turn left at Tarbet, speed up the Rest-and-be-Thankful, and swing down Gleann Mor on the road that twists delightfully from 1,000ft. through oaks and birches to the finest fiord in the Southern Highlands, Loch Goil.

Here indeed is a rival to the big sea lochs of the north-west, even to a roadless hinterland. It was the rugged eastern shore rising in a spine of peaks fancifully known as Argyll's Bowling Green which held our interest, for they crown the narrow peninsula which separates Loch Goil from Loch Long. To strike on to them we merely parked the car in Lochgoilhead village, walked down the urbanised east shore, and struck off uphill where a forestry track angles off through tall spruces.

This resin-scented path meets a forest road, and at this point we struck directly uphill through larches to find a ridge leading us rightward into open hillside. And it was just as we were turning the trees we met a dog fox who froze long enough to give us a vivid impression of staring brown eyes in narrow grey face, coat shining red and yellow brush of tail outheld. Then in a sinuous bound he was into the wood, leaving us to the slope of Ben Reith rising in rock outcrops.

Exhilarating to get up 2,142ft. on the summit for a mighty view, below us the point of the peninsula separating the long and the forked lochs shafting into the Clyde estuary.

The hills of Arran, Ben Cruachan, Ben More in Mull, the solid rampart of peaks walling the neck between Loch Lomond and Loch Long—it was hard to know where to look!

Argyll's Bowling Green! How did such a piece of knobbly country, rugged even by Wester Ross standards, get such an undescriptive name?

It was nothing to do with some early duke's sense of humour, merely the corruption of a Gaelic name Buaile na Greine, which means the sunny cattle fold, a place where the dukes and duchesses used to rest their horses on Loch Longside after crossing from Lochgoilhead.

It was their route to their castle of Rosneath. In 1735 the map maker Carington Bowles applied the name to the whole peninsula, except that he showed it as Argyll's "Bowling Green."

And rough as that peninsula is, it was much traversed by cattle drovers coming from Loch Fyne by Hell's Glen to skirt Loch Goil, cross the ridge to Loch Long, and ferry their cattle across to Portincaple.

We descended north now to follow the wavering ridge with many ups and downs leading us to the top of Cnoc Coinnich, a mica schist summit of 2,497ft. offering nice wee scrambles if you felt inclined. It was the best place for deer, with a herd of over fifty stags and hinds.

We were nearing the home stretch now. All we had to do was drop down the narrow north-west ridge and hit the right-of-way path which descends by the Donich Burn and leads easily to Lochgoilhead.

Our walk had taken just over five hours. How nice if there had been a paddle steamer to take us back to Craigendoran, but that civilised way of travel finished a long time ago and we are the poorer for it.

Early Birds

"There's been more lion than lamb this month," said the farmer grimly. "Look at the hedges, everything's behind!"

Not quite everything. March 15 and 20 gave me the earliest dates for summer bird migrants I have yet recorded in Scotland—three sand martins on the 15th fluttering over the ponds like bats, picking the surface and finding microscopic food items, I hope. By the 18th their number had risen to seven, and I had discovered that a keen local observer had recorded his first sand martin on the 12th, and been flabbergasted by this unusually early arrival.

I was glad I had not heard of his observation at the time, or it would have weakened the thrill of my own discovery. The surprise of the 20th was finding the first of the warblers in my own garden. And not just one but two of them, chiff-chaffs advertising themselves in silvery reiterations of song which consists of two notes, chiff-chaff, chiff-chaff, chiff-chaff.

They sang against each other, and there was a territorial clash when one flew into the tree occupied by the other.

Conditions were windy, with fierce hail showers and sunny intervals, but they had chosen the sheltered foot of the slope above the burn. One is still singing as I write, so the energetic olive-green mite has kept alive on the pickings of bud and bark and any insects it can find.

The unanswered question is what brought these migrants here so early? It looks as if they are accidentals, birds that have been caught up in the big southerly winds and carried here before their time.

Last Sunday in the caller air which brought overnight snow I had another treat as I stood on the edge of a gully on a poster-colour world of glittering summits, blue loch, brown islands, and green shores.

Out of the wind the sun felt warm and my eyes were idling when a bird shot over my shoulder and disappeared into the gulley. I could hear the feather scuffles of a chase. Then out of the gully flew a slim bird, pearly grey on the mantle, with ebony black wings and tail edged with white. And as if to show off, it perched on the topmost bough of the nearest tree displaying the black eye patch and hooked bill of a piratical great grey shrike.

We get these bold birds on Loch Lomondside from time to time, but they are always an event. Only once did I see an actual kill. The shrike was in a gorse bush when down it went to ground and rose again carrying

71

a wren in its bill, flying off with a tail of scolding chaffinches behind it.

A visit to the heronry gave a more accurate picture of just how backward the season was, since these early nesters usually have young in the nest by mid-March. This year we estimate they are a month behind normal, and instead of a coming and going of dozens of herons I found just half a dozen nests, only two of which held incubating birds.

But the unexpected could happen. Numbers might build up yet, for the heron has a protracted nesting season. It looks though, as if the weather has been hard on them.

Mull of Galloway

Bennan Head was in sunshine but we saw it through veils of rain as buffets of wind rocked the car.

Below us the waves were crashing on the rocks of Ballantrae Bay. Snug inside our tin box we could enjoy the rainbows. In Portpatrick at dusk I went off along the shore to examine a pinnacle and had a climb up it, enjoying the eerie feeling of seeking hand and footholds above the suck and slunge of the waves.

A rock traverse led me directly to the battlements of Dunskey Castle, pitch black within except for wee bits of glimmer easing through rents in the stonework. Lighthouses flashing from the Isle of Man and Northern Ireland heightened the lonely atmosphere of the place. With a shock I realised it was 10 p.m., time to get back to a good fire and supper.

Ah the mystery of the night. In the morning the ruins were just ruins, but chuckling with jackdaws, darting impishly past me with moustaches of nesting material. Fulmar petrels sat on rock ledges, tube-nose to tube-nose. Who would suspect that such large-eyed, gentle looking birds would squirt you with evil oil at nesting time if you disturbed their peace? Celandines like gold coins shone on the ground.

The benign day of bright sun, soft breeze, and rich colour on the red ploughland sent me thinking of the Mull of Galloway, so off we went inland on the wee roads that serve the farms on a softly undulating headland that is seldom more than two miles broad.

What a place for Ayrshire cows! But the farms come to an end as you reach East and West Tarbet where the leg of land narrows to an ankle with no more than a projecting toe beyond, on which sits the pencil stalk of the lighthouse.

Ringed by cliffs it feels as airy as Cape Wrath in the far north west though this is the farthest south. From the table-top edge of the bowling green turf the rocks plunge to the sea, and almost involuntarily you draw back as bursting waves explode and shoot spray high up a face dizzy with the blizzarding wings of kittiwakes screaming their names in neurotic chorus.

These most oceanic of gulls will master-build their nests of grass and perch them just out of reach of the sea above an echo chamber of caves and overhangs.

Honour compelled me to rock-climb down to them and stand as near as I dared to birds and bursting sea. It was not bravery. I was merely proving to myself that I wasn't frightened of the place, which I was. But its effect was stimulating. It made me feel so good once I was up on top enjoying the sights of gannets wheeling and plummeting into the sea one after another.

Loch Lomond Birds

Here I am, seated comfortably in the shelter of the drystane dyke, enjoying the warmth of the sun and the buzz of the bumble bees dusting themselves with yellow pollen from the scented willow catkins.

Gnats dance in the air above the whins, and along the wall from me a cock stonechat in splendid black cap, white collar, and pink breast pretends to be a flycatcher as he darts back and fore from the wall to snap insects out of the air. We are joined by his dowdy mate, then by a yellow hammer and a reed bunting which sit droopily and give out wheezing calls.

Behind me I can hear the woodblock-rattling of a pied woodpecker, the usual short burst lasting only a second, but it goes out three times per minute. After ten minutes I reckon it must be getting a sore head, since each "roll" is composed of eight to ten blows of the beak in quick succession.

High above my head is another maker of music by artificial means, a snipe whirling above in wild zig-zags and constantly changing direction on whirring wings. Climbing ever higher it suddenly goes into a diving glide, outer tail feathers stiffly spread to let the air twang through them, and floating down to me comes wind-borne vibrations of sound altering pitch with the dive.

Plenty is going on below. Two pairs of Canada geese fly over my head with trombone honks. These exotic birds will nest wild and produce young, and so shall some of the greylags which are flying around the woods in pairs, making noises of barnyard geese. Low cackling laughter comes from vivid black and white ducks flighting to the river to splash in and show off crimson bills and russet belly bands.

These are sheld duck which are rather special here on Loch Lomond. They nest in burrows below ground, sometimes as far as two miles from the water—which reduces the chance of breeding success.

Herons fly back and fore across the marsh, squawking in alarm at times as attacking carrion crows force them to take other flight lines to their nests. The big grey birds twist and turn, then glide smoothly on, stork-legs like long sticks behind them and necks folded to give them a pouched appearance. A loud squawk startles a couple of brown hares who collide comically with each other. A mute swan sits on eggs, but nine whooper swans are still with us on 16 April. It is time they flew off to Iceland.

As I rise to enter the wood a mistle thrush flies from its nesting tree. A wren ticks like a clock before bursting into ear-piercing song. A jay "rasps," and I notice that starlings have taken over the hole where the woodpecker raised a noisy brood. An outbreak of alarm calls sends my head up. The cause is a barred bird with longish tail and rounded wings—a sparrow hawk carrying small prey.

Galloway's Granite Hills

The granite of high Galloway is the biggest surprise of the Lowlands.

You don't expect a combination of the Trossachs and the Cairngorms in South-West Scotland, and it strikes you forcibly whether you come by Girvan on the Clyde or by the Cree from Newton-Stewart on the Solway.

Spring is earlier here than in the Highlands, and it was fine to see the butter-yellow of primroses and the shining gold of celandines holding their heads to the sun, crinkled green leaves contrasting cheerfully with the brown of withered bracken. Glen Trool Forest Park is the biggest in Scotland and you strike off the A714 at Bagrennan to reach its heart.

Park your car where the road ends at the Bruce Stone. Take a look around and you will see that I have not exaggerated the Highland character of this colourful place. Get your boots on and continue eastward on the farm-track through a natural avenue of oaks and birches to the cataract of the Gairland Burn.

For the best high-level walk in Galloway you strike up the west bank, following rock slabs and waterfalls to Loch Valley and Loch Neldricken.

Notice the words "Murder Hole" on the map, at the boggy western extremity of Loch Neldricken. It commemorates a fictitious act in a book called "The Raiders" written by the Galloway novelist S.R. Crockett.

Due north in a rough mile you come to Loch Enoch, highest in Galloway at 1,617ft, set in a real rock basin of smooth slabs spattered everywhere with nature's curling stones, blocks of rounded granite swept along by the glaciers and dumped on the edge of the ice-fall.

The loch was scooped to a depth of 127ft. and was the deepest in Galloway before Loch Doon was dammed for hydro-electricity.

The whole setting of Loch Enoch is impressive. Above you on the right are granite escarpments culminating on the knobbly peaks of Craignaw and the Dungeon. Due west is the hulk of the Merrick. Straight ahead above the north shore of the butterfly-shaped Loch Enoch is Mullwharcher, a lift of only 650ft. for the reward of standing on the most central of the pure granite peaks whose roots are in Loch Doon.

Alas, this very region of the most splendid scenery is where geologists hope to drill the hard rocks to test their suitability for the disposal of nuclear waste. Local people have been vociferous in opposition, disgusted at the very thought of processing radio-active waste at Windscale to dump unwanted residues in Scottish hills for safe-keeping.

They fear that if the Mullwharcher rock is found suitable it will be used, since Windscale is just across the Solway, and the threat of such use seems to them to have come nearer if Parliament gives the go-ahead for a £600m extension to Windscale to enable it to process nuclear waste imported from overseas countries as far away as Japan.

So get up there and enjoy the purity of high Galloway while you can. The best way home from Mullwharcher for a hill-man is south along the tops by Dungeon and the rocky top of Craignaw—my favourite—holding the broad ridge for a mile to come down by Cornarroch Strand, which is a miniature Lairig Ghru between Snibe Hill and Craiglee. Due west from there will take you back to the Gairland Burn foaming out of Loch Valley.

The round trip described is about twelve miles with some roughish walking but easy climbing. I included the top of the Merrick when I did it last time, but it is less interesting than the other summits. Red deer, wild goats, golden plover, ring ouzels, buzzards and merlins keep up the wild life interest.

Blairlogie and Dumyat

All the best wee hills in Lowland Scotland are volcanic necks, and none is more striking than Dumyat, rising abruptly above the most picturesque spot in the Ochils, Blairlogie, which is easy to miss by reason of the way it tucks itself under the crags.

From Stirling take the A91 past the Wallace Monument and the old-world village is only a mile and a half before you get to Menstrie.

I went by service bus the first time, hardly knowing what to expect; so my delight was all the greater when I had the feeling of stepping into another century the way the houses snuggled into the rocks connected by wee lanes and tracks.

Ironically enough the village was built for tourists 200 years ago when every one of the thirty houses lodged visitors who used to come to drink the milk from the goats which grazed on the rocks above the village.

Yes, Blairlogie was a famous goat-milk spa in the days when milk was considered beneficial in the treatment of tuberculosis. You can still see the goats' drinking trough in a village garden, and in former times Blairlogie Square was on the main road from Causewayhead to Dollar.

In my view the most interesting way to climb Dumyat is to turn right along that old road, go through the iron gate, then turn up the scree slope immediately to strike a leftward sheep-trod path passing behind the village in the direction of sixteenth century Blairlogie Castle, the highest inhabited house.

Now you have to cross a wee ravine in order to continue on your way up the glen which cuts hard right towards Dumyat, whose summit is out of sight until you get over the lip of the ridge above you. The feeling is of being in a narrow green corrie, and below you the perched houses of Blairlogie look like a Swiss village, yet just out there beyond it stretches some of the flattest land in Scotland where the Devon flows into the sluggish windings of the Forth below Alloa.

Bird life is good, jackdaws chuckling, kestrels hovering, wheatears bobbing, and it's a great place for yaffling woodpeckers sounding. You could branch off to a wee peak of 923ft. on your left for an impressive view down to Blairlogie and the campus of Stirling University before swinging right for the very definite top of rocky Dumyat 1,375ft.

From up there you see the Ochils for what they are, rolling uplands with gentle tops, ideal sheep country stretching east for nearly thirty miles and bounded by the A9 to the north. So you stand between the Highlands and the Lowlands enjoying a mighty panorama of peaks and plains, looking down on the Kincardine and Forth bridges.

No need to retrace your steps back. You have a choice of ways, you can have an adventurous descent by the Warlock Glen, whose sides are sheer rock, but the going is easy enough if you keep to the burn. Or you can strike east from Dumyat summit for Menstrie glen. I recommend the former though the final descent is down steepish screes and through prickly whins.

Make the Most of May

There are too few months of May in ones lifetime and no chance to be out and about should be lost while this one lasts.

Right now is a very special time in the Highlands, with winter snows still mantling the high tops while spring has brought the birds back to the nesting grounds.

To enjoy this fullness, nowhere is better than Loch Tulla, even if it means sitting at the wheel and resisting the joys of Loch Lomond by pushing on by Glen Falloch and Strath Fillan to Bridge of Orchy for a loch that most people notice only distantly from the Glencoe road.

Turn off left at Bridge of Orchy over the hump-backit brig and you are on the drove-road that carried the traffic before the new Glencoe road was opened in the '30s.

Now it is walkers country and no vehicle can be taken further than the Forest Lodge at Loch Tulla's western edge. My picture shows the setting, ancient Caledonian pines and pearly water reflecting the white peaks of the Black Mount.

But what it can't do is capture the joyous sounds of that still morning, the thrumming of snipe, the fluting of redshanks and curlews, the bubbling of blackcock, the crying of gulls, and the songs of skylarks.

How best to spend a perfect day like this? For me it had to be a walk to Ba Bridge to enjoy the resin scents of the pines and the singing of redpolls and siskins. Then the bareness of the high granite country.

The track climbs gently from 600 feet to 1,000 feet in four miles to Lochan Mhic Pheadair Ruaidh on the very western edge of Rannoch Moor, but the biggest corries in Scotland rise above you on your left in a snowy horseshoe of peaks, just the setting for a golden plover to be mournfully calling from the tussocks showing off its smart breeding dress of trim black waistcoat and gold-spotted back. No feeling of "Desert wide and wasted" here, but of life, with meadow pipits love flighting and stonechats "chipping."

Ba Bridge is just a mile beyond the lochan, spanning a wee red-granite gorge, and it's a grand lonely place for a picnic on the warm rock banks. I always have a wee walk in the corrie on an old track that follows the north side, for that big bowl has great atmosphere and I've seen golden eagles there a few times.

Once at Ba Bridge you have some nice alternative ways of finishing your day. If you can split the party, one lot could walk on north, and in another five miles come out at the Kingshouse Hotel road-end, to be picked up there by the others, who would go back by the way they came and drive round to unite with the party over some refreshments. I did that with my wife and sister not so long ago.

For the well-shod and fit who are good map-readers I recommend my own favourite way back to the car. From Ba Bridge push into the corrie for two miles following the river, then strike south at the nameless burn that comes down under the west ridge of Stob a' Choire Odhair.

You climb up the attractive little glen, cross the ridge at the lowest point, and in a short distance south, pick up the deer-stalkers path leading down the Allt Toag to a wee schoolhouse just over a mile from Loch Tulla. Enjoy yourselves.

Pied Flycatchers

I would call my cheery friend John a broth of a boy if he was not an OAP, for he has chosen to spend his retirement on a mountainside with a mile of treacherous loch to cross to reach the nearest road and neighbour.

Moreover, he had to ferry heavy building materials and do his own renovation of the cottage to make it habitable ten years ago. No postman comes to his door for the only way to his lonely house on foot is by tracks.

When I crossed the hill shoulder to meet him the other day he immediately took me on a wee tour of his nest boxes cunningly sited on tree trunks edging tumbling burns spouting white off the hill. This he has discovered is the kind of habitat favoured by pied flycatchers.

By living here he has unwittingly become an expert on a bird which is uncommon enough in Scotland to excite birdy folk. He put up the boxes to attract them.

But he resists the blandishments of serious ornithologists who would like him to catch his birds, put rings on their legs, examine the eggs, and study the young. He will have none of this because he regards the pied flycatchers as his guests, and he so respects their privacy that he won't even keek inside the boxes until they are finished with them.

Each spring John takes me to their locations, for the pleasure of hearing the sprightly cock birds sing their little jingles as they dart restlessly in the trees.

At close range the singer is a tiny beauty of black trimmed with white, whose hen is mainly inconspicuous brown. What they have in common is an ability to shoot like bullets from a distant branch straight into the nest, which makes them hard to pin-point. Unless you know the distinctive little song it is very easy to miss these birds.

They arrived at John's on the last day of April, together with the cuckoo, tree pipit, red-start, and willow warbler. "It's never happened before to see them and hear them all for the first time within an hour."

Few slopes in Scotland rise more steeply from the lochside than the ones above John's back door. They go up to a peak of over 3,000 ft., and next week John will be climbing to the top to celebrate his seventieth birthday. From his barn, occupied by nesting pied and grey wagtails at this moment, the route will be up the edge of a gorge to the rocks where the ring ousel nests and the purple saxifrage flowers. Then through a corrie beloved of red deer to the snow-patches which are the haunt of the ptarmigan.

John is the son of a farmer and his work as an engineer made him a city dweller until he came here. His old roots quickly re-emerged as he dug a garden, planted fruit trees, made a vegetable plot, and taught himself to be as independent as anyone in the kingdom.

He bakes his own bread, bottles his own rasps and gooseberries, brews his own beer, and can produce a very nice home-made wine. He has radio, but no television reception is possible, so he makes do with books.

Life is never dull for him for there are always mysteries to be unravelled. Who, for example, was stealing his mousetraps baited with carrot which he had set outside for short-tailed field voles. The thief was a stoat anxious to eat the vole that had been caught in the trap.

Voles have to be trapped or else he would have no vegetables. He has foiled the stoat by wedging the traps inside pieces of piping, so it has to catch its own now, which is all to the good for John.

John's Birthday Climb

Just last week I was out with my old batchelor friend John who wanted
to test himself by climbing Ben Lomond by its steepest side. He had even
baked himself an alcoholic fruit cake for the occasion by injecting sherry
into it with a syringe. And on top, picked out in almonds, were the figures
"70," for it was his seventieth birthday.

The route he chose was by the Cuilness ravine, up the edge of the
noblest woodland gorge known to me, then across a wide corrie to hit the
soaring north-west ridge.

On that perfect day the summit was crowded. More were arriving as
we stood on top, children holding the hands of parents, teenagers
cavorting about full of the joys, mature climbers lolling in the sun beside
their discarded shirts and boots.

We had seen nobody on our side of the mountain. John had felt certain
he could make it by the hard way. He didn't relish the descent. "The
jolting gets my back," he complained.

His delight was all the greater therefore when he hardly felt a thing,
and didn't even have a twinge of stiffness next day. Great to be young at
heart, but adventurers tend to be like that.

John's outdoor career began with scouting, and no doubt an armful of
badges showing competence in a range of skills he has never forgotten.
He had absolutely no doubt of the profound importance scouting played
in his positive attitude to life through the deep enjoyment of the outdoors
and the lasting friendships resulting.

Adventure-scouting is the name of the game today. Education depart-
ments carry on the same principles from outdoor pursuit centres.
Commercial organisations offering adventure holidays provide a specia-
lised product to those wanting to widen the scope of their own lives into
adventure.

As a leader I have been drawn into this net myself, sometimes
voluntarily, sometimes as a paid servant. I have never done it as a way of
life.

What I do know is that it has done me good to go out with folk lacking
experience or initiative to take on the outdoors by themselves.

The first time was about eighteen years ago, when a climbing leader on
an "endeavour" course failed to turn up and I took his boys up the
Cobbler.

They were industrial apprentices from the Midlands, and one of them
was clearly a misfit, withdrawn, and expressionless. He had no boots,
only stout shoes with hobnails.

None of my three apprentices had any previous experience of
mountains. I roped them up for the South Peak and watched with interest
the face of that dull boy become alight with pleasure. Where the others
were finding it difficult and clinging to the rock like limpets, he held his

body out in perfect balance and moved with the rhythm of a natural climber.

Down on the col I suggested we do the arete and handed over the lead to him, saying: "I think your father must have been a cat burglar."

The calculated risk I took in giving him responsibilty of the lead was amply justified when he wrote to me afterwards enthusing over the climb and saying it had been the most marvellous day of his life. Maybe it was the first time in his life he had found something in which he excelled, and something challenging and exciting at that.

Adventure leaders cannot hope to make skilled performers of their charges in the brief time of a course. What they can do is stimulate interest in the pursuit and point the way ahead for those with the urge.

I remember speaking about the nature of challenge to Commander Victor Clark aboard his adventure ship *Captain Scott.*

He told me: "You meet it positively or negatively. Accept it and you take on your mountain whether the challenge be Ben Nevis or Mount Everest. Refuse it and you are shrinking away from it.

"In the twenty-six days that each of our courses run we aim to show that there is no such thing as 'I can't'. Out of thousands of young men I have only met one in eleven years as Master who was not prepared to try to overcome his fear of going up the rigging of this sailing schooner. I ordered him off the ship."

Sorrowfully, however, the *Captain Scott* ran out of money and had to be sold. But you can have an equivalent challenge a lot nearer to the waves —in a canoe—demanding every resource of judgment and skill, especially if you aspire towards the tide races and skerries of the Hebrides.

Think of timing your arrival to go through the whirlpool of Corrievreckan on the slack, or setting off in the Atlantic swell for distant St. Kilda. Yachtsmen know that Scotland offers as challenging sailing as anywhere in the world.

Whatever your sport, be it sea-angling, hang-gliding, climbing, ski-ing, water ski-ing, slalom canoeing, or fishing the high lochs and burns for trout, the opportunity is there, if you want it, right here at home.

May Birds

May is the month for bird song on Loch Lomondside, especially on a glass-calm morning with reflections of the last snow-patches on Ben Lomond, in a terrain of frothing white blackthorn blossom, yellow whins, oaks, birches, and marshlands.

I was feeling cock-a-hoop, for I had just found a singing blackcap in my garden. In front of me now were sedge warblers and whitethroats, showing themselves occasionally when, carried away by their spluttering songs, they shot vertically into the air to come singing down. And on my

Early days on the hills. Tom Weir (left) and Matt Forrester, 1933. *(Photo: A. Hamilton)*

West from Balmaha to the Luss Hills, Loch Lomond.

On the wild Craigroyston shore of Loch Lomond. Ben Lui in the distance.

Tom Weir (left) and Lakeland climber Frank Nelson in Skye, 1936.

Matt Forrester cooks breakfast on the Craigroyston shore, 1955.

The summit of An Teallach above Loch Toll and Lochan.

On the narrow crest of pinnacled An Teallach.

Tom Weir on Doune Hill of the Luss group, Loch Lomond.

The Head of Loch Hourn in Knoydart.

Iain Smart, companion on many a jaunt, on the Black Pinnacle of Braeriach.

Remote Loch Avon between Cairngorm and Ben Macdhui.

Mid-winter in Glencoe. The high peak is Stob Coire nan Lochan.

Loch Tulla and the peaks of the Black Mount, January 1980.

Early morning on Braeriach. Frank Nelson enjoys the forest mists in the valleys below Lochnagar.

Seton Gordon at the age of ninety, photographed at his home in Skye shortly before his death. On the left are some of the books he wrote.

Seton Gordon at Uig in Skye with another golden eagle enthusiast, John Murray, former taxidermist at the Royal Scottish Museum.

Blairlogie and the peak of Dumyat in the Ochils.

Meall a' Bhuridh at the top of the ski-tow on a day of crisp visibility when Ben Nevis and its neighbours stood out icily against a clear sky.

The run down Happy Valley from the top of Meall a' Bhuridh, superb conditions.

Remotest Scotland. Looking down from A' Mhaighdean on the swirling mist over the Fionn Loch, Wester Ross.

Red deer hind and calf a few days old. Wester Ross, June.

Glen Affric pinewoods, wooded habitat natural to red deer.

Red deer stag in velvet, July.

April on Ben Nevis. Note the two climbers on Tower Ridge, right of centre.

The Auld Wives' Lifts. Tom Weir shows the scale. Note the sculptured head (inset).

Gannet with young, July.

Gannets wheel over the cliffs of St. Kilda. Behind rise the great rock stacks where they nest.

Border country. Delightful hill walking at Broughton, Peebleshire, where the river Tweed flows.

Dunnet Head, the most northerly point of the British mainland, photographed from a trawler.

Ardnamurchan Point, most westerly point of the British mainland, where Atlantic waves pound the rocky shore.

right, as if to show how it should be done, a tree pipit was rising high above its perch on a beech tree to come diving and giding in a cascade of melody ending in "tree-tree-tree."

I go over to the wood but the welter of song bewilders the ear. No problem about the cuckoo, or the squealing laughter of a green woodpecker. By concentrating I sort out the stutter of wood warbler, the jangle of a red start, that mixed-up sweetness of marvellous variety is coming from greenfinch and goldfinch. Cutting across it is the mew of a buzzard, and the broad winged bird swings into view with a swearing carrion crow tumbling after it.

A thrush dives into a holly bush and I see it has eggs in the nest. A tree creeper's needly sound leads my eye to a branch with a crack in it, and I am just in time to watch the final part of the climb, as a head pops out of the crack and takes the beakful of insects in a quick snatch.

Different sounds on the marsh among the snipe and redshank. Shrill whistles everywhere, but I think I can hear something else. It could be imagination for I have been listening out for it for a while. Now there it is, unmistakable, the thin reeling of a grasshopper warbler, more like the music of an insect than a bird.

The skulker is a ventriloquist which will "reel" for minutes at a time, but you don't know where to look. And when you see it—a little brown job—you see that it turns its head perpetually to send its grasshopper notes in every direction.

Listening to it I am diverted by the shivering seven-note whistle of the "May Bird", the staccato phrase 1,2,3,4,5,6,7 is repeated again and again, each note exactly the same as the other. Without the whistle you would take it for a curlew. They pass through here on their way northward, mostly to Scandinavia, like the white wagtails which are fly-catching on the sandy shore.

I go down there and glass the water hoping for an osprey. We get them fishing here from time to time. No luck, only familiar things, cormorants, red breasted mergansers, shelduck, wigeon, mallard, shoveller, goldeneye duck and tufted duck, greater black backed gulls. Then I notice that only a few feet from me are three warm brown wading birds that seem to have no heads—three dunlin having a nap.

I try to see how close I can get before they wake up. Out pops a longish curved bill as I get to eight feet. We survey each other and it utters an alarm "scape" with immediate effect on the others. A short shuffle forward, and they give me a grand chance to admire their splendid breeding dress of jet black below and warm brown above flecked with buff.

But instead of taking alarm they begin to display, one goes up on shivering wings to come gliding down again with a series of trembling vibrating sounds impossible to describe, but joyous to hear.

St Kilda

I'm writing about St Kilda and thinking it is just twenty years ago this May since I sailed there across forty-five miles of storm-tossed ocean in a pitching landing barge with provisions and equipment for the 5004 Airfield Construction Squadron who had been on the island since 16 April.

Their task was to establish a beach-head and build a road to enable wheeled vehicles to operate there for the first time.

Groggily I tottered ashore on a storm beach where soaking men in denims were gathering boulders to feed into noisy stone crushers. Below the drab misty cirque of hill a village of tents stood near the church manse. "Weather. No wonder the islanders left!" was a general opinion of those working a thirteen-hour-day with pick and shovel. In the previous three weeks tents had been hurled down and Atlantic breakers had undone yards of work on the beach-head.

How different it all was from my memory of St Kilda when it was a desert island, when ten of us had pooled our money to hire a fishing boat from Tarbert, landing with provisions for a three-week stay. Vegetation then was brilliant green. The sea was Mediterranean blue, and the sun hardly stopped shining.

Hirta was very much as its people had left it in 1930, except for the decay of the houses by weathering. We were there to study its wild life, and at sunset took our sleeping bags to Carn Mor to lie out waiting for the arrival of the shearwaters and listen for the purring notes of Leach's and stormy petrels. Dawn brought us spectacular fly-pasts of puffins—thousands of them.

That May visit was notable for birds in a different way, migrants making landfall on their long flights to the Arctic. Research ornithologist Kenneth Williamson was in residence, and we had exciting times netting whimbrels, Icelandic wheatears, pipits, white wagtails, redwings, corncrakes, snipe, etc. After three weeks I felt I had St Kilda out of my system, and resisted later invitations to go back.

Then came the chance of a flight to the islands from Plockton in a small Piper Aztec. Within minutes of being airborne it was magic, playing tag among the clouds swirling round the Cuillins, and trying to recognise fragments of ridge I have scrambled over.

Clear of the peaks we were in the sun and ahead stretched the Long Island. It was all too sudden, lochs of South Uist, causeways of Benbecula, the sands of the Monarchs—ten hours by landing craft reduced to twenty minutes by air. Before my eyes, unbelievably close were these islands that haunt the imagination—St Kilda.

"We'll go in close," came the pilot's voice over the intercom. "Get yourselves ready for photography in the tail. It'll be bumpy over the stacks. Watch your nose on the perspex."

Then it all happened. A pointed top like the Matterhorn came rushing up to meet me, but the snow was gannets, thousands of them. No time to register Stac Lee for the 600ft. pinnacle of Stac an Armin gas rising from the bursting spume, gannets pouring from it like spindrift. Then up we rose over the top to Boreray, pinnacles plunging 1,000ft. into the sea. What a thrill to be a St Kildan poised to leap from a heaving boat to lodge on the stack and climb it to harvest gannets for the pot.

By comparison to that, Village Bay on Hirta was anti-climax. It was interesting to see the finished road climbing up to the big white egg of the radar station perched on the roof of the island, and see the garrison buildings and new pier beside the old manse.

Below me were buildings housing some of the most sophisticated gadgetry in the world for tracking destructive weapons, and close to them bee-hive houses built by the first men who came here 1,000 years ago, perhaps bringing with them the Soay sheep. These animals which have been described as "living fossils" still roam the garrison fields.

Stepping Out on Border Hills

It's a holiday weekend in Glasgow. How to make the most of it? For the cost of a telephone call to the Weather Centre you can get a fairly true idea of where to go if you want the best weather. So where better than the Border hills if the forecast is bad in the north and good in the south, as often happens in May.

In fact, you can keep a lot of options open if you drive by the Clyde Valley taking the low road to Lanark beyond Hamilton for a look at the orchard country which gets more and more lush every day. The plum blossom is in bud and should be bursting white about a week from now so don't miss it while it lasts.

Meanwhile, the destination is Carstairs for Peebles with Tinto on your right and an ever-upland landscape of smooth sheep hills spaciously wide as you leave the Clyde for the Tweed. With the trim town of Peebles behind you the destination is Melrose, signposted by the triple peaks of the Eildons, so loved by Sir Walter Scott.

For an enjoyable traverse of these knobbly little tops you don't even need a map for the route begins at Melrose railway station car park. Step on to the hill, whose lower slope is a golf course, and you are on your way, with a flying start of 400ft. above sea-level and less than a 1,000ft. to climb. You will want to do more than this, however, if you traverse the three tops.

So begin with North Eildon, height 1,327ft. and, only a mile distant, turfy, easy walking, with red grouse in the heather higher up. Notice how the top, just before it narrows, has what looks like an overgrown field dyke all the way round it.

That dyke was the outer defence of a prehistoric fort, protecting a village on its top side. You can see the flat village on the eastern side before the final rise to the summit. Archaeologists tell us that 300 houses were built inside that hilltop fort at a troubled time when it was safer to sleep up there than be an easy target for your enemies down below.

What a command of the Vale of Tweed you get from the top, rolling country stretching to Cheviot and across to Gala and Lauderdale! You can sort out the topographical puzzle on the centre peak, for there is a summit indicator, and you can have great fun pin-pointing the villages dotted around and the hills and woods of a gentle landscape.

Don't call a halt there. Follow the ridge to the third of the Eildons, 1,216ft. and not much of a rise from the col. Having done the traverse you realise what a neat little world of its own the volcanic rise of the Eildons makes, totally different from anything around. But you needn't finish there just yet.

Look west and you will notice a wee loch below, and beyond it Cauldshiels Hill, only 1,076ft., two miles from where you stand and reached by sheep tracks across Bowden Moor, easy going and very little climbing for an attractive summit whose rocky outcrop is crowned by the ring of another ancient fort. The Borders were aye a troubled place.

Your way home is down to Cauldshiels Loch whose small track brings you out on an old drove road. Turn right, and right again at the first junction and you are on a minor road to Darnick, with Melrose a mile east along the disused railway track. Four hours is plenty for this little outing, which gives you time to stroll round the finest of the Border abbeys before you drive home.

Something for Everybody

What luck to get the finest day of the year on a special Monday holiday in May.

I was glad not to be driving any farther than across the Erskine Bridge for Johnstone and the A737, to turn off on the Lochwinnoch road. I was looking for a new object on the landscape, a 30ft. tower built of Norwegian timber. And there it was with the Royal Society for the Protection of Birds' sign, and some weel-kent faces standing outside it. For this was its official opening, and it was many a year since I had been at the Barr Loch.

From the top of the tower you can really appreciate the character of this birdy bit of country of reed beds and water, bespeckled with little islets. Straight out in front was a swan on its nest, and beyond it a cormorant like a gargoyle perched on a branch, with tufted duck and great crested grebes swimming beyond it. The reeling of grasshopper warblers and the cry of a tern mingled with gull and wader sounds.

An attractive path goes along the reedy shore of the Aird Meadows, to low-set timber hides, ideal for viewing the water birds. You'll enjoy a look at the displays in the Nature Centre—good for a wet day.

I was specially interested in the Barr Loch, which in older maps is shown not as a loch but as an extensive marsh a mile long by half a mile wide, reckoned at one time to be the main stronghold in Europe of the water rail and grasshopper warbler, according to Dr J.A. Gibson. The intention now, when funds permit is to drain away the water and restore this largest marsh in the West of Scotland.

There is limited scope for walking here, so after an hour or two I moved across to Castle Semple Water Park for a chat to the rangers who help the visitors to enjoy the surroundings and keep an eye open for conoeists or dinghy sailors in trouble.

This was my first contact with the Clyde Muirshiel Regional Park which in time will extend from here right over to the Clyde when access agreements with the landowners are finalised.

I was in luck again. A new bit called Parkhall Wood had just been acquired and I was invited to take a stravaig over it by supervisory ranger Terry Robinson, ex-Royal Marine, water sport expert, and parachutist. Working hours never bother him because he loves the place, and Parkhall in particular. Along the lochside for a quarter of a mile, we struck north over the disused railway to delightfully open deciduous woodland on the flanks of a wee glen.

Then turning east we came to the sixteenth century ruins of Castle Semple Collegiate Church, with grey tower and walls still upstanding. But the old ice-houses nearby interested me more.

Out to the edge of the Black Cart we climbed back by a ridge giving fine views over the loch and the soft green hills which hem it. From the car park you can walk to the top of Windy Hill in an hour, a climb of 1,000ft., visit a waterfall on the Calder, or find yourself a picnic spot.

By the Bonnie Banks of Clyde

Ask me to describe the loveliest views in the orchard country of Clydesdale and I'd tell you about the stretch from Crossford to Hazelbank, and that the best way of enjoying them is to leave the road, get over to the east side of the river, and follow the tracks which run high along that side.

You are walking through a man-made landscape under the Braes of Nemphlar, and if you are a gardener you will marvel at the intensive use the small farmers make of their ground with plums, pears, apples, gooseberries, red and black currants, rasps, strawberries, vegetables, lettuces, tomatoes, and flowers all crowded into their few acres. They say it was the Monks from Lesmahagow who brought fruit farming here in the eighth century and made it the garden of Scotland.

There is so much to enjoy, with scents and bird sounds, that you hardly notice you are covering the ground until you hit the white square of a power station, Stonebyres. Now the Clyde is more of a racing river, challenging to canoeists, though the Linn has been tamed by electricity workings. You continue by crossing the Clyde by the weir, with permission from the power-house attendants.

Kirkfieldbank lies ahead, and when you get there you have walked about four miles and a wee bittock. From this hub of the valley where the Clyde runs under two bridges, New Lanark is only a mile ahead. Once it was the biggest tourist attraction in Scotland. People came from all the airts to see the very first industrial estate, a cotton mill using the water power of the Clyde falls and Arkwright's spinning frame which achieved a record in productivity—in the late eighteenth century.

Stroll through the village which employed a thousand people, housed them, paid them wages above the normal for the time, and introduced nursery schools and evening classes. David Dale and his son-in-law Robert Owens were justly famous as reformers and social experimenters.

From the far end of the village you keep by the river and follow the track climbing alongside the big pipes which descend to the power station. Up there you look down on Corra Linn, though it is hard to believe that the slim waterfall echoing up from the sheer rocks is the Clyde.

The narrow path continues along the unfenced edge of a canyon plunging 100ft. to the river, an edge which was a natural flower garden of white wood anemonies, violets, celandinès, and yellow kingcups when I was there.

Bonnington Linn lies at the farthest reach of the walk, where the river makes a sharp right angle and would plunge over a considerable cataract were it not for the pipes which swallow it and lead it to the powerhouse by another route.

From up there you look to the cone of Tinto, dominating the heathery uplands of Lanarkshire where the Clyde has its source.

I recommend the walk to the topmost linn, because there is a footbridge for crossing to the other side and you can return to Kirkfieldbank by Corehouse for a new look at the Gorges of the Clyde.

On the Braes of Balquhidder

May had never been merrier, and I had been making the most of it.

Certainly I never saw Callander look better than on the morning I met Pat for a day on the hills with the crags rising over the town in a feast of colour, grey rocks, red bracken, the flourish in white blossom, and the new leaves of beech, oak, birch, and rowan every shade of delicate green.

Pat, shanked in the kilt and wearing his tackety boots, was ready for anything, but like me he favours a combination of attractive glen and rocky hilltop rather than sterile moorland. A glance at the map decided us on Leum an Eireannaich, 1,800ft. up in the hills between Balquhidder village on Loch Voil, and Luib in Glen Dochart.

This is an ancient hill-pass which was a main route before there were any roads. And in the days of the old Oban railway it made a perfect walk. You got off the train at Strathyre Station, kept to the west side of the River Balvaig for Balquhidder, climbed up the Kirkton Glen to the bealach, descended easily over the other side, and caught the train at Luib Station for the run back to Glasgow.

But times have changed as you see at Loch Lubnaig, where everything is organised for the motorist—landscaped laybys, picnic spots, and a new timber-built information centre with free literature by the Forestry Commission to enable you to enjoy the paths and woods. Our intended walk was listed, I noticed, as "fairly strenuous, on forest and hill path from Balquhidder climbing to 1,800ft."

The commission suggest that you take the signposted path from the old kirkyard where Rob Roy is buried, and advise that if you go right over the pass, make sure you have arrangements made to be picked up on the other side.

Pat, who knows this country well had a better idea, and led me a mile west of the village to a steep open hillside flanked by the deep cut of the Tulloch Burn edged in a fragrance of birch leaves. And as we went up the edge enjoying the flash of waterfalls and a silver of bird song, down the steep face came a pair of shepherds bearing in front of them a cascade of ewes and silky white lambs—an idyllic scene—given a feeling of timelessness by the stabbing notes of a cuckoo endlessly calling its liquid name.

We kept climbing, enjoying this open hillside in preference to the normal pass of the Kirkton Glen where you are enclosed in gloomy spruce trees for all of two miles. Up there Pat took me to a secret spot where a waterfall sprayed out over a bulge, and behind it was a cave. Splashing in I found a delightful lookout through the sparkling water curtain.

Above it were the cattle grazing grounds of long ago, with the ruins of summer shielings, relics of cheese-making times when the clansfolk moved up there in the summer.

The old track we followed led us to where these folk, long gone, cut their peats, and on the moss we were among red deer, black as buffalos from wallowing in the wet dubs to cool off. We were high now, and climbing north-westwards. At 2,000ft. we had sight of a long-winged hawk elegantly buoyant as it crossed in front of us, a hen harrier.

From the crest of the ridge there was a fine impression of the wild west of Balquhidder, its most shapely peak Stobinnein, still considerably snow-patched at 3,812ft. The Gaelic name meaning "Anvil Peak" neatly describes the way its narrow top is sliced flat.

But we had no eyes for it when in a step or two the ground fell away, and across the gap rose the great rock face of the "Irishman's Leap"—a beetling nose overhanging the oval of a grey lochan.

We were on the crest of the pass, enjoying the magic of the place, and the reward of remoteness and everything that goes with it, grandeur, tranquility, verticality, roughness. Even the boulder by the loch shore which rock climbers call Rob Roy's Putting Stone is 40ft. high and has no easy route to the top.

Yet Balquhidder is only two-and-a-half miles below, and a very short descent down the corrie path leads you to the forestry track twisting down through the big spruce trees. There is a great moment when the pointed crag of the "Leum" towers over the feathery tips of the forest, looking like something out of the Dolomites. We had been gone only four hours and our faces were burned red by the sun.

Gigha

Here I am on *Gigha,* God's Island—most accessible of the Hebrides, if you have a motor car.

From Balloch you can be at Tayinloan in two-and-a-half hours, and if you time yourself to catch the ferry you will be across the water inside another half hour. But why rush in the kind of weather we have been having and with a Jubilee holiday to celebrate? Why indeed with scents of bluebells and May blossom coming in the open windows and brilliant tree colours wherever you look. The sweet of the year was never sweeter.

Small islands have special delights. Gigha is only six miles long by one-and-a-half miles wide. Only three miles separates it from the mainland but it is immediately Hebridean, terns splashing or flickering above you, swallow-tails spread; gannets wheeling and crash-diving, eider drakes bobbing and coo-ing like pigeons, oyster catchers, redshanks and peewits wherever you look.

Hire a bike, free-wheel north along the narrow road and the fertility hits you in the greenness of the fields and the profusion of flowers in the ditches. On every ridge the whins make a tide of yellow. Bird song fills the air. Within half an hour of landing I was heading north for Tarbert, which suggests a neck of land between two lochs. So it is. Here the island is nearly cut in two by opposing bays.

I choose west for the sake of the rocky scramble northwards, and dumping the bike, traverse through spikes of yellow iris to the little rock skerries where the terns nest and everywhere around me are sprays of seapink framing the view across to the Paps of Jura. But the place I am making for is *Eilean Garbh,* Rough Island.

It is not really an island, nor is the little strip of silver sand leading to it a tidal strand. But the island is certainly rough, and if you are agile and keep to the shore you are in for a lot of fun on big boulders and little pinnacles where black guillemots perch like tiny red-legged penguins. Great to rest among the ox-eye daisies and look down into the clear green Atlantic on reptilean cormorants and shags fishing.

Not so good is the clamour of the herring and lesser blackbacked gulls in a storm of protest over a pair of islanders raiding their nest for eggs. The seapinks here are marvellous, growing from rocks Picasso-yellow with crotal. Violets grow among white scurvy grass. Ledges of clean bare rock above the sea invite traverses and give exciting little climbs.

The highest hill on Gigha is Creag Bhan, a mere 331ft., a spine of ice-scored rock projecting above the rampant whins. Small of stature, the view is wide, to Ireland, Islay, Jura and Kintyre. On its east side the Vikings anchored their fleet, and they named the island Gudey, which is the old Norse for Good Island. From up there you see how good it is, with fields which the farmers say are as fertile as any in Scotland, giving milk rich in cream for the making of cheese which is the mainstay of its 180 inhabitants.

And, of course, there is the garden created by Sir James Horrlick, fifty acres of brilliance showing what can be done when money, creative imagination, botanical skill, and the soft Atlantic climate come together. Most day visitors to Gigha seldom go beyond the gardens.

Hire a bike and you will find that the island is just as marvellous as the garden.

Twixt Loch Etive and Loch Tulla

It was fine to abandon the car, shoulder weekend packs, and step off the road end into a trackless glen in the wilds of the Black Mount between Loch Tulla and Loch Etive.

It was 7.30 p.m. on one recent flawless evening, and we had four climbing miles ahead of us to reach the badger sett under the rock where a golden eagle has an eyrie, and where the dawn chorus is from wheatear, ring ouzel, and meadow pipit.

Rucksacks were trimmed to a minimum. Tent, light sleeping bag, gas stove, and food for twenty-four hours. No change of clothing when high pressure was still being forecast. No midges or clegs to worry us either, as we worked our way along a burnside with grey wagtails, yellow as canaries on flanks and underparts, tempting us to watch their elegance as they danced on the boulders.

A family of young dippers—water ouzels—spurted ahead of us trying to imitate their swerving parent. Under a tussock was a pipit's nest with two eggs, revealed when it darted from under my boot.

Even more exciting was the arrival of a sharp-winged arrow of a bird with grey wings and flashing white rump. "Whoosh," and it just about lifted the sun-hat off my head as it dive-bombed us again and again, giving out loud triple cries—a greenshank, joined by its mate.

Landing near us they kept up a shrill piping. "Yes, we know you have young." I said, as we moved off into the territory of a wailing golden plover running ahead of us from one tussock to another to lead us away from its hidden chicks.

The crag we were heading for was getting nearer and already we could scent the fragrance of white rowan blossom flourishing on its ledges. That scent gave us more than aesthetic pleasure for it meant that the breeze was strong and blowing directly from the badger's sett to us. Even so I hardly expected to find a badger already outside the sett at 9 p.m., before the sun was off the slope.

It was having a snooze outside one of the holes which lead below the ruins of a summer shieling. I could have stalked it with the camera, but preferred to sink down and watch it turn its tummy to the sky, wave its short legs in the air, and wriggle its back energetically on the ground like a big grey terrier scratching its back.

It was restless, turning on its left, then its right side, before sitting up and shuffling towards where we sat, 100 yards away.

With binoculars trained you could appreciate every subtle detail of colour and shape in the rich flood of sunset—the striped face, white from pig-snout to forehead, flanked by jet-black, ending in white tips of ears, the dark trousers of the incredibly short legs setting off the grey back which is as long as that of an Alsation dog.

Ambling with that curious hunch-backed motion it turned to a pile of grass, yellow as hay, and treated us to a show of how it gets its bedding underground as it rolled up big tufts to tuck under its chin, press the bundle against the chest, and back into the hole with it in the first of a few journeys.

By the time we pitched the tent it had gone off to hunt with various members of its clan which had emerged from other holes in the base of the shieling. We could hear them mumbling gruffly as we lit the gas stove and lay back well content to wait for the water to boil.

The badgers were having worms but we were having soup—out of a packet.

Deer Forest Delight

It was marvellous to be away from main roads and traffic sounds.

First, badgers before supper in the high camp and now I came to wakefulness with the chuckling sounds of a wheatear. Even as I listened to the gritty sound there came the "whee-whee-wheee" of a ring ouzel—the mountain blackbird which has a white collar on its neck. But it was a thin coughing, clearing of the throat, just through the tent fabric at ear level, which sent my head peeping out. It was a tiny spotted red deer calf tottering to join its mother about twenty yards down-slope.

It was then I became aware of the quality of the morning, for although the tent was still in shadow, the whole corrie was a bowl of golden light dotted with feeding deer, truly red in the sunrise.

The drift of the beasts was towards the enclosing ridge, which was perfect, for while they were making their leisurely way into the next corrie we could have breakfast and explore the birches and Caledonian pines growing high across the opposite burn.

In a treeless country, it was the kind of oasis where you expect to find a few willow warblers, chaffinches, goldcrests, tits, hoodie crows, and the like. Everything was as I expected, except a thin unbird-like squeaking coming from some thick undergrowth.

The maker of the sound was a roe deer fawn, no bigger than a hare, trembling with effort as it tried to stand upright. What a little beauty it was, brown coated with yellow spots, and big dark eyes that matched its lump-of-coal nose.

I left it in peace hoping its mother was well and would come back soon. The fawn should not have been squeaking but lying curled up and absolutely still. Then neither I nor any other creature would have been likely to see it.

A golden eagle came flapping and sailing above the ridge as we climbed back to the tent. It looked big, until it was joined by the female, when it looked small by comparison. They soared above an eyrie which, the first time I visited it, held two fox cubs, a leg of lamb, and a grouse, beside a white chick just beginning to sprout black feathers.

This time I didn't look to see if the eyrie was occupied, not having applied for a permit to do so. We climbed past it, and on the crag top sat looking down on lonely Loch Dochard and across to the pink rocks of Ben Starav and the snowy point of *Stob Coire Albannach,* The Highlandman's Peak.

Cautiously we went over the lip and looked into the corrie of the deer. The wind was still in our favour and at a suitable distance, binoculars to eyes, we could sweep across the hundred and more feeding animals, slim hinds, quite unaware of our presence, some with spotted calves keeping close to their mothers as if attached by invisible threads. Others were seeking below for the milk bar.

Young stags with small antlers of shiny bone were feeding with the hinds. They are always slow to cast. The adults which had dropped theirs in April now sported handlebars of new growth covered in the rough brown of "velvet." The adult stags were lower down the corrie, among the peathags, lying in the moist dubs to keep cool, presumably. Come late July the antlers will be fully grown and the velvet rubbed off.

Blackcock Lek

Who wants to go to bed on one of the longest days of the year, when the fiery red in the north-west has banished darkness and the broad mirror of Loch Lomond is suffused with pink?

Ben Lomond is cut in ebony above the grey islands and I am thinking of a blackcock lek where I can put down a tent, have a catnap, and let the birds wake me up with a noisy dance.

A short drive, ending with four miles of rough road, and I am at the place. A woodcock is flying around like a bat, and a grasshopper warbler is loudly reeling as I pitch the tent.

I doze, and seem hardly to have shut my eyes before there is a thump on the tent canvas and a rattle of whistling wings. Turning on my side as silently as possible, I peer out and note that within easy vision I have a dozen or so plump shapes.

The fun begins with a few cat-like whimperings. Then almost as if an engine has been switched on, I am surrounded by a rhythm of vibrant rookooing sound, which I can only describe as a pulsation of blackcock. Excitement is mounting. The noise is now punctuated by violent sneezes, tushoos, the sign for battle.

Great—the light has strengthened enough to see the whole neurotic show. Cocks stand face to face, hopping as if on hot bricks, necks swollen, and stretched aggressively towards each other, the wings poked out from the body like little arms, white tail feathers standing up straight in the form of a fan.

Back and fore they sway, bubbling, making the cat-like whimper, advancing and retreating like boxers preparing to deliver a punch. The sneeze results in action. Heads clash; wings beat; red wattles over the eyes bristle. Partners change and the whole thing looks like a weird dance.

But I have seen nothing yet. Suddenly, as if at the touch of a button, a wild skirmish breaks out as blackcock criss-cross each other's tracks. Birds get bowled over. Beaks clash; claws meet; feathers fly. The excitement is due to two delicately stepping females who have moved in as if to watch.

I have the good luck to see how mate selection is made. The hen initiates it, perambulating the lek, but never standing long enough on one spot to give anyone ideas. Then she circles a particular cock, causing him to almost burst with vibrating satisfaction, wings quivering in a kind of St Vitus's dance affecting his whole body.

The excitement seems to communicate itself to the hen who twitches her neck with sharp jerks and crouches down from time to time, but jerks up again every time the cock bird thinks his moment has come. Then when the two birds are almost touching the cock shoots away about twenty feet, pirouetting gracefully to come back at the same speed, this time to be rewarded by a willing hen who lets him tread and flap his wings for a few seconds.

The general excitement among the other cocks is almost like handclapping, and I almost applaud myself at such a graceful culmination to a balletic dance. Of the twenty birds on that lek, it is on the cards that all the hens which visit it will be mated by the same one or two cock birds. The others won't get a look-in. It is nature's way of selecting the dominant males to father the next generation.

Hill Man of Glen Artney

It was Saturday morning and the scents and bird-song in Sunny Glen Artney had a blissful freshness. I was thinking of leaving my car at the head of the road and taking the right of way path which continues in four miles to the Ben Vorlich ridge when I got a wave from Pat the Shepherd, and his wife Isobel, who were gardening in front of the house.

So I had to stop, expressing surprise to find such a keen hill man at home at this time of day when he is normally out on the hill. "And a good job too," nodded Isobel forcibly. "He's been working sixteen hours a day for weeks, up at four in the morning. It's a good job he retires in November."

Pat grinned. "Come in and we'll have a bite," he said, "and I'll take you to a hill I bet you've never been on. I need a wee holiday."

So off we went, short-haired collie at heel, through the grassy parks where cattle drowsed, then past the sheep fanks to the higher ground where peewits squeaked and golden plover piped telling their chicks to keep their heads down. Partridges ran ahead of us, skylarks sang, wheatears jangled, and hundreds of black-headed gulls screamed as they made a blizzard of white wings above their marsh nests where it would be easy for a man to drown.

Up on the heather we were on boot-width tracks grooved out by Pat's boots—£25 a pair and he only gets a year out of them. "Aye, this is the walk I take first thing every morning, to the top there at 1,622ft., to look at the sheep and move them to different ground. Ewes giving birth often need a hand. Now this is what I want you to see. This is what we call "Grand Corner" where the marches of three different estates meet.

93

How's that for a view?"

Beneath us was the Findhu Glen and the deer forest of Glen Artney and the inviting track leading to the lonely house of Dubh Chroein 1,400ft. up on Ben Vorlich, where Pat at the age of fifteen lived alone and did his first high hill lambing. "Hard work for a boy," he said.

I could tell the peak still fascinated him, and told him of two of us getting off the late bus at Comrie one Saturday night, and walking up to the middle glen to sleep out under the stars to enjoy the dawn chorus of the birds. Then to Ben Vorlich, arriving on top at a time when I am normally in bed for a mighty view of the Highlands and Lowlands, the Forth, the Clyde, the Lawers range, Perthshire peaks, and Arrochar Alps.

The world was ours that day, unlike a more recent trip the quick way up from the side of Loch Earn by Glen Vorlich and the north ridge, only three miles—a mere 2,700ft. of climbing for a big reward. On that occasion the summit was speckled with climbers, many of them children.

"Aye," said Pat, "I like to see folks who have the good sense to go to the hills and enjoy themselves. It's the dogs we don't like to see. People moving quietly do no harm, but romping dogs are a menace."

I knew that Pat was not over-stating the case, for I've seen it so often myself. Indeed, since my jaunt with Pat, I've had a talk with another shepherd friend who had to talk to seven parties with free running dogs in one day. "They were nice reasonable people but not one of the dog owners was aware of the potential harm they were doing, scattering the sheep, separating the lambs from their mothers and causing general commotion.

"It's not just money. That ewe in the park there had a lovely lamb until a few days ago. Some children told me what happened. A dog separated them, the lamb went into the loch trying to escape and was drowned.'

THIRSTY WORK ON THE CUILLIN

It was 10 p.m. on a superb evening when Iain arrived at our rendezvous point in Pitlochry. "Look how they're grinning at the prospect of being free of their wives," said Iain's wife as she drove off.

We pointed the car north and deferred decision of what we should do until Dalwhinnie. Iain was thinking of Sutherland, but I was oriented towards the Cuillin. We swung west, agreeing to sleep on it, camp somewhere on Loch Lagganside and decide in the morning.

Midges in hordes resulted in the tent going up in record time and ourselves into the sleeping bags without so much as a cup of tea. A breeze in the morning made breakfast a delight, and since it came from the north-east with sunshine and crisp visibility, we headed for Skye, determined to be climbing by lunch-time.

No stops for photography, though it almost hurt to whisk down Glen Shiel without halt and force the pace to Kyle for a quick bout of shopping, then over the ferry and on to Sligachan. Marvellously, there was only one tent on the wee site just north of the hotel, and in no time we had our camp down and a quick snack inside us. Now for the cloudless Cuillin.

"Great to be setting off for a new peak," said Iain. "I've never been on Sgurr nan Gillean, nor Am Bhasteir, nor the Bhasteir Tooth, so what could be better on a day like this?" For myself, I thought it was almost too good to be true, for on dozens of summer days spent in these finest rock peaks in Scotland I have invariably been unlucky for weather. I had never known what it was to be thirsty on the Cuillin, though I had heard plenty of the sufferings of other climbers in heat-wave conditions. In the next three days I was to learn.

Only the cool breeze saved us from being broiled as we plodded over the moor at midday, enjoying the sight of a greenshank piping agitatedly from a boulder, telling its young to keep down among the white tufts of waving bog cotton. Glimpses of twites and wheatears were other excuses for stopping, and soon Iain was suggesting a five-minute snooze and a sandwich in preparation for the Sgurr nan Gillean pinnacles which had gradually strung themselves out in bristling profile.

On the move again, his stride had a new swing as he exclaimed on the marvel of the rock. "A hold wherever you put your hand. I had forgotten it was so rough." Each taking a different line, we met on top of the third pinnacle to look down the vertical line of descent, and Iain was so impressed that be began uncoiling the rope.

As is the way with gabbro, the climbing is easier than it looks, but there is an awkward step on the steepest bit here where any unroped man must take great care. The best climbing lies ahead now, straight up the fourth pinnacle and down into the gap for the top of the Sgurr itself, rising in a bristling wall. Then came the great moment when we stepped over the top and the view ahead burst upon us.

What bliss to peel an orange, slake our thirst and look along the grey rock spine rising and falling above shadowy corries in ten miles of sinuosities with thousands of feet of ups and downs between one end and the other. Across the glen in amazing contrast to the gabbro, the smooth crowns of the Red Hills were glaring pink, becoming abruptly purple in the splinter of Clach Glas and the elephantine bulk of Blaven. In a glance we could look from the white houses of Portree beneath The Storr, to Harris and the Uists.

Our route now lay along the Western Ridge, over the gendarme of Sgurr nan Gillean, where you have the fun of swinging from his head above a mighty big drop and enjoying it all the more because of the size of the holds. The rocky way continues with a delightful scramble leading you to the top of Am Bhasteir, beyond which is the Bhasteir Tooth.

The "Tooth" is below you, but to get to it means overcoming the beetling wall. We chose different routes. Iain eased his way down the awkward bulge nearest to the Tooth on the edge of a big drop. I chose the Lota Corrie side, which involves delicate traversing of a steep wall.

The Bhasteir Tooth was climbed for the first time in 1889 by Dr Norman Collie. By the time we arrived on top the bronze light of evening was setting in. The Outer Isles were silhouettes and the lochs at our feet pale blue.

We would have lingered for the full glory of the sunset, but for thirst. Saturated with sun, our thoughts turned to water with lemonade powder in it. So we hared over the tops to come down under the pinnacles of Sgurr nan Gillean, to slake our thirst below the gorge.

The marvellous breeze was still blowing when we awoke to the sunshine of another perfect morning. We knew where we were going, to the Glen Brittle side for Coire Lagan and its superlative rocks. This is where Iain had done his first climbing in the Cuillin, as a medical student, living frugally in the Youth Hostel and brashing Forestry Commission trees to get money for what he did eat. His main memory of the Cuillin is hunger!

We gravitated to the Western Buttress of Sron na Ciche, for its shade and also because this is a face where two of my most memorable climbing adventures occurred. The first was on Mallory's Slab and Groove, when I had to abseil (double the rope round a knob of rock and slide down) for the first time in my life as a matter of life or death. The second was a war-time climb with an officer of the Scottish Horse named Ramsay, when we embarked on the 1,000ft. face on a day when wise men would have stayed by the fire.

The date was mid-September 1943, and the wind was thundering on the crags and the rain battering as we roped up for the Median Route. Heaven knows what we did climb, but benumbed and battered, we each led our pitches until a line of overhanging chimneys blocked the way and Ramsay took over. This fine cragsman was killed in the war. His lead was certainly heroic that day, and even to follow stretched me to the limit.

Yet we went over Sgumain and Alasdair after that climb. We were indeed in the act of going for Thearlaich when an even more violent gust of wind than we had so far experienced hit us with the equivalent of several pails of icy water. At which even this hard man blinked and said, "Perhaps we should go down."

So, now that Iain and I were here on a perfect day, why not for old times' sake, get into the cool by having a wander on that face and trying to find the Median Route. In fact, however, the extraordinary depth of shadow made it impossible to pick out features on the dark gabbro, so we followed our noses and after a few hundred feet knew we were well off line by the difficulty of the terrain.

Iain had led to an overhanging impasse, and now called me up to see what I thought of the way ahead. It was a Captain Ramsay sort of situation, black roofs and clefts blocking upward views. Unwilling to commit myself until I had explored other ways, I tried a line I had noticed on the way up to join Iain, an airy, slanting crack.

It was the open kind of climbing I love, exposed, steep and interesting without being too difficult. Moreover, there was a continuation, with a choice of ways opening up, and the last rope-lengths were up a splendid basalt arete, delicate balance climbing offering food for thought in places. Iain had the pleasure of the last pitch, and as I looked up the rope I saw his body become a halo of gold as he moved out of shadow into sun and give a yell of delight at what he saw as he came over the top.

No wonder. The little harbours of Soay were immediately below us, edged by birchwoods, a pancake of greenery. Beyond it over the blue sea were the near peaks of Rhum above the white sands of Kilmory, with blue-grey Canna on one side and Eigg on the other.

A quick drop to the col to dump the sacks, and now we could do a direct ascent to the top of Thearlaich and perch above the great hollow of Coir-Usig, envious of the streams we could see pouring into it.

I thought of the lucky men who were the first to climb these peaks, and who were immortalised by having tops named after them; of Sheriff Alexander Nicolson, the Skyeman, who, at the age of forty-six, in 1873, worked his way to the top of what is now called Sgurr Alasdair; of Charles Pilkington, who made the first ascent of the Inaccessible

Pinnacle and for whom the peak upon which we were sitting—Thearlaich—was named; of John MacKenzie of Sconser, the first British mountain guide and native-born rock climber, who climbed the Cioch with Collie in 1894 and is for ever remembered in Sgurr Mhic Coinnich.

What a discovery for the alpinists to make, long after the Matterhorn had been climbed—a range of difficult and unexplored mountains in Britain. Sgurr Thormaid is called after Professor Norman Collie, an outstanding mountain explorer of the biggest mountain ranges, who so loved the Cuillin that he settled permanently in Sligachan in 1939 and is buried with John MacKenzie in the little cemetery at Struan. To come back to the present. Never did man see a bonnier evening than that in the Cuillin as we leapt and slid down the Great Stone Chute to celebrate in lemonade the quenching of a noble thirst.

Past the loch, through the dancing bog cotton, and down into the glen we thought we had seen the best of the day. We had not, for as we topped the pass in the car we looked down on a crimson Loch Harport and the red ball of the disappearing sun. Even that was not the finish, for an astonishing vision came into view as we swung into shadowy Glen Drynoch. Coming round a bend, there, in front of us, in an unearthly terracotta against the green sky, were the jagged pinnacles of Sgurr nan Gillean and the Bhasteir Tooth.

Curiously, despite another ten-hour day, I felt neither tired nor hungry. Morning saw us off again, this time into Corrie Tairneilear for some fun on the face of Sgurr a' Mhadaidh. What makes this corrie so superb are the little alpine meadows of flowers and ferns amidst such a cliff-walled cirque. Now and again we sat down just to enjoy the scents of thyme and drink from the numerous springs.

Mhadaidh's four peaks stretching to Bidein Druim nan Ramh give perhaps the most sustained bits of up and down rock climbing in the Cuillin, with some route-finding problems. Striking along to the southerly peak, we met two climbers just about to leave its top. Their first question was about the next bit of ridge, and what lay beyond to Sgurr nan Gillean.

Then they told us a remarkable story. Leaving home in Yorkshire at 6 p.m., they had motored all night, crossed over to Skye at 9 a.m., dumped their car at Elgol and walked to Coruisk by the Bad Step, arriving at 4 p.m. A two-hour halt for a meal, then off they went with bivouac kit to the top of Gars-bheinn to snatch a few hours' sleep before setting off to do the whole ridge at 5 a.m.

When we met them they had been going for thirteen hours, were saturated with sun and suffering agonies of thirst. Their thoughts were fastened on a high spring of cool water on the Fionn Corrie, alas, still several hours distant. I thought they were too heavily laden with gear for a push involving 10,000 feet of clambering, and, indeed, they themselves voiced the thought as we went along the ridge together.

98

At least we could do them a certain amount of good by saving them time on route-finding. Also, since our thirst was less than on other days, we still had two oranges which we passed to them, and it was better than eating them to see how much these were enjoyed by two men who desparately needed them. I regret now that we did not stay with this couple, for it was after the main peak of the Bidein their route-finding went wrong. Time was lost, and it was 11 p.m. before they could ease their sore throats at the Fionn Corrie spring.

Not surprisingly, they decided to bivouac there, setting off again at 3 a.m. down Lota Corrie, intending to climb Collie's route on the Bhasteir Tooth which Iain and I had descended two days before. But they failed to find the way, and after an hour's searching came back to the col, missed out the Tooth by climbing Am Bhasteir from its easier side, then set off for Sgurr nan Gillean.

But things went wrong here too. They failed to find the route along the Western Ridge, and after various intimidating verticalities bailed out with an abseil, retreated to the Bealach na Lice and abandoned the tops by Lota Corrie for the weary trudge down Glen Sligachan and over the pass to Coruisk to arrive at noon. They had been on the go for thirty-one hours.

Nor could they sit back, for Frank Milner had business appointments in Yorkshire the next day. So they had to pack up immediately and see about getting back to their car in Elgol. Luckily they got a lift across Loch Scavaig in a tourist boat, and motoring all night arrived home at 6 a.m., not having been in bed since they left four nights and three days before.

Well, not many men in their prime could survive that pace and output of nervous energy. But reflect that one of the pair was sixty-two years old, and he told me he did not climb his first peak until he was forty owing to "a seven days a week job." Moreover, he has done very little rock climbing, though he and Frank have been winter climbing in Scotland every year for the past ten years.

Stan Bradshaw, the veteran from Padiham in Lancashire, and Frank Milner who is just over half his age, are keen to have another go. In a letter to me Stan says, "How about joining us? It would be so much easier, I think, with someone who knew the route intimately. We lost such a lot of time route-finding."

It is true enough, I do know the ridge, but despite having been on every peak of the Cuillin more times than I can remember, I do not claim to know it intimately. Memory for routes is a fickle thing, and, in fact, I was amazed at how little I remembered in detail of the Cuillin ridge.

I think the secret of doing the main ridge as a single enjoyable expedition is to keep your equipment down so as to be able to move swiftly over the long sections of moderately difficult rocks. What I would do is leave a rucksack of spare clothing, etc., at Sligachan Hotel, book a room there, and get driven round to Glen Brittle, timing my plod up Gars-bheinn to arrive there about daybreak.

The boots I would wear would be light. In addition to food, I would carry a plastic bottle holding about two pints of water, and I would carry climbing line rather than rope, for it would be used double only for abseiling. I would expect to be out for about fifteen hours betwen Glen Brittle and Sligachan. For me the ideal weather would be breezy with shifting mist and sun. I'd certainly like to do it before I get too old.

Footnote 1

Stan and his friend Frank achieved their ambition by doing the main ridge of the Cuillin in a day just a year after their gallant failure. Beginning in Glen Brittle at 3.30 a.m. they were in Sligacan at 11 p.m. in a joyous 19½ hour day.

In a letter to me immediately after it Stan wrote:

We had a cache of food planted at the Inaccssible Pinnacle, and once we got it we felt sure nothing could stop us. We were tired when we got to the Bhasteir Tooth, and once again we couldn't find the route, although we had made a reconnaissance in advance. We wasted a bit of time and energy, but once we were up we could relax, for we knew nothing could stop us getting to Sgurr nan Gillean.

It was beautiful! Everything about us was grand—the colours, the sea and, swinging away from us the marvellous ridge and the corries we had traversed."

At sixty-three years of age the jaunty wee man had done it, and he is busy ticking off the Scottish Munros as I write this. And I'm sure he'll do them before he's seventy. He's the youngest old man I know.

Footnote 2:

The astonishing Eric Beard at the age of thirty-one ran the Cuillin Ridge from the top of Gars-bheinn to Sgurr nan Gillean in 1963. His time from first top to last was 4 hours 9 minutes. At the time he did it he was holder of the English, Irish, Scottish and Welsh fell-running records. He was killed in a car crash in 1969. In the last letter I received from him he had cycled out from Yorkshire all the way to the Alps to climb there.

Footnoote 3:

As this book goes to print (Sept. 1980) I hear that Stan has now climbed all the Scottish Munros and achieved his ambition.

MEN OF THE TREES

Packing to drive north for Beauly and Cannich, I took my ancient Ordnance Survey map with me, bought for three shillings in the 1930's. I was an eager youngster then and had hatched a plan to camp at Benula beneath Lochs Mullardoch and Lungard and reap the harvest of the highest summits north of the Great Glen. Yes, I was a Munro-bagger in these days, but a keen wildlife man as well and I took my holidays in May when the shrilling of wading birds mingle with the songs of warblers and the quarcks of wild duck busy with their nesting.

Most of the Highlands were unknown to me then, and I had never met anyone who had been to Glen Cannich. I wrote to the postmistress at Beauly and discovered that by changing mail cars at Glen Affric Hotel I could get to Benula, and might be given accommodation by Mr Maclennan the deer-stalker. Alas, he could not oblige. Visitors were not encouraged by the estate.

I arrived with a tent and had the effrontery to send up a parcel of food addressed to myself care of his name. The journey from the sea winding along the tree-clad gorges of the Beauly River and into Strath Glass enchanted me, but it was the sterner stuff I craved, and this came with the changing of mail cars and a rough climbing road. Sun-brilliant birches clustered green in the gullies, and gnarled Caledonian pines spread over the hill shoulders.

Loch Mullardoch was grim by comparison, hills hidden in grey clouds and a general impression of coarse peaty shores. At the end of it was Benula Lodge and the keeper's cottage. The man who came out directed me to a nice little camping place half a mile along the road on the edge of a pine wood. "Come to the house if you get lonely," he invited me.

Those days of discovery can never be recaptured, but I still remember wakening to the piping of greenshank and the drumming of snipe, watching a bobbing sandpiper in the burn and listening to the cascading songs of willow warblers.

The clouds still wrapped the peaks and no wind stirred as I headed up Ben Fhionnlaidh for Carn Eige and Mam Sodhail. My climb in the mist was enlivened by a ptarmigan which just dodged being tramped on to disclose seven warm eggs. My reward came when suddenly the clouds rolled and blue peaks solidified from the greyness. The heart sang as I recognised Liathach of Glen Torridon, Sgorr na Ciche of Knoydart, Ben

101

Nevis, its cliffs clearly textured, and around me a bewilderment of near ridges and cloud-filled glens.

In my week in that glen I had sudden switches from warm summer sun to a bleak winter wind driving snow before it as I mopped up peak after peak as far distant as fabled Sgurr nan Ceathreamhnan—an expedition memorable for the fact that I forgot to pack the substantial piece I had made up, only discovering my oversight when I slung off my pack to have a bite on the summit.

Food or no food, I traversed the six tops in what my diary describes as a snow-blizzard high up and rain low down. Soaked, and weak with hunger, I won't forget the big tightener of soup and eggs and ham I put down when I got back to camp.

Nor shall I forget my last day, getting up at 4 a.m. in a downpour and climbing up by Gleann a' Choilich where the rain changed to snow. At 2,300 feet it was almost impossible to believe the month was May in the driving blizzard as I sought the way down to Glen Affric and the lonely house of Alltbeithe, in those days inhabited by a deer-staker's family. I was taken in there and pushed into a seat of honour by the fireside while the teapot was filled and at a shout, in trooped a family of boys and girls with their own private school teacher. Clearly, I was a welcome interlude, and I would have stayed the night but for the fact that I was meeting a friend down on Loch Duichside at 4 p.m.

Why do I write about these distant events now? Because I wanted to assess as objectively as possible the changes of the past quarter of a century as a result of large-scale hydro-electric operations and Forestry Commission plantings. As luck would have it, I had the company of Donald Maclennan whose brother had given me permission to camp all these years ago.

Donald was an estate deer-stalker in the early days. Today he is a Forestry Commission ranger, which means his first duty is to the health of the growing trees, whereas before, his interest was with deer as sport. Together, on top of the big concrete dam which blocks the head of Glen Cannich, we contemplated nine miles of windswept reservoir under which lie three shooting lodges and their cottages.

"We call that wee headland you see down there Cape Horn," said Donald, "and on a wild day in a boat you're glad to get round it into shelter. You need a boat to get up and down for the road and the paths are under the water. You couldn't do the walks you did in the past. I've been out on it in rougher days than today. It's no wonder they call it the Atlantic."

The 2,385 ft.-long dam with a height of 116 ft. is the biggest in Scotland, and when the waters built up to amalgamate Loch Lungard and Loch Mullardoch it meant that the drove road, a right of way from the North Sea to the Atlantic, was severed—a great route lost. The developers should have been compelled to build a substitute footpath.

Glen Cannich was unlucky on another count. Too many of its Caledonian pines fell to the axe in order to make room for commercial stands of timber. The Forestry Commission have admitted that they made a mistake here. Even so, they have done a fine job, and there is a fine mixture of old and new trees stretching up to the rocky corries, with a rich sprinkling of larch.

Cannich village didn't exist when I came the first time. It was the site of the work camp for building the Glen Affric power scheme completed in 1951, and the present settlement of attractive modern houses, in the form of a square, dates roughly from that time. Donald lives here and finds it a lively community, composed equally of forestry and hydro-electric workers.

It was from here I went exploring Glen Affric and Guisachan Forest with District Forestry Officer Finlay Macrae and Donald, his head ranger. Finlay is a Skyeman who began as an ordinary forest worker in Glen Brittle below the Cuillin in 1947, graduating B.Sc in Forestry at Aberdeen University where he was a student of professor H.M. Steven, a fierce advocate of the regeneration of the Caledonian pine.

In these early days in forestry he could hardly have foreseen that seventeen years on he would be given the task of putting his training to use and undertaking the regeneration of the Caledonian pine woods of Glen Affric from Loch Benavean to Loch Affric in a mountain setting without compare in Scotland.

Here was a challenge indeed, for the major loch had been turned into a reservoir with an artificial shore line and the scars of a new road reducing the aesthetic appeal of a hitherto unspoiled gem of wild mountain and loch scenery. True, the damage had been kept to a minimum by tunnelling the waters of Loch Mullardoch through the mountains from Glen Cannich thus avoiding pylons and enabling the powerhouse to be put down at Fasnakyle.

The existing pines were beautiful to look at, an open forest flowing over the foothills, but they were ancient trees without successors, offering marvellous shelter to sheep and deer which grazed down every young seedling which reared its head. Finlay's first job was to fence off large sections into reserves to give the young trees a chance.

Donald's job is to maintain the fencing and keep out all grazing animals, no easy job with over 200 miles of fencing around 4,300 acres of pinewood reserve. Motoring up the road, Finlay explained the strategy. "The deer must have somewhere to go, so each side of the road is open forest which is theirs, but look at the wee trees inside the fence and some of them not so wee.

"The old road, you remember, took a delightful line through the shore pines and was submerged when Loch Benavean was raised. People who loved Glen Affric were bitter about the felling of the pines and the ugly scars, but see how the birch has taken all along the shore without fencing and young pines are even colonising the new road."

I've seldom had a more stimulating drive as feature after feature of the pinewood reserves was pointed out. Hundreds of trees had grown up from seeds cast by the aged parents, while in other areas hand-planting had been resorted to, where the natural fertility had been degraded by neglect. In some cases chemical fertiliser has been put down to good effect.

We parked the car and took the new river walk which has been laid out by the building of little stairways and cunning stone-walling of bouldery gaps. The delightful circuit took only twenty minutes, sweeping down to a curving waterfall and picnic place, then up through the trees where red deer stags were browsing. An indicator-type plaque with engraved map shows the marvellous walking opportunities available on a superb network of tracks.

"We want the public to come and enjoy Glen Affric with minimum restrictions. The area is so vast the public don't need channelling. The only other path we have specially laid out is at the Dog Falls at the beginning of the glen, for visitors who want away from the car but don't want anything too strenuous.

"The real back-packers can find their own way. It's about eighteen miles through the hills to Kintail, I did it with my daughter last year and it was pretty tough," said Finlay. "That house you mentioned— Alltbeithe—it's now an open Youth Hostel, but the Association are threatening to give it up because the folk who use it are tearing it up for firewood."

Donald had left us to go to the head of the glen and talk with his brother at Glen Affric Lodge. "You're invited up to the house for some tea," he said when he joined us, so up we drove to the only habitation in the length of Glen Affric. Lonely? Not a bit of it for Duncan and his wife who have been living there for over thirty years.

"I never want to leave the place, nor do I want to retire, though I'm close enough to the age. They'll have to carry me out!" His contented wife smiled as she handed us tea and fresh-made scones and pancakes. "The winter passes for us too quickly, for it's the only time we get to do things for ourselves. Now it's the lambing and all the outside jobs until the end of the season."

Duncan and his two deer-stalker sons are also shepherds, and Donald the forest ranger used to be here, too, so there is a fine balance of interests between the old estate and the new owners, especially since Donald still does a bit of deer-stalking on adjacent territory for guests of the Forestry Commission.

One of the many things I didn't know about Glen Affric was that until 1947 birch trees were cut for manufacturing into bobbins for the Indian jute mills, an industry which came to an end when that country became independent. Nor did I realise that the village of Tomich, just south of the mouth of the glen, was built as a model hamlet for the Great Guisachan House, now a ruin.

We drove through the grounds of the former mansion next day on our way to see what Finlay believes to be as fine a stand of Douglas firs as you are likely to see in Britain, planted, perhaps, by the first Lord Tweedmouth who built the mansion in the latter half of the nineteenth century. What a glorious parkland they created above the river, not only Douglas firs, but great redwoods over what were no doubt green lawns when this was a haunt of Liberal politicians gathered together for "the season."

In fact, when these trees were planted, the sport of stalking deer with the express rifle was about to reach its zenith, with ornate lodges being built in glens all over the Highlands. It was then that many of the roads, paths, bridges and bothies we take for granted were built; the British Empire was secure, wealth created more wealth, and there was no war on the immediate horizon.

Fate, however, had something in store for a young man who came here to visit his aunt, wife of the second Lord Tweedmouth. Her name was Lady Fanny Spencer Churchill, and the name of her nephew who came in 1901 was Winston, who amused himself learning how to drive a car in these grounds.

Two miles along that track where the future Sir Winston had practised his driving and we were hard against the river, with great Douglas firs towering up over our heads like a fragment of the American wilderness. Finlay was in his element as he led the way with Donald across the half-submerged stepping-stones to a path climbing up through them.

We were contouring a steep bluff above a deepening gorge, becoming noisy with the sound of thundering waters. Ducking under branches and feeling our way, it was not possible to see much until suddenly we were in the clear and facing one of the most glorious waterfalls in Scotland, a great cascading spout of white, falling over 100 feet in one vertical plunge before breaking into two parallel falls. On the map it is shown as the Plodda Falls, and it is a place for the sure-footed to seek out.

"Now these Douglas firs are at their best, but the time has come for them to be cut. It's sad to say it, but every tree has its prime. The Caledonians, too, will have to be cropped when their time comes, but that's what forestry is about. In Glen Affric and wherever regeneration of Caledonians is taking place, the important thing is to have new generations following on—the forests of the future."

Finlay's dedication to his native pinewood reserve has now been justly acclaimed with the award of a statuette of a Phoenix rising from the ashes. He didn't get it in Scotland, though. He got it in Dublin from the Society of American Travel Writers. His work has also been honourably mentioned by the World Wilderness Congress.

High praise must be given to the Forestry Commission, too, for giving the right man his chance to do one of the most worthwhile things I have seen done in my lifetime. In Scotland there are thirty-five locations of

105

true Caledonian forest remaining. Over a score in private hands are in deer forest and have no future unless fenced. Now owners are being encouraged by a grant of £225 per hectare if they will undertake conservation. I sincerely hope they will respond.

THE TROSSACHS

High on the south huge Ben Venue
Down on the lake in masses threw,
Crags, knolls, and mounds, confusedly hurled
The fragments of an earlier world . . . .

So wrote Sir Walter Scott, and you could say that this is where the romantic vision of the Highlands was born. The word 'Trossachs' is said to be derived from 'bristly', which is a good description of what is perhaps the finest bit of small-scale country in Scotland. It was here that Sir Walter got his inspiration for *The Lady of the Lake* and *Rob Roy*. And it was the publication of these books 150 years ago which brought the first tourist boom to the Highlands.

Earlier travellers did not write so ecstatically of the Bens and Glens. The usual impression they brought back was of a disagreeable country of ugly scenery, where roads were bad and the accommodation worse. As for the Trossachs, despite its proximity to the Forth and Clyde valleys, it was one of the last bits of the Highlands to be civilised, thanks to the warring MacGregors, whose most infamous son, Rob Roy, was still a legend even in Scott's time.

Rob Roy had died an old man, peacefully with his boots off, in Balquhidder in 1734. Living in a Scotland weakly governed from England, Rob began imposing his own discipline of law by guaranteeing protection for those who could pay for it. In that time money was scarce and cattle was the true currency of the Highlands, so Rob, having set himself up as a cattle dealer, could ensure that a drove could get to market if protection money was paid. If not, then the cattle would mysteriously disappear.

Many tales exist about Rob's exploits, and although Sir Walter Scott was not born until thirty-seven years after the death of Rob, the outlaw was still very much alive in folk memory when Scott first came to the Highlands as a lawyers clerk to superintend an eviction. Rob would have hated life in the Highlands that Scott was seeing, with the clans disintegrating and the Highlanders being forcibly evicted from their lands to provide sheep grazing.

Law and order was on the march. Thomas Telford was building the Caledonian Canal and a road network of nearly 1,000 miles, and Clydeside had become the centre of the new steamship building industry, thanks to James Watt's revolutionary discovery of the principle of the separate condenser.

107

Sir Walter Scott was living during a time of industrial revolution, and though his mind dwelt on the romance of the past, new discoveries were opening up the Trossachs.

The subsequent tourist traffic provided a business opportunity for the Loch Katrine MacGregors who plied boats for hire between Stronachlachar and the Trossachs. In 1843 they showed that they were still the wild MacGregors when a small iron steamer was launched on the loch threatening their livelihood. They responded by towing it away during the night and sinking it.

By this time however, Glagow Corporation had plans to raise the level of Loch Katrine and bring its Highland water to Glasgow. To do this meant building the biggest aqueduct in Britain, and when the soft water flowed at the turn of a tap in 1859, the consumption of soap was halved in Glasgow. At the same time a slate quarry was opened above Aberfoyle which was to be the third largest in Scotland. It continued to function until 1951.

I wonder what Sir Walter would make of the changes if he came back today? One thing I am fairly sure about is that he would find the Trossachs just as beautiful as when he wrote his poetry. Take the forest. At the time when Scott was writing of this territory, trees were mainly used to provide charcoal for iron smelting, while the bark of the oaks was utilised to tan leather. For these purposes the Duke of Montrose planted 1,200 acres of timber in twenty years. He also built the toll-road from Aberfoyle, still known today as the Duke's pass, though it was rebuilt in the thirties and has been free to the public ever since.

On that high road from Aberfoyle to Loch Katrine you travel through some of the best modern forestry in Scotland, now part of the Queen Elizabeth Forest Park. Here you can appreciate how nature and man manages to mix natural oaks and birches with American spruces and European larches. To see it at its best, leave your car at the little parking place near the summit at 796ft. and take a walk up to the indicator view-point. In autumn there are few more colourful places in all Scotland when the deer grass is crimson and rock peaks and lochs are patterned with the gold of larches and birches.

I have a particular affection for this bit of country because I grew up with its spruce trees. Indeed I knew my way over Rob Roy's territory even before the Forestry Commission began their work around 1940. Today the woods are so vast that I think even Rob would have a hard job to sort out all the trails, with something like 170 miles of forest track. My own feeling is that the Trossachs is a much more interesting region today than when I first got to know it.

The wild life is so much richer today, especially the birds of prey, hen harriers, short eared owls, sparrow hawks and buzzards which hunt the woodland fringes, while in the clearings you can listen to the liquid bubbling of blackcock at dawn, and at dusk, listen to the churring of nightjars. There are also crags where peregrine falcons nest, and a familiar sound on a still evening is the thin reeling of grasshopper warblers.

It is indeed fortunate that this forest with a highly scenic road passing through its middle has never suffered a serious fire. "The public are the best vigilantes," say the Commission. Early alarm, quick communications and a dependable regular fire service has taken away much of the worry. Most of the timber is now beyond the vulnerable first ten years, so the fire risk is less. The "Park" has its own Roving Ranger who patrols constantly in his vehicle. The Ranger is employed to help people enjoy themselves, and he does his best to encourage them to make full use of the opportunities for fishing the lochs, walking the hills, learning about the trees, or hiring a pony to go trekking the trails. The Commission take a lot of trouble to provide the maximum recreational facilities for the public. On the timber productivity side, they expect to harvest something like 70,000 tons by 1992. The present labour force is about sixty-five.

Loch Katrine is eight miles long with an average width of one mile, and half its total length is over 400ft deep, with a maximum depth of 500ft. One of the best ways to see it is to take a sail from Trossachs Pier in the *Sir Walter Scott.* The first part under the crags and knolls of Ben Venue is especially fine, but there is never a dull moment on the 1¾hr. trip. The big pylons you see striking across the hills of the upper reaches of the loch are those of the Cruachan Pumped Storage Scheme. Incidentally, the sail is very cheap due to the fact that the *Sir Walter Scott* has been plying the loch since the beginning of the century and has long since paid her way.

Notice that Ben Venue throws down a bouldery north-eastern spur, forming a narrow pass peppered with boulders high above the loch. this is the *Bealach nam Bo,* the Pass of the Cattle, which Rob Roy used to drive stolen cattle to secret hide-outs. It was also one of his routes to Inversnaid and the Craigroyston shore of Loch Lomond which was another MacGregor stronghold. When I visited Rob's grave at Balquhidder one day and heard that thieves had stolen the bronze railings and the chains from round his grave, I could almost see in my mind's eye the image of Rob looking up at me. I seemed to see a powerful red-headed man, slightly bow-legged, with abnormally long arms. He was shaking his head at such a mean action, unthinkable for one like himself who was of noble blood. And true enough, the real story of Rob Roy is one of generosity. He shared his bounty with the poor, and never killed a man although he dearly loved a fight.

Perhaps this is what appealed to Scott, a highly civilised man with forebears who were Border rievers. As an adventurer with the pen, Scott had no equal.

When he built Abbotsford, his mansion on the River Tweed near Melrose, it was worthy of the man he was. He earned more money from his pen than anyone had ever done before, but he died in debt, and he probably killed himself by overwork trying to pay off his creditors. The debt was due to the failure of his publishers. What a spirit he had. If there is life after death then I know of two red-headed men who should be great company for each other.

TROSSACHS TO KINTYRE

There is a very special kind of winter day when suddenly the countryside has a spring look. Everything seems to have a shine on it: beech bark, silver birch, the warm colour on the oaks and bluish sheen on plantations of sitka spruce. That's how it was one frosty morning as we set off for Ben Ledi, revelling in the glorious clarity and enjoying the warmth of the sun through the car windows.

Great to be early and have the road to ourselves, not another car to Aberfoyle, then the exciting bit twisting up the Duke's Road in and out through the grey rocks and crimson bracken before the moment of revelation—the view over the undulating Queen Elizabeth Forest to Brig o' Turk and straight ahead to the blue slit of Loch Katrine between lumpy Ben Venue and the spike of Ben A'n. Bristly country, the Trossachs, as you realise in the descent to Loch Achray.

It was a good place to appreciate that spring was on the way in the pink branches of the birches bristling on every knoll, the hazy look that comes with the rising sap in the lengthening days. Now we swung round the far shore of Loch Achray for Brig o' Turk where a wee road climbs steeply to Glen Finglas.

This is real MacGregor country, and the name is still common hereabouts below the west face of Ben Ledi which we were going to climb from the wee loch which lies on its flank.

The older "Loch Lomond and Trossachs" O.S. map does not show this reservoir, created a few years ago to top up the waters of Loch Katrine. There are new bull-dozed roads, too, so we had a word with the young shepherd at Gleann Casaig.

"The best way is along the side of the fence by the birchwood," he told us. "Follow it to a gate, go over and you'll find a bit of a path across the rocks of Stuc Odhar. It's a better way than by Gleann Casaig—at least, I think so." It was good to be going a new way to Ben Ledi, for usually I've gone up from the steep eastern flank by the Stank Glen for the sake of the rock-climbing. But that side would have been in shadow today, whereas we were in the sun and it was grand to be on the move. Everything underfoot was crisp with frost, and the route which traversed a series of knobbly knolls was varied. I liked the views of sparkling white Crianlarich hills and the Arrochar Alps. We were almost exactly on the Highland Line as I realised when I took to the rocks for a scramble and

111

found myself on pink Lowland sandstone, yet just above it was the schistose grit, the grey Highland rock.

Forging ahead, it was the sight of a falcon passing on my flank that made me look back. The bird was a merlin, flying low and fast. Beyond it was the jumble of the Arran peaks standing high above a sea of shimmering cloud between me and the Clyde.

Soon we were on boulders and ice-hard snow patches where a white ptarmigan rose croaking from our feet, the first I recollect seeing on Ben Ledi. And up there we began to feel the bitter wind. On the ridge the grasses had sheaths of crystal ice, tinkling against each other as they shook, a glittering sight as magical as the panorama which suddenly opened before us.

To detail all that lay before us would be a recital. What made it was the contrast. Below us was the wee town of Callander and the Carse of Stirling extending to the big smoke of Grangemouth and Arthur's Seat. And down in deep shadow lay the Pass of Leny, while the glittering snows of the high Highland hills rose to the north, their peaks stretching from Cowal to Atholl. Here was height and depth and every shade of colour.

We struck north to the next little summit before descending west to Gleann Casaig where all the red deer stags and hinds seemed to be concentrated, enjoying the warmth well out of the wind. The biggest herd numbered about fifty, and after the icy top it seemed a different world as we plunged downhill in the pink-tinted light of a perfect afternoon.

Returning by Callander, we had still a last treat in store—one of the most marvellous winter sunsets I have ever seen. The feature of it was the red blaze of the sky echoed by the Lake of Menteith while everything else was in black silhouette. I would call that an absolute stunner of a day, when just to be alive was true joy. And we knew how lucky we were, for before returning home we visited a friend newly out of hospital after a difficult eye operation. For weeks she had lain blindfolded, unable to move her body. Now she could see a little, and we wanted to tell her of our day, knowing she would be able to visualise it and share our experience, for she, too, loves the hills.

I told her all about a visit to Kintyre I had made just a short time before when we again had the good luck to get a great day for an exploration of the peninsula which is the longest in Britain, its tip as far south as the Farne Islands in Northumbria.

We started off in Carradale, and I had forgotten what a lovely situation it had, with its fine salmon river coming down from unmistakably Highland hills, then through green parks to discharge into a two-mile sweep of the finest bay in Kintyre. You get a feeling of prosperity and vigour in this community which has at least four strings to its bow—fishing, forestry, agriculture and tourism.

There was only one fishing boat tied up at the modern harbour, and it was just about to go out and join the other dozen or so boats already out taking advantage of the fine weather. We learned from one of the crew that although gales had made catches difficult, prices for prawns and white fish compensated, and the hundred fishermen who fish out from here were in good heart.

Then in the forestry office we met Ranger Peter Strang, who led us along one of the nature walks through thirty-year-old Sitka spruce which he had seen planted as seedlings. Seventeen Commission workers are employed in Carradale Forest, and Peter helps visitors to enjoy the walks when he is not doing his main job of deer control.

I hadn't realised that this is one of the few places in Scotland where all four species of deer occur in the woods—roe, sika, fallow and red. The first two can be a nuisance in the 7,000 acres or so of plantations. Peter keeps their numbers down with the gun. No snares or traps are used.

He told me there are only about thirty fallow deer, and that they used to be confined to the projecting arm of Carradale Point. The Point still supports a herd of wild white goats in the rocky area tipped with a vitrified fort. To reach this part you go through the attractive parkland of Carradale House, the home of Lady Naomi Mitchison.

I had long wanted to meet this distinguished authoress and traveller who has described her recreation as "Accelerating the Mills of God," so it was a real pleasure to step into her spacious living-room-study looking out on the hills of Arran beyond the sweep of Carradale Bay. When I remarked that it must be nice to live in the old house of Campbell of Carradale, she looked a bit doubtful.

"Well, I'm not awfully keen on the Campbells. You see, my people were Stuarts and you know how we feel about one another. Of course, there are good Campbells, too, but Campbells in general make me feel a wee bit awkward, and, of course, there are quite a lot of ghosts and one thing and another about."

"Haunting the house?" I queried.

"Well, I wouldn't say no, but since we had a fire in the house the Grey Lady who used to be a terrible nuisance, has not reappeared. People were always saying to me, 'I see you've got a cook at last,' and it wasn't a cook, it was just the Grey Lady! She was always on the back stairs before they got burnt."

Knowing what an active part she has played in the Carradale community, and of her work on the Highland Panel, and acting as Tribal Advisor to Bakgatla, Bechuanaland Protectorate, since 1963, in addition to writing her books, I asked her how she found time to do all the things she did.

"Oh, that's often quite a problem. Quite often I go to sleep thinking of all the things I haven't done during the day. But we're a hard-working lot, we Haldanes, and somehow we usually manage to get through at least twice what other people do. I've a lot of friends here and they help to keep me on the right path."

We talked about her work on the Community Council, and of the small caravan site in her grounds which she set up to help the village tourist trade. "It means more people coming to the shops, using the village hall, hiring boats and so on. A good deal of the future of the Highlands, and especially Kintyre, depends on this rather naughty thing of deploying their beauty to strangers, and although one doesn't entirely like it, I think it's got to be done. It is very beautiful around here. If only we could be sure of having a hot line to the Almighty to get a bit of fine weather during the summer!"

Listening to this small, white-haired lady talking, I found it hard to believe that I was with someone born in 1898 who had written over forty books, was an *Officier d'Academie Francaise* as long ago as 1924, and eleven years later had stood for Parliament as Labour Candidate for the Scottish Universities Constituency.

Now we drove south by Torrisdale Bay under the highest peak in Kintyre, Beinn an Tuirc (1491 ft.), named after a fierce wild boar slain, according to legend, by Diarmid, progenitor of the Clan Campbell, hence the portrayal of a boar's head on the Campbell crest. Looking to the hill from the ruins of Saddell Abbey, I felt a deep sense of history for this is where the great Somerled was laid, the King of the Isles who drove the Vikings from Kintyre and the Southern Hebrides when he engaged them on an early January morning in 1156. Slain himself two years later, his body was brought to this monastery which he had begun. It was his son Ranald who built this Cistercian Abbey of Saghadail to enshrine his father's body.

I liked the look of Saddell Glen, its greenery leading into the brown hills where sheep and cattle grazed on high knolls with traces of old lazy-bed cultivation around them showing it must be good ground. Forestry Commission trees give variety to the hill-shoulders. Near the sea-front was the village, many of the houses having wee boats in their gardens ready for a quick launch into the Kilbrannan Sound.

The short day was slipping away so fast we had to skip Campbeltown, inviting as it looked, seen across its deep loch marvellously sheltered on the seaward side by Davaar Island, with views out to Ailsa Craig. Our destination was Southend to meet up with Angus McVicar, who, at seventy years of age, has written seventy books.

A quick cup of coffee with this couthie man and his wife, Jean, then off we went a short distance down the coast to look at St Columba's footprints. The site was impressive, a big cliff with fulmar petrels sitting on their nest ledges, paired, waiting for the spring, while above them chattering jackdaws swirled about, taking no notice of a buzzard hovering on the slipstream. Below us, eider ducks bobbed on the water.

"These are the footprints," said Angus. "But look—they are both right feet, one facing the east, the other to the north. One of these is genuine, and it goes away back before St. Columba. It is the one to the east, and probably it was used by the chiefs of the ancient tribes for swearing faithfulness to the tribes. It has been dated by the Royal Commission for Ancient Monuments to the first millennium B.C.

"I think that St Columba did use that footprint, for he was a statesman as well as a Christian missionary, and it was his principle to base the new teaching on the foundation of the old. So I think he would pay homage to the beliefs of the tribe here by placing his foot in the print. The other print was made by a mason in his lunch-hour about last century, I believe."

We talked then about Dunaverty, the rocky protuberance just across the bay where the Lords of the Isles built a fortress in the 13th century, though it did not become notorious for another 400 years when in 1647 the Marquis of Argyll with 3,000 Campbells laid siege to 300 MacDonalds within the castle.

Angus has a great gift for storytelling, and we would love to have stayed to hear more but for an appointment with the head lighthouse-keeper over a road which climbs to a thousand feet with a hair-raising descent through the rocks on the other side.

Principal light-keeper, Mr John Harrow, took us up to the lantern and talked to us as the turning beam shone towards a red sunset and we could see the answering light on the Irish shore looking astonishingly close. "That road with the gradients of 1-in-5 doesn't scare us," he said. "Some days of the year in snow it can be difficult, but a few men with shovels can work wonders. My wife and family are very happy here. We've enjoyed it for the four years we've been here, and I just hope I can finish my time at the Mull. My two assistants and their wives are very happy here too, we've no complaints.

"It's not isolated. The women can get away shopping into Campbeltown two days a week, and the men when they have their time off can do the same. The sea can be quite frightening on a wild day with a good gale of wind for anybody on the water. They say that seven tides meet here at the Mull of Kintyre. In these conditions big ships can look as if they were hardly moving they've got such a struggle to get through it. But on the calm days of summer it's just beautiful here."

The lighthouse is perched 260ft. above sea level. It rarely gets salt spray, so for gardening it's a good place. It's the best I've had in the lighthouse service, said John. There's nothing that I can't grow—tomatoes, cucumbers, green peppers and other things in my wee home-made greenhouse, and in the garden itself every vegetable you can think of. It's a sun-trap and it's just beautiful. We don't need to go to Spain, this is such a charming place."

Sitting below the light in the snug sitting-room, drinking tea and chatting to the family, we were loth to leave. One thing we were very sure of: Kintyre is a superb place to live, and there are some very contented people there.

SUMMER DIARY

Schiehallion

That pointed peak Schiehallion, such a landmark in the Central Highlands whether seen from east or west, derives its name from *Sidh Chaillean,* the Fairy Hill of the Caledonians.

Ptolemy realised its topographical importance by including it on his second-century map of Great Britain. Over 1,600 years later the Astronomer Royal was drawn to its geometric regularity in 1774, using the conical shape of the mountain to calculate the density of the earth with great accuracy.

The heathery mountain is indeed a beauty, situated between Loch Tummel and Loch Rannoch and Loch Tay, with a road from Keltneyburn lifting you to its shoulder and crossing it at over 1,000ft. So you have the prospect of an easy climb to reach 3,547ft. Simply park your car off the road by Glengoulandie Farm, follow the path up the Gleann Mor Burn to the shoulder of the hill, and keep on going as the heather gives way to an airy half-mile of boulders ending at the summit.

Let clarity be with you for a view to give you a panorama extending southwards across the Lowlands to North Berwick Law and Arthur's Seat, and westwards across Rannoch Moor to the Glencoe Peaks and the jostling summits stretching from Ben Nevis to the Cairngorms, with all Perthshire at your side, lochs and moors and summits.

A day of sunshine and showers offers the best chance of that view, though my best day ever was in winter snow.

On our last hill outing a few days ago, Pat and I resisted the summit of Schiehallion and swung down to Loch Rannoch, keeping along the south shore for the pines known as the "Black Wood." It was Ptolemy again who coined the name Caledonian Forest for the trees that covered most of the land in Roman times.

There was mystery and danger then, from the brown bears and wild boars and wolf packs. The caribou and the great fallow deer browsed with red deer among the trees, and beavers built their dams along the streams.

That this fragment has withstood the ravages of time and neglect and exploitation is remarkable. Just in time we have realised its value and the Forestry Commission in the past decade and more have done a fine job to preserve and regenerate it.

They have also been signposting paths and laying out a camp and picnic sites around the Carie Burn where walks through the forest have been signposted. These range from one mile to five miles of really exciting terrain, and you won't even get your feet wet though the name "Rannoch" comes from a Gaelic word meaning "watery."

In fact we chose the soggy ground by going farther west to the Camghouran Burn where the wood gives way to two saucer lochs called Monaghan and Finnart surrounded by quaking bog, great for birds, and we had a fine sight of the red-throated divers we expected.

Complete contrast now when we headed east into the wild forest for a rough traverse at a height of 1,000ft., climbing over knolls bright with white stars of chickweed wintergreen and blue with milkwort, then across a burn where a family of wagtails, yellow as canaries, were spiralling in acrobatic sorties catching flies.

Scents of bog myrtle, birch, and pines were heady. Wood and willow warblers and redstarts sent down cascades of song on us. Red deer moved through the trees and a red squirrel peeked down on us, tip of bushy yellow tail sticking above its feathery ears and bright eyes. It was luxury to lie up there, eat a "piece," and sip a glass of sherry which Pat had brought along. He played me a tune on the chanter too.

In front of us over the forest and across Loch Rannoch was the grey hump of Ben Alder, still flecked with snow, the hill where Prince Charlie hid out his last days in Scotland with Cluny MacPherson.

Netting Salmon

The time is 8 a.m. and I am stepping into a salmon cobble crewed by a team of five to go round the salmon nets set under the big cliffs of Troup Head, the most spectacular bit of the Moray Firth coast.

The rock strata is sandstone, bright pink, and it shines above the steep village of Gardenstown perched above the sandy curve of a bay.

We have ten nets to haul, together with forty fathoms of lead, for it is a Saturday and no net is allowed to remain set over the weekend. The attraction for me is the prospect of viewing the seabirds at the bottom of the cliffs where the caves and overhangs carved by the sea are impossible to reach by climbing.

I have made a few hard climbs here and I want to see at close range the places where puffins buzz about like bees in a hive, and the ledges where guillemots stand in rows like bottles in a press. And I want to see into the big cleft above the sea where the kittiwakes make a tumultuous din round thousands of crazily perched nests.

On such a morning the life of a salmon netter seems good, chugging from one set of coloured buoys to another, looking down into the bag-nets floating in the clear water trying to see how many salmon are swimming inside.

Gathering the edges, the men lift together and sweep up varying bags of salmon which flash with blue and green scales.

Everything is sweetness and light, until the sun is veiled by a sudden pocket of mist. Greyness enshrouds us. The glare makes us screw up our eyes, so we know the sun is not far away. But meantime we can see only a few feet on each side of us.

We cut down speed, and now the sounds seem magnified above the small tick-over of the engine.

The skipper is listening closely. Safety on this rocky coast depends so much on observation and attention to unseen things—instinct as well as vast experience of wind and sky and the behaviour of the sea. I wonder how the skipper knows where we are as we drift on, and find a buoy.

"You can always tell where you are if you're close to the rocks and can hear the birds," he says. "You know where the different ones nest, and in the summer time it's a big help. You often get this kind of haar on fine mornings." Now that is something I had never thought about, navigating by bird sounds—practical ornithology.

With the last lead lifted we turn for home, and joyfully there are clearings, inspiring moments when great bulges of cliff rear over your head, dark or softly glowing with colour. The mist is thinning all the time as we turn the corner for home with thirty-four fish averaging eight pounds each.

They will be sold on Monday, and between then and now the free-swimming salmon have a chance to seek out the mouths of their home rivers unmolested. Upstream they face their new enemies—game-fishermen and poachers.

Eriskay

Eriskay, the love-lilt island is my favourite of the Outer Hebrides. Only 3½ miles by 1½ miles, it has everthing that I look for, and much that has been lost elsewhere in the Long Island.

It has a thriving population who net a good living from the sea. The everyday language is Gaelic. Ponies slung with panniers still carry down peat from the hills, and although the ground is poor, lazy-beds are still dug and vegetables cultivated in hollows among the rocks.

Children everywhere give a fine feeling of vitality to this community of 200 living on the flanks of two rocky hills where their forebears were driven at the time of the clearances in the mid-nineteenth century.

The dispossessed were allowed to stay on Eriskay because the land was thought to be too poor for sheep. But Eriskay has a rare blessing for a small Atlantic island. It has a good harbour on its eastern side, rocky, dangerous to enter, but sheltered. So in the absence of cultivatable land to support them, the destitute folk turned to fishing, and survived on the herring and mackerel which shoal around the Sea of the Hebrides.

A week ago I was on Eriskay, hearing about the wonderful weather they had been having since the beginning of May. If they had any complaint, it was that the ground was too dry. True enough the flowers were not so good as on a former visit three years ago at this time. Nevertheless, clover and thyme still scented the air, vetch and trefoil and silverweed were yellow at the roadsides; marsh-marigolds and primroses were still in bloom.

For an island with so little cultivation, and no trees, it is a surprise to waken up to a familiar dawn chorus of blackbird and thrush, corn buntings and cuckoo. Black rabbits darted about amongst the crofts. Snipe, nesting in the wet places had pepper-and-salt young, but Arctic terns were still on eggs.

The famous beach of Eriskay is *Coilleag a' Phriennsa,* the Prince's Beach, the one where Bonnie Prince Charlie landed on 24 July, 1745, making his first footprints on Scottish soil. Islanders will take you there and show you his flower, Calystegia soldanella—the sea convolulus.

The tradition is that he planted it to mark the historic moment of arriving in Scotland. I am all for Charlie having his flower, but I have to tell you that it is not the only place where it grows. It can be found on nearby Vatersay, on Coll and Tiree, on Islay, and even in Ayrshire. But Eriskay remains its most northerly station. Had he turned back for France as he was advised it is probable that Eriskay would be an empty island today.

Mingulay

It is 7 a.m. The sea is glass-calm, and off the starboard bow shine the curving sands of Tiree. To port, the slim pinnacle of Skerryvore lighthouse shoots up like the jet of a spouting whale.

Dark Manx shearwaters skim the surface in little weaving packs, almost touching the water as they bank and turn. Razor bills and guillemots float ahead of us until the bow of the yacht is amost on top of them before they dive under or scutter away with paddling wings. Kittiwakes, fulmars, and gannets swing around at mast-height.

Tiree is not entirely "land beneath the waves," an ancient description of the flattest of the Hebrides, Ceann a' Bharra rises from its south-western tip as an impressive wall of rock. Barrapol just to the north is where the Mingulay fishermen used to wait for favourable winds to bear them home under lugsail and jib. Alas the wind is not in our favour and we have to use the engine or we would never get to Mingulay before tomorrow morning.

We get there in the evening, and at 9.30 p.m. I am leaping from the dinghy on to the shelving white sand of a lovely little bay. I move fast, otherwise the rubber boat might be broad-sided and swamped by the tidal swell.

A scramble up rocks and I am at the derelict schoolhouse whose playground is now a sheep-fank. I follow a broad grass track to the ruined village which was home to 150 people 100 years ago. Blowing sand is filling up the roofless squares of drystone which were once houses.

The Gaels abandoned this little corrie above the sea to try to find an easier living because they had no safe place for their boats. They did a bold thing. They grabbed land on Vatersay and some went to prison. I walk up through the rich greenery of their former fields, the rigs clearly visible inside grey dry-stone walls. I can't afford to linger if I am to reach the highest point on the island and watch the sun drop into the ocean which extends 2,000 miles to Labrador.

Too late. A black cloud is swallowing the last half of the red sun as I get there. Skylarks singing and snipe bleating are the only sounds. My eyes are held by Berneray, separated from me by only a tide-race. The Norse name Berneray is derived from "end piece," a good description of the tiny hummock on which perches the Barra Head lighthouse, the last flash that ships heading to America will see.

I have climbed 891 ft. and I am on a grassy top which could be a border hill. But this is the Biulacraig and I go carefuly as I descend westwards knowing that suddenly the slope is going to sheer away as if sliced by a knife. The moment is even more impressive than I expect, since the cornice of grass actually overhangs the black wall dropping a sheer 700 ft. to the sea.

The Mingulay bird hunters feared this cliff, and climbed for seafowl on the off-shore stacks of Lianamul and Arnamul, which meant leaping from boats and scrambling along rock-faces generous with ledges and jam-packed with birds. Theirs must have been an adventurous life, with a lot of spice to mitigate the hardship.

Mother Carey's Chicken

Although I am a lover of islands and seabird cliffs, I have to confess that I avoid boats whenever I can.

I feel happier on solid ground than acting as a target for the malevolence of the ocean. So I was surprised to find myself enjoying being on watch with the skipper of the yacht at 1 a.m., and taking over the wheel while he went below to consult the chart for the course to steer once we won clear of the Sound of Islay.

"See if you can see a bat," he said, before leaving me in the cockpit. "It's been following the boat for the last two hours. I've never seen such a thing before. There can't be any insects here for it to eat."

My curiosity was whetted, especially when I saw there was more than one flickering form circling the ship at rail level in the semi-darkness.

I didn't think they were bats, but went down for a powerful electric torch when the skipper took over the wheel. A few flashes at the elusive shapes and I had caught enough glimpses of white above a square tail to be certain they were stormy petrels.

Then as I held one in the beam it fluttered on to the deck, crouching as

I advanced on it, a tiny bird hardly bigger than a swallow in my hand.

In the torch-beam it looked glossy black, from webbed feet to steep forehead and tube-nosed bill.

"Where was this wanderer nesting?" I wondered. Perhaps as far away as the Outer Hebrides, for these birds are ocean travellers, staying away for a few days and only visiting their nests during the hours of darkness.

The nightless days of June are best for watching them on the lonely skerries where they nest. On Carn More of St Kilda I have had them criss-crossing in front of my face at midnight, and actually brushing me with their longish wings. I reckoned what I was seeing was an orienting flight, for it can be no easy job finding a tiny burrow on a big cliff on a dark night.

You know you have found a burrow when you hear a loud purring coming from underground. On St Kilda they breed from May until October, nesting under stones and in burrows. Leach's petrel which nests beside them is a rarer bird in Scotland with only four known breeding stations. It is easily distinguished by its fork tail.

Seafaring men call the stormy petrel Mother Carey's Chicken for its habit of following ships, feeding on plankton disturbed by the propellors. The word petrel is said to be derived from the Apostle Peter.

These birds take a long time to rear a chick, thirty-eight days to hatch out the egg, then eight to nine weeks before the chick is ready to face the ocean.

Hebridean Sailing

Happiness may baffle pursuit, but even an old yachtsman like our skipper can find it at the wheel, watching mainsail and jib stretched from a 72ft. mast to make the streamlined craft cut the water at eight knots. Everything was right for comfort. The wind was not too strong, and it was bearing us in the direction we wanted to go—eastward to the Small Isles.

Halfway between Barra and Skye there was plenty to look at with the Cuillins throwing off a white wrapper of cumulus. First you could see only the grey scoops of the big corries, then one by one blue-jagged fragments thrust through, The Inaccessible Pinnacle, Sgurr Alasdair, Mhic Coinnich— and across the sound from them, the high platform of Canna overtopped by the Cuillin of Rhum.

We were looking forward to anchoring in Muck in mid-afternoon, but the Atlantic swell was too much, and there was no point in going into Canna since we had been in that snug anchorage a fortnight before.

On that occasion I had the pleasure of renewing acquaintance with naturalist Dr John Lorne Campbell who farms this basaltic platform which is six miles long by half-a-mile broad and has about two dozen inhabitants, all Gaelic speakers.

Dr Campbell is an Argyll man who bought Canna thirty-nine years ago and in the interval has vastly increased its natural history interest by planting pine, larch, spruce, oak, wild cherry, alder, hazel and willow.

In early June when I was there, the island was singing with birds and from the fields came a rasp-rasp of corncrakes. I even found a siskin in the house policies, round the corner from 600ft. cliffs buzzing with seabirds. Bluebells made a haze on the slopes.

Playing a lone hand, this naturalist has shown that if you reinstate former habitats you get the wild-life. By allowing a lochan to reform and by planting its shores with bull-rushes, bog myrtle, and some trees, he has induced three different kinds of dragonflies to colonise. Pollen analysis in the peat reveals that trees once grew extensively over Canna, so he planted fifteen acres with some of the species that formerly grew there.

Dr Campbell is a working farmer, which came as a surprise to me for I only knew him as a scholarly writer on all matters Highland and Gaelic. Nor did I appreciate the extent of his contribution to the study of butterflies, moths, and insects of the Hebrides.

Yes, Canna has good land, a healthy stock of sheep and cattle, excellent sea-fishing round its shores, and lobsters in the creeks, yet farming it successfully becomes increasingly more difficult as freight charges go up and the shipping service goes down.

But Dr Campbell refuses to give up, though he is certain in his heart that the Government would like nothing better than for the people of the Small Isles to move out, lock, stock and barrel and save it the bother of administration.

The Luss Hills

When you get a haymaker of a morning of hot sun with a cooling north-wester moving the white clouds gently along, you know you are in for something good on the tops, for that combination spells hard visibility and good contrasts for photography.

No need to waste much time travelling when there is a shapely range of a dozen peaks beckoning between Loch Long and Loch Lomond.

These Luss hills are favourites of mine. Go up the glen behind the Colquhoun Arms and in the first mile you are ringed by them, the first truly Highland summits near Glasgow, and the first to be taken over by the southern flockmasters when they brought their black-faced sheep to the glens following the failure of the '45 Rising.

The natural trees and the steep north corries hemming the Luss Water give fine character to the steep single-track road which ends below Ben Eich in 2½ miles. This was our chosen peak, so we parked at the sheep farm of Glenmallochan, packed the "piece" and a flask of tea, walked the private road to the top farm of Edentaggart, and struck up the grassy slope of the east ridge immediately above.

Plenty excuses for rests, with a wide view opening behind you as you climb, an unusual one for it is entirely Lowland in character, gentle shores and wooded islands, the water of Loch Lomond seeming to lap the big agricultural patchwork of Strathendrick. And if you follow the ridges of the Campsies leftward you see the grey pinnacle of the Wallace Monument backed by the Ochils.

And you can trace your own river too by the tower blocks of Clydebank and the oil tanks at Bowling right down to the estuary. Your eye will light at the hump of Ailsa Craig, and, far out to its right, the grey-blue ridge of Arran's Sleeping Warrior. To be here at 2,302 ft. for the price of about an hour and a half of climbing is a fine reward indeed.

Nor are we alone on the summit, for a criss-crossing throng of scimitar-winged missiles hurtle back and fore above our reclining bodies. Always banking from side to side, wings beating alternatively, they are the fastest of all insect catchers—well-named "Swifts." We can hear the wind whistling through their feathers as they arrow past. Our cheese rolls tasted the better for them.

Refreshed, we head down the other side of the ridge for Beinn Lochain—a misnomer, for there is no loch, only a wee marsh. But as if to justify the description there is a cavorting of common gulls around it. Over the top and on we go for Doune Hill, 2,408 ft. and the highest in the range. The surprise here is a clamouring squadron of rooks, about 200 of them, the first I ever remember seeing at this height on a Scottish hill.

We can look down on the West Highland Railway now where it cuts into Glen Douglas before threading along Loch Longside to Arrochar. Opposite is the pass across to Lochgoilhead with the rocky waves of the Cobbler range dominating the MacFarlane country. MacGregor's Glengyle looks no less wild in rocky bumps.

The Beauty of the Cobbler's Wife

We're lucky in Glasgow to have one of the most challenging rock peaks in Scotland within easy reach of rail and road—the Cobbler—three elegant prongs thrusting into the sky above the head of Loch Long and commanding an unobstructed view of the Firth of Clyde from each of its airy tops.

Airy, yes. But the right-hand top, the North Peak, requires nothing that could be construed as rock climbing, so the pleasure of noble and exciting mountain scenery can be yours for a climb of 2,800 ft. in three miles from sea-level.

Historically the mountain is important, for it sparked off the very first true climbing club in Scotland, whose worthy object was ". . . to climb the Cobbler and whatever worthy hill could be reached in the course of a Saturday expedition from Glasgow."

That was away back in 1866. But even then it was also part of the objective to "crown the labours of the day by an evening of social enjoyment." New waves of climbers have found the same old delights since then. The route I recommend is as follows.

Take to the hill at Succoth at the head of Loch Long, near the mountain rescue post, where a path rises steeply to a broad track running west above the trees to the Allt a' Bhalachain concrete dam. Strike up the burn and in an easy mile you'll reach two boulders which have given a roof and draughty overnight shelter to many a keen party.

Even if you climb no further than this you have the full glory of the three peaks before you, Jean on the left, the Cobbler's Wife on the right, and the Cobbler with upraised arm in the centre.

The Wife is the lady for you if you want the easiest conquest. Simply head up towards her on a steep path to reach the gap between the Cobbler and his Wife. From there it is an easy scramble to the sensationally exposed top with a great overhanging beak of rock below on the biggest sheer wall on the mountain. Don't look over unless you have a head for heights.

Given a day of visibility, consider traversing across to the Cobbler himself for a perch below his grey pow. Don't climb the last bit unless you are sure and steady on exposed places.

Nor do I advise continuing along the narrow ridge to the south peak called Jean, for it is a wee bit rocky and in dampish weather can be slippery. Mica schist rock always requires extra care when it is wet because of a lichen which grows upon it. Yet the Cobbler is a kindly mountain, for its distances are short and because of its situation, you see any changes of weather taking place before your eyes.

So choose a good day, not only for the prospect of views, but because you should see some bold rock climbers on some of the seventy routes which make this one of the best hills in Scotland for practitioners of this baleful sport.

We all have our strange addictions. Bill Murray, one of Scotland's most respected climbers got his by climbing the Cobbler one April day in the early thirties. He chose it because it was the only mountain he knew by name.

Alone and wearing his ordinary city clothes, shoes, collar and tie, he made the top block and went on to do the steep side of the south peak. He told me later of his fear of a slip, but the joy of it all, and the sight of the mountains all around raised in him the desire to be a mountaineer.

For those who want to see the Cobbler corrie without going to the tops I can recommend a little round tour. From the Shelter Stones go up to the Bealach a' Mhaim and strike east between Ben Ime and Beinn Narnain to reach a good track to Coiregrogan above Inveruglas.

From the old farm track strike south down Glen Loin on a wooded path which brings you out at Succoth from where you started.

Barra

Here was a cheery sight for July—three athletic birds of prey plainly visible in a rock eyrie only 50ft. above the Cockle Strand in Barra where the daily plane lands.

You might have described them as jumping for joy, especially the biggest one which not only danced up and down but was fanning its big brown wings so vigorously that it was becoming airborne, at which it would make a wild grab with its yellow talons, hang on to the heather, and slide back into the nest.

They were young birds, and I wasn't surprised when the most active performer, plainly anxious to leave home, had disappeared next day, leaving one still dancing and flapping, while the smallest one crouched abjectly as if missing his elder brother. Buzzards need a good food supply to raise three chicks, in this case rabbits which are everywhere among the grassy dunes.

Compton Mackenzie the author lived beside the Cockle Strand in his Barra years, but that windy dwelling is now a factory which crushes cockle shells to be sold as grit for harling houses.

A big herd of cattle shares the strand with the cockle gatherers, and at plane landing time it is fun to watch a man driving about in a tractor driving off the beasts to give the little aircraft a free run on what looks like water. The first sheets of spray, however, show that the firm sand is only a few inches below surface. The plane disgorges its passengers on the dry sand beside the airport terminal with easy informality.

Everything about Barra is easy. It has fourteen miles of ring-road and enough off-shoots in the form of rocky hills, sandy bays, and crofting peninsulas to keep any explorer happy for a long time.

From the top of Heaval, 1,260ft., you look down on Castlebay and get a bird's eye view of Vatersay across the water. In the great days of the herring fishery the two miles of water between these islands used to be filled with sailing boats from all over Scotland. But between 1914 and 1930 came the decline and slump, with fresh herring galore being dumped back into the sea.

Things are changing again. At North Bay on the Friday evening when we anchored the boat at Ardveenish there was a queue of fishing boats unloading prawns and whitefish at the new factory.

A few minutes in the dinghy took us to two interesting features, the first, a statue of St Barr on an island below the road, an eye-catching piece of modern sculpture 10ft high, bearing a crook above his head and gazing to the sky.

127

Just across the road is the only woodland of any density in Barra, no more than a small plantation of conifers, but an oasis which excites a bird man. One colonist I did not expect to find there was Britain's smallest bird, a goldcrest, carrying green caterpillars to a swaying hammock suspended from the lower branches of a Sitka spruce.

That find was even more suprising than the collared doves feeding on the grass round the Barrahead lighthouse, and the pair of swallows hawking flies round its tower, which is windier and higher than any other lighthouse in Britain.

Red Grouse

I suppose I can claim to have tramped as many miles over the heather as many a grouse-beater who will be out every day for the next few weeks waving a flag to raise the coveys from underfoot and send them skimming towards the waiting gunmen at the butts.

"Not much sport in that!" you might exclaim. In fact the red grouse is rivalled only by its mountain-top cousin, the ptarmigan, when it comes to wildness and hardiness. And it has to be even more aggressive towards its own kind if it is to survive.

A sea of heather is as necessary to a grouse as the ocean to a cod, except that the moor where the bird is hatched is its invisible cage. The chances are that the grouse will be dead within a year-and-a-half of hatching, nor will it reach even half that age unless it can battle with its neighbours and win itself a territory, a living space.

What size of territory? It takes a shooting season to provide the answer, because it is the grouse themselves who share out the moor according to the health and nutrition of the heather. In years of good heather-growth each bird can do with less moor. In poor years each requires more moor, and the unsuccessful are driven off, to die of starvation or be killed by predators.

These facts which I give so glibly were unknown twenty-one years ago when Dr. Adam Watson and Dr. David Jenkins began work trying to discover for the Scottish Landowners' Federation why grouse numbers were declining. Glen Esk was the first base for the work, which later moved to Banchory to become the Unit of Grouse and Moorland Ecology.

In science, conclusions are hard-won and have to be tested. Kerloch Moor, in poor conditon when rented to the research unit, was divided in two. One half was treated with calcium and ammonium nitrate. The result was brilliant heather and an increase in shoot-length, where grouse laid earlier and reared four times more young than on the untreated portion.

However, the basic quality of the heather is reflected by its underlying

128

rocks. Granite is infertile, and birds on it need large territories, whereas on schists and the like they will squeeze up. The hardiness of grouse conceals the fact that a moor may be offering little more than starvation diet in bad years.

Once on a ski-trip in Glen Clunie I counted over 800 grouse in one whirling pack. That was in January. Come April the hen birds were incubating eggs at 1,500ft. in temperatures around freezing point.

Paradoxically, however, the cold and late spring of 1977 has favoured these high-nesting grouse, since they lay their eggs later than birds of the lower moors. Thus they caught some warmth and sunshine, so favourable to producing good coveys.

The Treshnish

Gurly was the sea, grey the skies, and the wind strong as we sped south from the island of Coll, at eight knots, with sails spread, towards the Dutchman's Cap, its steep crown an old volcano, its brim a flat oval of the lava we call basalt.

With the Atlantic swell no landing was possible, but adjacent Lunga, largest of the scatter of rocks known as the Treshnish offered hope, and our experienced skipper nosed his way in, finding reasonable water on its sheltered eastern side to drop anchor, launch the dinghy and drop us off on a storm beach of slippery boulders, haunt of nesting storm petrels.

A historic moment for me to be landing here, because twenty years ago a plan of mine to land with tent and provisions was defeated by August gales and I got no farther than Calgary in Mull. My desire to go there had been fired by reading Dr F. Fraser-Darling's *Island Years*, tales of adventure and pioneer studies of the Atlantic seals in the 1930s by the famous ecologist.

So it was no ordinary moment going ashore in the footsteps of the master and climbing a volcanic staircase to face the still unclimbed pinnacle of Dun Cruin, a bird fortress split from Lunga by the narrowest of sea alleys echoing with an Atlantic boom of waves and the cries of seabirds.

I knew now what I had missed, for here was a concentration of island wild-life on a horizontal and vertical plane within immediate eye range. Below my feet nothing but space, yet the wall of Dun Cruin was so close that you almost shared the ledges with the puffins, razorbills, shags, fulmars, and guillemots crowding its ledges and decorating every protuberance and usable stance.

Oh for a movie camera team to put this on film and show the excitement of the place with auks scurrying past at eye-level, paddling the air inexpertly on short wings, victims rather than masters of the up-draughts, because these paddles are for swimming below water rather than for flying.

Like penguins, their element is the sea, and they come to land to lay a single egg, rear a chick and depart to spread themselves over the ocean.

Darling spent three months on the Treshnish to watch and record these annual events, and how envious of him this teenager was in the 1930s, wishing I could be there sharing his discoveries and opening up a new era of natural history research.

But he had written so well of Lunga that I felt I had been here before. The rabbits were thick on the ground, some of them black as he had noted. Fat cattle still grazed the Dorlinn—a volcanic tableland girt by cliffs— and I almost saw his tent beside the ruins of houses where people lived 120 years ago.

And it was there that Fraser-Darling made one of his first wild-life discoveries on Lunga, namely the ability of house-mice to endure without their hosts, for he had barely settled before his tent was plagued with lodgers. Sorrowfully he records reducing their population by seventy-five. It had to be done. It was a matter of survival, theirs or his, which is how nature works.

Staffa

Here we are, all sails spread and turning round the end of Staffa for my first close view of its rock pillars, like dark hanging icicles, smashed by the black gash of Fingal's Cave.

It is late afternoon, showers sprinkle the hills of Mull, but the sea is not too rough for a landing, so down goes the anchor and off we go ashore, glad to have the place to ourselves.

Ah, how I would like to have been Sir James Banks who sailed with Captain Cook in the *Endeavour* and who was the first tourist to land here in 1772. He came with tent and food for two days, having been told that ". . . no one even in the Highlands had been there." Banks came to look at the pillars, described to him as being like those of the Giant's Causeway.

Scrambling up to the crown of the island he found a bothy, and in it a herdsman living a solitary life, looking after cattle grazing on the green crown of the island. It is the next bit I especially like. The herdsman insisted on Banks and his companion sharing his hut. He set down fish and milk before them, then regaled them all evening with Gaelic songs.

They spent the night scratching themselves, and by morning they discovered they were lousy, and Banks mentioned the matter, expecting some sort of apology to his reproach. At which the herdsman bridled, telling them with some asperity that they must have carried the vermin with them since there were none before they came.

The ruin of a bothy is the only sign of habitation today, but stone steps for the convenience of tourists lead up the cliff, and concrete has been laid, and iron stanchions, fixed in the MacBrayne era to safeguard the tourists traversing from the jetty into the great cave penetrating the gash which extends for 228ft. into semi-darkness.

I was more impressed than I had expected to be by the scale and the rock architecture exposed by the hammer of the sea. Describing it, Banks asks the rhetorical question: "Compared to this, what are the cathedrals or the palaces built by man?" Banks was told it was called the cave of Fhinn, Fhinn MacCool, hence Fingal's Cave.

But long before it got that fanciful name it was known to the Gaels as *Uamh Binne*, the cave where the sea makes music. And no doubt it was the sounds of the sea among the fragmented pillars which impressed itself on the perceptive Mendelssohn, resulting in his Hebridean Overture written after his visit in 1829.

There are other splendid caves shattering the basalt at this south end of Staffa, but none has such high portals or stretches back so deeply as Uamh Binne. From the pillars of lava, shaped into hexagons at the joints where the hot material cooled, nature has produced a masterpiece of architectural form, for when you look out from the farthest point in the cave you see the most sacred isle of Christendom on the horizon—Iona.

A friend of mine canoed to Staffa from Iona. He expected to get back to base the same night. It was a week before the sea gave him a chance. We were glad of our sails.

Lochnagar

One fine thing not to be taken for granted, is the good relations which have always existed between the Queen's Balmoral Estate and rock climbers and hill-walkers.

Even now, when the royal standard is flying and deer stalking and grouse shooting are in full swing, the most sporting route to the summit of Lochnagar from the Spittal of Muick remains open, and this is where we are going today.

Route finding could hardly be easier. Drive from Ballater on the narrow road which climbs up Glen Muick to 1,400ft. and you find yourself at a car park.

No problems from here, for the path is signposted, and there is even a Scottish Wildlife Trust information centre with a friendly ranger in attendance to tell you anything you want to know. In fact a whole chunk of Lochnagar, including Loch Muick, is available to the public under a Nature Reserve agreement with marked paths and picnic spots.

These facilities do not diminish the wildness of Lochnagar however, for this is not so much a mountain as a range of eleven tops over 3,000ft, covering sixty-three square miles, with some of the sheerest cliffs in

Britain walling its wild corries.

For a first visit there's nothing better than the easiest way to the top, distance 4½ miles and only 2,600ft. of ascent. Allow yourself six hours for the return journey.

You can see where the route goes by looking at the cliffs of the north-eastern corrie just across the glen. You cross to the white shooting lodge beside the burn, follow up through the trees, and continue to a junction of paths. Your way is obvious, steeply uphill in a westerly direction to a gap between two mountain spurs.

My advice to you is to make a wee divergence from the normal route by climbing the right hand of these spurs called the Meikle Pap. Why? Because of the sudden revelation of the horse-shoe of crags encircling the black lochan from which Lochnagar derives its name.

In all Scotland there is no better example of a wild mountain corrie, cliffs 750ft. high, curving in a mile, and riven by gullies, chimneys, pinnacles, and flying buttresses.

From this position at 3,211ft. you will realise the truth of Byron's "The steep frowning glories of dark Lochnagar." The poet was only fifteen years old when he climbed the mountain in 1803 and was inspired to write these noble lines.

His gillie records the quiet boy sitting on the edge of the cliffs saying nothing, but stopping often to take in everything in sight.

Back to the path, you climb by a series of zig-zags known as "the ladder" and so to the grassy plateau. We were lucky, in that our ascent was made in showery August weather which had cleared the humid air to give sharp visibility and lustre to everything in view.

Through binoculars we could see the Great Tower standing out from the top of Ben Nevis. Caithness was pinpointed by the sharp peak of Morven. South of Ben Lomond were distant summits beyond recognition, but the Sidlaws, Pentlands, and Lammermuirs were beyond doubt.

The highest point, at 3,789ft., is at the far end of the rock horse-shoe, and on the way to it you should enjoy the cliff edge and walk out along some of its airy projections to enjoy the rock sculpture and plunging buttresses curving sensationally to the lochan 1,200ft below.

The two highest peaks lie close to each other, nippled with rockpoints like Bennachie. And here too the original place-name makers found their descriptive imagery by naming the mountain we know as Lochnagar as *Beinn Cichean*, mountain of teats. Nothing could be more natural.

OOT O' THE WARLD AN' INTAE FINTRY

More than forty years later, up here at the source of the River Carron high in the Campsies, it's interesting to trace your obsessions. Mine were with this place, half way between Lennoxtown and Fintry where the Crow Road climbs to the Toll House. As a lad I used to walk here from Springburn every Sunday, and when I got a bike I was here during the week as well. What was the attraction? I didn't try to analyse it. Just to be among the hills, hearing the sounds of the burns and the wild cries of whaups and peewits was magic enough, in a world where even the clouds seemed alive, casting their sailing shadows on the green slopes. My destination was usually the Toll House where the streams flow north instead of south, indicating the direction of Fintry, as fascinating as Tibet, because it was unknown.

Jimmy McEwan who lived at the Toll House would be a man of forty-six then, black haired and vigorous. He sold bottles of lemonade in these days and I always envied him his job as roadman, free to work his wee croft and fly his pigeons—a man contented, so long as you didn't have to move him more than walking distance from his lonely house. Sadly I have to report he died not long ago aged ninety-two.

He was too poorly to appear in public by the time I made a television programme about Fintry beginning at his house by the source of the Carron and following its path to where the high road swings away north to begin the exciting descent between the bold hill-shoulders, combining a feeling of fertility and grandeur. Then came the first fields and woods. Cattle interspersed with sheep, and below, the Clachan, the ancient part of Fintry built round the kirk. Newton of Fintry lies a mile on, a village built to house cotton spinners around 1796 when 20,000 spindles kept 260 hands at work.

Bob Aitken who farms Bogside is the very man to talk about Fintry past and present. "Aye, the cotton mill failed and so did a woollen mill, because they were ower far frae Glasgow and the coal seams. Even a distillery couldna pay its way here. You can see the ruins behind the garage on the main street. The water was there and it was supposed tae be the best o' malt whisky which was produced frae 1816, but it fizzled oot."

We looked at the old mill, still in remarkably sound shape and being used as a workshop, and the track of the lade which supplied water power. Bob opined that the remoteness of Fintry was against it even in

133

the railway days when trains served Lennoxtown, Dumgoyne, Killearn, Balfron, Buchlyvie, Port of Menteith and Kippen. "Every one o' these stations was the same distance frae Fintry," said Bob, "seeven or eight miles, so they didna help."

I asked Bob if anyone in Fintry remembered the days of the great droving trade. "Aye, I mind an uncle o' mine walking a filly hame that he had bocht at the Falkirk Tryst. That was aboot 1895, but it wisnae much o' a fair by that time.

"Fintry must hae been an awfy busy place when Falkirk was the biggest cattle market in Britain. I mind a story I heard aboot Corrie-choille—you'll hae heard o' him, the biggest o' the drovers. He made a bargain wi' the man at Fintry Toll and struck the price for hauf an oor. He had a lot o' cattle an' sheep and he rushed them through at sic a speed that he cam oot best. The toll keeper was coontin' an' saw he had been diddled oot o' £5. by no chargin' each beast individually. He should have kent better than to bargain wi' Corriechoille."

Two events occurred at the right time to create the opportunity for cattle trade between the Highlands and Islands and the Lowlands. The first was the Union of Parliaments in 1707 and the arrival of more settled times. The second was the growth of London, the Midlands and the North of England towns, not to mention the wars which lasted from 1727 to 1815 and created a demand in England for lean Scottish cattle for fattening.

The wild clansmen were used to lifting other folks' cattle and walking them through trackless glens to their hideouts, so it was natural for them to become drovers, fording swollen mountain torrents, ferrying beasts across lochs, taking shortcuts through roadless countryside with hardy animals which were able to transport themselves to market. In 1827 at Falkirk, 130,000 cattle and 200,000 sheep were sold at just two markets.

June to October was the droving season, and the trade was so important to England that drovers were allowed to carry weapons for their defence even during the 1745 Jacobite Rising. "Aye," said Bob, "they were hardy men and hardy cattle. At the sale they might fetch £7 a beast. We dinna breed cattle like that the day. The heavy cattle o' today couldna walk and for a bullock I would expect £160 to £200 for a guid yin o' aboot nine hundredweights."

We talked about the improved land management, the introduction of the turnip and the rotation of crops which had led to the breeding of heavier cattle, resulting in the wonderful breeds of today. Bob's own cattle are cross Herefords, but his first love is horses, Clydesdales descended from the ones he used to work at the plough. Prize-winners at the Royal Highland Show, their ancestry going back to vol. 1 of the Clydesdale studbook.

You can take a walk into history by going a little east of Endrick Bridge and following the old drove road past the ruins of Fintry Castle to

Spittal Hill Farm which was a "stance" where the drovers rested their cattle. Or drive along the Carron Valley to Falkirk. How paradoxical that the Carron Iron Works were going full blast when the droving trade was at its height, smelting iron for use in the Napoleonic wars, building the first steam engine for winding coal, and building an engine for the first steamship to be launched on the Carron River in 1789, so that the ships of the Carron Company were soon plying to London.

It was paradoxical because these products were to outmode the droving trade as the age of the steamship and the railway was ushered in. It is also interesting to remember that whole forests as far north as Glen Moriston, were consumed to provide charcoal to feed the iron furnaces of Falkirk.

The Highlanders were being pushed out of their cattle grounds by alien landlords to make way for sheep at this time, so, instead of one big market at Falkirk, a variety of smaller markets were set up in the north where some drovers continued to walk their beasts although increasing numbers travelled by rail and ship.

Eventually, a very adventurous trade, where robbery was only one of the many dangers to face on the long walk through a troubled country, died out. As for the old Toll House on top of the Crow Road, I learned that it used to be a shebeen. At 1,100 ft. up in the hills it was always a good place to enjoy a drink of lemonade. Jimmy, who used to sell me the bottles, was a teetotaller.

THE LAKE OF MENTEITH

After a run of drizzly days, when it seemed as if the world had suffered a power-cut, suddenly the light was switched on and the golden lamp of the sun was lighting snowy Ben Lomond across the great mirror of the Lake of Menteith, its reedbeds shimmering against the long escarpment of the Campsies. Never did that hollow of low country look so enchanting, or ring with such a medley of exciting sounds, for as far as the eye could see, the lake was dotted with birds, flighting, calling, landing or taking off. A great baying of almost human sound came from the grey geese, thousands of them, an undulation of musical noise like you hear coming in waves from a school playground at play-time.

As we drove along, we could see the geese were strung out along the whole shore in water and in fields. There were other sounds too, the chirruping and whistling of ducks as teal jumped into the air, flights of wigeon took-off, and wherever we looked there was movement of mallard, pochard, tufted ducks, goldeneye and coots.

A mile along the narrow road and I came to the Port of Menteith, wondering if I could find a ferry to take me over to the island. I needn't have worried. The ferry runs summer and winter to the monastic ruins of Inchmahome. "You'll have the place to yourself," said the ferryman, as we chugged off on the short crossing to the island where Mary Queen of Scots had been taken after the disastrous Battle of Pinkie in September 1547.

Looking at the reflections of the white washed village houses and church spire in the limpid water, I asked the ferryman how it came to be called Port of Menteith. "It comes from the French word *puirt.* It means the taking-off place. And it must have been busy when the monks were coming and going to the Priory."

Within minutes I was stepping ashore and walking amongst graceful arches of what is said to be the best preserved of all Augustinian monasteries. There was a feeling of hallowed peace as I walked among the carved stones brought here in the thirteenth century to build into arches and aisle piers. It was in 1238 that Walter Stewart, ancestor of Mary Queen of Scots, was authorised by the Bishop of Dunblane "to build a House for Religious Men of the Order of St. Augustine, in the Island of Inchmaquhomok."

I walked into the Chapter House to look at the joint tomb of this 4th Earl of Menteith and his Countess Mary whose effigies lie together in a fond attitude. The leg of the Earl crossed below the knee indicates he was a crusader. It set me thinking about Mary Queen of Scots who came here nearly 300 years after these ancestors were laid in their island tomb.

The Queen was five when she was brought here with her four "Maries". She spent only three weeks on Inchmahome but was not allowed to be totally idle, for she was promptly put to school by the black-habited Augustine monks. I strolled along to her bower, through an avenue of gnarled Spanish chestnut trees, limbs twisted with age. The bower lay beyond, a little den encircled with box hedge. It is said that Mary planted it. Perhaps she did, but the present bower is not the same one, though it stems from cuttings taken from the original bower.

Mary may have seen the monks making play at an unusual kind of fishing. First they secured one of the mute swans that are common on the lake, then they tied a long piece of line to a leg with a live perch baited on the end. The swan was then released, watched carefully by the monks to see if a pike would take the bait. If so, they would know instantly by the swan's distress and all they had to do was row out and pull in the line to get their Friday dinner. It is also said that local farmers practised the same technique except that they used tame geese instead of swans, which swam home towing their catch behind them.

Robert the Bruce seems to have liked Inchmahome, for he visited it three times, first after his coronation at Scone in 1306, when he found a self-supporting community of monks baking bread, brewing beer, catching fish, and working their orchards and vegetable gardens. Many of the monks were farmers and employers of labour who preached in Parish churches and helped the needy. They were also bound by deed of gift to pray for the soul of their patron, his kindred, and other persons named by him.

Mary's short stay in 1547, 237 years after Bruce, took place in the century that saw Inchmahome Priory fade into obscurity. In the very name Inchmahome, there is an echo of an even more distant past, for the words spring from *Innis mo Cholmaig,* the Isle of my Colmac, St. Colmac who lived on Inchmahome. Standing on the edge of the island I looked over a narrow strait to *Inchtalla,* the Castle Island, which was a stronghold of the Earls of Menteith after the annexation of Doune Castle by James I. The ruined castle occupying a tiny island is almost lost among the tall trees, and it must have been a grim place to occupy. In fact, it was so distasteful to one countess that she removed herself to Edinburgh because of the croaking of the frogs.

Nearby there is another tiny island, Inchuan—*Innis nan Con,* the Island of Dogs where the Menteith Earls kept their terrier-like dogs.

Strolling back for the ferry which was due to leave at 3.30pm, I had a look at the grave-stone of a remarkable member of this house who died in my own lifetime. Robert Bontine Cunningham Graham, Scottish laird, South American gaucho, writer, socialist and Scottish Nationalist, whose body was brought over in a Graham tartan plaid to the sound of the pipes and laid to rest.

Among the long line of Menteith Earls there are noble figures and sinister ones, but only one who died as a beggar. This pathetic figure of royal blood had tried to be a medical student and failed. Poverty turned him to begging. The year was 1783 and there was no priory of hospitable monks to offer him succour. Half-crazed, he died by the roadside not far from the lake.

But why the name "lake" in a country where every other comparable sheet of water is a loch? Was it because the monks used Latin and the word *lacus* to indicate a sheet of water? This would be convincing were it not for the fact that long after the monks had gone, Menteith was not called a lake but was known as the Loch of Inchmahome (Timothy Pont 1654). Or could it be that the Lake of Menteith became a common reference towards the end of the eighteenth century when increasing numbers of travellers came to Scotland and described its scenery in books. The low-lying area nearby was known as the Laigh of Menteith, (Laigh: low-lying) and this may also have caused a misreference.

The very gentleness of the scenery here, compared to the wild Trossachs just over the hills from Aberfoyle may have oriented them towards the unselfconscious use of the English word lake. After all, Sir Walter Scott wrote Loch of Menteith, and he was not born until 1771. It is a puzzle I leave to you.

As for the lake itself. It was formed by the weight of a great lobe of ice, which slowly melted, filling the depression it occupied, and in its history it must have been lapped by the North Sea by reason of the marine shells found in moraines. The Lake of Menteith is 1½ miles long by 1 mile broad. Its maximum depth is 77ft. Its height above sea level is 55ft.

138

FLANDERS MOSS:
SWORDS TO PLOUGHSHARES

Let me put a proposition to you. Forget for the moment that you are living in the present; imagine you are living 200 years ago and pretend you are a Highlander, living in Balqhidder or Callander. The failure of the Jacobite cause has left the country full of broken men. Black faced sheep are taking over the glens, and you are being encouraged to emigrate like thousands of other destitute folk. But suddenly, you have the offer of a new life on a notorious peat moss between Stirling and Doune. You are given the chance to take over eight to ten acres of the moss with a wooden spade to dig it. For this work you will receive no weekly wage, except two bolls of meal. But you will get the timbers to build a house, and a lease on your ground for thirty-eight years. Your task is to dig down to the good clay soil which is known to be underneath the peat, and reclaim it for agriculture. You will have nothing to pay for eight years, and little more than a small token payment will be demanded until the nineteenth year. After that you will be expected to pay for each acre in cultivation, plus 2.6d (12½ pence) for each acre which is still in peat.

How would you react to such a challenge? Would you pledge your best years to try and make the moss yield food to feed you? Hunger is a hard taskmaster. You are being asked to try something that has never been attempted before. Lord Kames of Blair Drummond had dreamt up a scheme of reclamation. He had conceived the idea that if the peat covering the moss could be chopped up and thrown into ditches, then the power of the water would carry it away.

You are being offered the chance of a new life because the success of the scheme depends upon a plentiful supply of cheap labour. The beggars of these desperate times could not afford to be choosers. The first colonists came in 1767. Others followed, and by 1774 thirteen tenants had disposed of 104 acres of what was known as the Low Moss.

The reclaimers, living in thatched huts were objects of scorn at first and termed "Moss Lairds". But within ten years, applicants had to be limited because of the shortage of water for carrying away the peat.

Landlords of the other mosses stretching westward from Stirling had also joined the band waggon.

The excavation of the peat unlocked many secrets. Antlers of deer, jaws of whales, great oak trees black as coal, bearing the cuts of the small Roman axe. These trees lay on clay, just above the roots, and the wood was still sound though it must have been lying there for all of 1,700 years. Other woods found in the peat were birch, hazel, alder, willow and some pine; all supporting the theory that the woods which once grew here had been deliberately destroyed by the Romans.

Why did they destroy them? Probably because they provided too much cover for the native Britons who opposed their occupation. The predecessors of Severus may have been trying to make a fortified line similar to Antonine's famous Clyde-Forth structure, but gave up in the face of ambush. They left many remains behind them, a road made of logs twelve feet wide in Kippen Parish—a Roman causeway on Flanders Moss, only nine miles from Alauna, on what was the Roman A.1.

The destruction of the forest would favour the formation of the peat-moss by making it more soggy and clogging the natural drainage channels, especially since the elongated plain between Stirling and Aberfoyle is hemmed by hills except to the east. Even in Roman times much of it would be quagmire, especially these regions where the peat is around 20ft deep today.

The period of peat development remains a speculation. What is more certain is that the sea once rolled over the Moss, and that its former shore line is where the villages of Kippen, Thornhill, Gargunnock and Buchlyvie are sited above the flat lands of the carse. Think about this the next time you motor along the Kippen-straight to Stirling on the line of the old Roman road. Notice too that a large bit of intractable peat-moss stretches west towards the Lake of Menteith.

The Highland Mossmen would have cleared the entire moss if it had not been that their methods were too successful. Hacking out the peat and floating it down the Goodie Water and the River Forth they did not see it again. But it was a different story when it got to the estuary where it floated about as a filthy pulp, destroying the oyster beds and the salmon fisheries. So in 1865 the method of peat-floating was declared a public nuisance. The reclamations were banned, and ". . . the most singular and considerable improvement yet accomplished in Scotland came to an end." (Statistical Account).

The cheap rents had also come to an end. Leases had run out and new land values had been created thanks to the industry of its creators. The squeeze was on and many of the small holders were unable to pay. They had to sell their leases. The era of the take-over bid had come to pass, but it is recorded that most of the "Moss Lairds" sold at a good profit. By 1847 the price of "Carseland" had risen to £2.7s an acre, but the MacFarlanes, MacGregors, MacLarens and Fergussons were still going strong. Houses were growing bigger, roads were being improved, and the present foundation of Carse farming laid.

I had the good luck to speak to one man whose family had farmed Fordhead by the Ford of Frew for over a hundred years. He claimed direct descent from Rob Roy and still had his christening robe in the family. We stood on the bridge over the Forth as he described an incident which happened to Rob when he had been captured by Government troops and taken on horseback into custody.

In those far off days Flanders Moss was little better than a morass, and the Ford of Frew, one of the only crossing places, was in dangerous flood. Rob loosened his jacket as his horse plunged into the water, and choosing his moment, tumbled into the depths of the river. The next thing the troopers saw was his jacket floating downstream and they went after it, while Rob, swimming under-water upstream, made his escape.

Rob's descendant, Buchanan More, showed me an old stone by the farm with the inscription "5 miles to Burnfoot". It is all that remains of the once important drove road over the Fords in the great days of the cattle droving which followed the 1707 Act of Union and made this such a paradise for cattle dealer and reiver Rob Roy, who knew these dangerous mosses better than anyone.

In Rob's time, the only cultivation possible on the moss was on the "spreadfield" where peat had been cut for fuel, and subseqent drainage completed. In other parts of the moss reclamation was done by digging trenches and lifting out the clay to spread it on top of the peat. A better way was by repeatedly ploughing the surface and burning it as it dried out until the underlying clay was reached. In just one hundred years of reclamation by the Moss Lairds the mosses had been transformed to fields of wheat and barley, hay and grass; the crops thinning out to pasture lands for cattle and sheep as you went west to the unreclaimed bogs. For many modern farmers it is Timothy hay seed which pays the rent, for Flanders Moss is its main source in Scotland.

A very good way of seeing how the unreclaimed moss gives way to carse is to head east from Aberfoyle past the Lake of Menteith for Thornhill. Stop about two miles along the A873 and look over Cardross Moss much of which is being planted with Lodgepole pines and Sitka spruce. This is the wheel turning full circle, since the origin of the word "Frews", so common on the moss—East Frew, West Frew, North Mid Frew, Mid Frew and Bridge of Frew is said to stem from "trees". The name Flanders Moss originates from the Flemish people who settled during the time of the reclamation two centuries ago. The word "Poldar" which occurs in place names on the moss is also Flemish.

Your road lies parallel and at a higher level than the Goodie Water which flows out of the Lake of Menteith to join the sluggish river Forth whose source is high on Ben Lomond, yet here it is meandering over some of the flattest land in Scotland. The B822 from Thornhill crosses the Goodie Water and the Forth, and if you pause on the latter bridge you are looking down on the Fords of Frew.

An exciting time to go there is in early April before the thousands of pink footed and grey lag geese which winter here have left for the Arctic. See them flying and listen to the torrent of skylark song mingling with the shrilling of curlews and oyster catchers against a background of snow-capped hills. I guarantee you won't be disappointed.

MAN WITH A FIERY CROSS

I knew before I swung down from the snow-patched heather of the high Brae o' Moray through the pines of the River Findhorn to Forres, that on this visit I was going to range far beyond the Moray Firth, for I was on my way to meet a man who had laid the foundation of his fame living and working in the Highlands and Islands of Scotland. None other than Sir Frank Fraser Darling, who, after his global travels as a world ecologist, has retired to live at Lochyhill on the outskirts of the town.

To be invited to spend a day with him talking about the past and the present was indeed a very great honour, for we had met only once before, at a lunch party, and hadn't exchanged a word, for he had lost his voice and couldn't even manage a whisper. That was before he left Scotland and went to America, where he never failed to acknowledge his debt to the Scottish Highlands which had taught him to see and think about landscape in a way that no one had done before. I know that the book which most profoundly affected my own outlook was his *Natural History in the Highlands and Islands*. It came out in 1947, and today is rightly regarded as a classic.

So you can imagine I was fairly excited as I drove through the farm steadings to a hilltop house fringed by pine trees. And as I got out of the car a tall figure in jersey and knickerbockers came out to meet me. The head of thick black hair, the friendly brown eyes and the kindly expression of the rather sombre face were as I remembered them. I complimented him on his view, over broad fields on one side, while on the other, Highland hills ranged above the Moray Firth.

"Yes, you can see Ben Wyvis with snow on it, and away to the right of the Sutors is Morven in Caithness. Ben Clibreck isn't showing today, but it comes up over the Black Isle on really clear days. We've never lived so close to a town before, but we feel in the country up here."

He led me inside to a blazing log fire, and within moments his soft-voiced Scottish wife was making me feel at home with a large cup of coffee, as three silky Pekingese settled down to keep us company. "We lived in Glen Urquhart before coming here," she told me, "and then I happened to see the advert for this house in the local paper. We bought it as soon as we saw it. That was four years ago, and we have no regrets."

Sir Frank is half Scots by birth, but wholly Scots by instinct. "It's inevitable that a cross-bred from Northern England will choose one side of the Border or the other. I knew I would come back finally to settle in

142

Scotland, but not to the West Coast. It's too wet. And it's too touristy nowadays. At seventy-one I have no career ahead, and this old farmhouse is a good place to be. I don't want to travel unless I can walk, and I'm not fit for that now."

Looking around me at the elegant Chippendale furniture, the beautiful bird paintings on the walls and the fine, hand-carved objects on his bookcase, I could not help thinking of Eilean a' Chleirich out west from Loch Broom, and the hut which was his first island home.

" . . . a tiny house with presses and shelves for everything, set down in your own fairy country beyond the reach of the external world. I had played and pretended this bit of escapism all my life, and here it was, as good as the pretending and perhaps a little better, for I had with me those I loved.

"As a philosophy of life, I doubt whether my pleasure at that time would hold water, but as a moment in a life-time it was perfect, reaching its apogee when a flock of barnacle geese came low in front of the window and landed a hundred yards away at the foot of the burn."

He had written that in *Island Years*. "You know," he smiled, "even when a hut was all I wanted, and lonely places were all that mattered, there was a side of me which still wanted beautiful works of man, highly civilised things, works of art.

"But there is a time for everything. That was all part of my first experience of putting the work I wanted to do before money. My dream was an island. But I began with the life history of the red deer. As a naturalist, I was happiest working in a field never touched before. Nobody had studied the life histories of Highland animals and bird flocks and the breeding cycle. My wife—I was married to my first one then— was really splendid. She accepted me giving up my job in animal genetics in Edinburgh, and she came up to Loch Broom to live with me on a Leverhulme Fellowship of £350 a year. And even that sum was guaranteed for only two years."

It was from Brae House, Dundonnel, that Fraser Darling launched himself on An Teallach and the big wilderness to the south of the Strath na Sheallag. And it was here that my own beginnings overlapped with his, for we had a mutual friend in Calum MacRae, the keeper at Carn More, who lived in what was possibly the remotest house in Scotland. Calum used to tell me about the big fellow from Dundonnel who lived like a deer so that he could watch what the beasts were doing night and day.

I had envied him greatly then, not only for the full life he was leading in these favourite hills of mine, but for his skill as a writer. I told him as we sat at the fire, how his books had affected me as a teenager. It was the kind of life-style I wanted for myself.

"Writing was the only thing I was ever good at," he chuckled, "I had a good tutor who pruned me down. I knew I could make money from writing, enought to keep a wife and child and live the kind of life I had chosen. It was the writing that paid for the work. And I've been a very lucky man, for until I was sixty-seven I never knew anything but youth. I never knew what it was to be middle-aged. Then, four years ago, I had a stroke. Suddenly I slowed up, and I've been an old man ever since."

I asked him which of all his island experiences he cherished most. The reply came without hesitation: "North Rona!"

He went on: "I felt completely fulfilled on Rona. The immensity of the ocean was so absorbing in itself. The seabird cliffs in spring and summer, one of the most thrilling things a man can have to watch. I remember how, on 10 August, they were gone, and at the end of the month the seals were hauling ashore and building up in thousands. It was by seeing so many deaths among the pups through overcrowding that I realised there could be too many Atlantic seals on one breeding island, and that there could be a way of managing them for their own good."

Here is a little vignette on Rona from Fraser Darling's pen:

"Enormous waves broke against these cliffs and the water was churned to white foam for seventy-five yards from their foot. It was the sort of sea of which people sometimes say, 'Nothing could live in this terrible surf.' So you would think, but close in to the rocks and where the waves broke most fiercely were our friends the great seals. They were not battling against the seas but taking advantage of them for play. . . They were keeping to the surface, nearly a hundred of them, enjoying the deep rise and fall of the sea and the spray of shattered waves.

"They were living joyfully, and I in my own way rejoiced with them. The sky was a shining vault of blue, the sea was a deeper blue, and as we watched, the surf grew even bigger. The whiteness of it shone in the sunlight, and the movement and sound of it all were glorious. In those days I think we were lifted out of our earth-bound humanity for a space."

I have a good idea of what the sea was like, for on a May day at the Clo Mor cliffs, Cape Wrath, I have seen the waves breaking white over distant North Rona. Listen to his description of a 4 December gale:

"When I went for water I had to crawl over the ridge on hands and knees. Fianuis was impassable for a short time. The sunrise that morning had been a magnificent show of blood-red and cerise, which always bodes ill. After the tantrums of the afternoon we had thunder and lightning at night; the thunder came in single claps just like great explosions and were rather frightening, because for the first two or three I saw no lightning and could hardly believe they were thunder, the sound being mixed with the great noise of the wind."

Yet in our conversation Fraser Darling did not dwell on the mental

Summer in Glen Coe. Stob Choire nam Beith above Loch Triochatan.

Hay-making on the Isle of Raasay opposite Skye. Blaven on the left stretching to the Red Hills.

Man of Knoydart, John MacDougall, whose long life was spent as a shepherd.

Pat Sandeman above Loch Voil on the Braes of Balquhidder.

Cliff-girt Mull of Galloway.

Dick Balharry, Nature Conservancy Officer in Wester Ross, enjoys a laugh with one of his Rhum ponies who seems to find amusement in a red deer calf.

Loch an Eilean in the Spey Valley. Aviemore can be seen in the middle distance.

A salmon cobble fishes below the kittiwake-haunted cliffs of Troup Head, Moray Firth.

The *Sir Walter Scott* sails beneath Ben Venue in the Trossachs.

The Silver sands of Eriskay in the Barra Isles.

Flanders Moss, where the River Forth runs through former marshland.

Day trippers enjoy an outing to Inchmahome on the Lake of Menteith.

In the heart of the wild country between Little Loch Broom and Loch Maree where Dr. F. Fraser Darling studied the deer in the 1930's.

Sea-pinks and puffins on the Island of Noss, Shetland.

Sir Frank Fraser Darling in retirement during the last few years of his life.

The escarpment of West Lomond dominates Kinross.

A new-born Atlantic seal pup cries like a baby and uses its hind limbs like legs.

In three weeks the young seal casts its coat and has put on weight at a rate of four pounds a day. It swims buoyantly.

Dougie Simpson on the Campsie Hills hunting foxes with his terriers.

After heavy rain the Falls of Clyde are reinstated. Normally the water is piped for hydro-electricity.

Loch Enoch, the highest and remotest loch in Galloway. Photographed from Mullwharcher.

Deserted island Eilean nan Ron in Sutherlandshire. Once it was regarded as a very fertile place.

The view south from Eilean nan Ron to Kyle of Tongue. On the right is Ben Hope, most northerly Munro in Scotland.

Isle of Jura, from the crofting township of Knockrome.

The Butt of Lewis. One of the most attractive parts of the Island.

The Old Man of Hoy frames the Orkney ferry boat *St. Ola.*

Guiser Jarl Jim Nicolson prepares for Up Helly Aa. His boys will accompany him on the great day as will this Shetlander from New Zealand.

Tom Weir climbing in Glen Lyon 1979. *(Photo: David Hutton)*

strain that these winds imposed, especially at night when the door of the hut bent and the roof lifted. For as the hut creaked and the crockery rattled, they were uneasily conscious of how narrow was the neck of land called the Fianuis on which they were perched. Only forty yards separated them from the nearest of the bursting waves, and only 100 yards westward was the mighty Atlantic swell.

After the storms came rare days of calm. One was specially memorable. They awoke, three days before Christmas, to a frozen Rona, white after snow squalls.

"Never had we seen the view so magnificent as on this which was to be our last morning. The sun was behind the far, clear line of the Sutherland hills and tinted the whole of our snowy world a rosy pink. The atmosphere was clear and still, and even as we watched I spied a dot thirty miles away between Cape Wrath and the Butt of Lewis. A ship undoubtedly, the first we had seen for a month, and it must be the cruiser coming for us.

"We may never see Rona again as we saw it that morning early. No one else alive has been there at such a time, but we felt in these quiet moments by the chapel that our farewell was not for ever."

Sir Frank took up the story:

"We went back for the summer birds, but not to study the seals for a second breeding season. We were living on Tanera of the Summer Isles by that time, and I was going to make that the base for my seal studies. My intention was to purchase a 40ft. 'Fifie' so as to be able to visit different seal nurseries, for I held that the separate stocks of Atlantic seals remain discrete."

The year was 1939. "We were at war, and I couldn't even go into the army, for back home on Tanera on my way to milk a cow I had a slip on the wet grass, my leg went crack, and I knew it was broken. I had enough sense to know that whatever I did I shouldn't try to walk the 300 yards home, that somehow I would have to crawl up the wet grass of the hill on two hands and one knee. No hope of calling a doctor with the south-wester that was blowing. My wife set the leg from instructions in a St John's Ambulance book, and in six weeks time when the doctor saw it he said it couldn't have been done better if I had fallen on the steps of a hospital.

"Lame for a year and out of the war, I decided we should stay on at Tanera, farm it as effectively as possible and be self-sufficient so as not to be a drain on the country. We were losing convoys at sea and I felt it dreadfully. By working the best land on Tanera intensively, and making the soil more productive so as to carry more stock, I could pass on the message via my writing. We farmed, and I wrote articles in the Highland papers, and published a little book about crofting agriculture.

"The Highlanders listened to what I was saying, because I wrote as a practising crofter, and as one who had been brought up to farming. Moreover, I liked the work. People tell me I have a lasting monument on Tanera—the hill still shines green after all these years. We changed it from heather by carrying up shell sand. Animals grazing on it have kept it good ever since. But there is little interest in crofting as a way of life today."

Island Farm tells the story of bringing life back to Tanera, and how the conviction was forced upon husband and wife that one family is too small a unit to live alone on a small island. The boy, Alasdair, was at Gordonstoun School then, and came home only at holiday times. He is now a doctor of medicine, and lives in the Midlands of England.

"When we left Tanera," said Fraser Darling reflectively, "I had to re-educate myself about division of labour. I had been used to trying to be at both ends of a baulk of timber. The move to Strontian on Loch Sunart, where we had a gardener, a cook, a housemaid and a team of people working together on the West Highland Survey restored the balance."

The book which resulted, *West Highland Survey*—an essay in human ecology—is the work I consider to be the most valuable single reference book ever written about the Western Highlands and its people. But Fraser Darling shook his head.

"I was very green when I put up the idea for that survey. I had been asked to nominate my own salary as director, and because of the war and the fact that I was making £2,000 a year out of writing, I put myself down for £600 a year. I felt I could not take any more money, considering the position we were in as a nation. But the effect of my action was that I depressed the survey in status.

"Also, the Department of Agriculture for Scotland loathed my guts because I had stolen a march on them. After years of work the Report was finished and six copies sent to them. They never even acknowledged their receipt, though I heard they were being well thumbed. Nor would they allow the Report to be published for another three years."

West Highland Survey is preoccupied by the human condition, which can be made better in every respect. *Natural History in the Highlands and Islands* describes the whole ecological range of our marvellous country, and it preaches the need for a "Wild Life Service" devoted to studying unique areas in order to conserve them and their wild life for posterity.

The Government took action by setting up the Nature Conservancy in 1949 for this purpose, but the man most fitted to be its Scottish Director from the standpoint of scientific attainment and experience in the field was not invited to take the post.

Sir Frank chuckled merrily as I aired that view. "I never applied for it! Later I became a lecturer at Edinburgh University, and spent a great deal of time travelling. But I did feel squashed by attitudes within the Nature Conservancy. I wondered if everybody else was right and I was wrong

146

about what was happening to the natural world. In America, when I went there in 1949, it was different. I lectured and met men who were as concerned as I was about population and pollution and the disappearing wilderness.

"I came back knowing I was right, and that great opportunities were being lost. In the early 1940's you could buy some of the finest scenic land in Scotland for 7s 6d and 10s an acre. And that would have been the time to purchase it for the nation and set up National Parks. I was a member of the Ramsay Committee in 1943, defining the five areas. I was also on the big committee which produced the good second report, but no action was taken. Now we can't afford to buy the land, but wilderness should have some legislative control. I hear that an Arab sheik has just bought a big sporting property in the North-West. I hope he will do better than the Arabs have with the oryx."

Breaking for the family lunch, I saw another side of Sir Frank Fraser Darling as he talked about his passion for building drystane walls, and the delight of having a glorious peacock strutting on his lawn. "I've had it for twenty years, and I wouldn't like to be without it. It's a bird of such splendour, I look at it every day, and still experience the same sense of wonder."

After lunch he showed me some of his treasures; a leopard cub in a curled position sculptured from Portsoy marble by Margaret Findlay. ("I knew I had to have it whenever I saw it.") On the same staircase was a realistic snowy owl in Danish Porcelain. He handed me a little short hammer, its smooth shaft beautifully fitting the hand; its adze was of slate held on by thongs. The next thing I held was a bronze dagger, green with age. Above these works of early man was a glowing Russell Flint painting of Spanish dancers with castanets and whirling skirts.

"See that rug beneath your feet. Notice the tassels hanging from the end of it. What do you think these were for?" I soon saw when he picked the rug of intricate Afghan design off the floor and opened it out to show it was in the form of a sack. "Yes, a camel bag, a pannier. Can't you just imagine the camel being unloaded at the end of the day, the goathair tent being set up and the rug tied inside as a draught-excluder and hold-all?"

Many of the things in the house are mementoes of travel. "Yes, it was the Americans who gave me the chance to spread my wings. Working for them was my longest time in single employement, thirteen years, and all with the opportunities to carry out one's ideas. I could even endure New York. The Conservation Foundation, of which I was vice-president, is financed mostly by rich men with open minds: no catch-penny terms."

In the U.S. he became a panoramic ecologist, looking at the world in totality, seeing what man was doing to it in America, Africa, Asia or wherever, advising, writing, helping to set up National Parks, sitting on United States committees as well as committees in Britain.

"And it was because I was known in America that I was picked to give the Reith Lectures for the B.B.C. Thirty years of work on government committees meant little, but what the U.S. gave to me in friendship and opportunity were the punch in my Reith Lectures, given my original convictions.

"I have never had very much ambition, except to live the life I wanted. I have no career ahead, and plenty of time now to think—one of the compensations of age. Perhaps I will still write something. There are so many threads. I suppose you could call me an anti-development man, and to be that is to be a misfit in this modern age."

Sir Frank Fraser Darling has done much more for Scotland than make a brilliant success of his own complex field of study, which is man in relation to his environment. The fiery cross he lit on the Summer Isles and North Rona has never gone out. It was Fraser Darling who inspired a student by the name of John Morton Boyd to become a biologist, and he is now the Director of the Nature Conservancy Council, Scotland.

Moreover, it was Dr J. Morton Boyd who carried on the seal work on North Rona, begun by Sir Frank Fraser Darling. I remember Morton telling me in Glasgow University that if he could achieve even a tenth of what Fraser Darling had done he would consider his life well-spent. And while Fraser Darling was in Africa studying conservation problems, Morton was appointed Regional Officer for Western Scotland, with St Kilda and North Rona as part of the study area.

And the two names came together again when the time came for a revision of *Natural History in the Highlands and Islands,* though the title has been changed now to *The Highlands and Islands*, so we see the fulfilment of the original dream. The vision remains, and other fresh minds will go to the high hills and the lonely islands and find an ecstasy that cannot be put into words.

As I left, Fraser Darling said, "Even for a pessimist, it is still a beautiful and wonderful world. Are we going to destroy it completely?

*   *   *

Sir Frank Fraser Darling's health was in decline when I interviewed him, and he died four years later, on 22 October 1979. To be recognised for what he was worth he had been forced to leave Britain in the mid-1950's, but by the late 1960's when he returned to Scotland, the land which he loved most, he was internationally recognised as a naturalist-extraordinary. Honours were heaped on him, but he remained a simple man, glad to stay at home amongst his books and mementos of travel and adventure, happy to look out from his garden across the Moray Firth to the Highland hills. Few who heard the great man deliver his Reith Lectures in 1969 with such fluency would credit that Sir Frank in the mid-thirties was plagued by a bad stammer, a speech impediment which did not deter him from mounting the platform and conquering it. He was that kind of man, courageous in everything he undertook. It is not too much to say that he changed our thinking about the natural world and our responsibility for it. He believed that ecological knowledge can be applied to the most ravaged and abused areas to bring them back to life. But first, man has to have the conviction and spiritual belief that it can be done. It was his gospel, and he preached it well.

AUTUMN DIARY

Salmon Leap the Pots

Last Sunday afternoon I was one of many salmon-louping enthusiasts taking advantage of the heavy overnight rain to visit the Pots of Gartness on the river Endrick in the hope of seeing a good run of fish. Nothing. Only dismay at the dank smell of pollution and the water running as grey as a glacial stream with silt.

Folk with concerned faces ask me for an explanation. "It's the result of the dry summer," I said. "The smell is the build-up of stuff that would have been swept away by normal rains, chemicals from the fields and other muck. By tomorrow it will be away, the river will be running clean, and the stimulation of oxygen will send the salmon jumping."

To test my words I went back the following morning after another wet night. Marvellous. My only regret was that the folk of yesterday weren't there to see the queue of dark fish hurling themselves in the rough direction of the cataract, some of them missing it completely to slap the rocks, others hitting it at the wrong place to be projected with some force back the way they had come.

But a proportion of the bigger fish were getting the perfect trajectory, arrowing out of the water like Polaris missiles, to hit the left side of the waterfall at three-quarters height, and maintaining a precarious position for as long as a minute against the rush of water. Cunning, because up there was a space, a ledge. From this resting point, not one failed to take the gush above in a single vertical glide, fins out at right angles to the body, tail thrashing from side to side in sinuous body movement.

You could hardly keep from crying out with excitement as they got to the top, spray rising from the tail, streamlined nose cleaving the waterfall like the sharp prow of a speed-boat. What power, what movement! All the more exhilarating when the sun blazed between showers, contrasting the dark backs of the fish against the sparkling foam.

These louping salmon were obeying the mysterious spawning urge, which brings them back from the wide Atlantic to seek out their home rivers which they left when they were tiny silver smolts.

What special directional aid enables them to find the Clyde, take the tributary of the Leven, follow it into Loch Lomond, then branch off up the Endrick?

Experiment has shown that the aid is their sense of smell, and in these times of pollution it must be a remarkable sense. But there is a sad end to the big journey from the sea and the surmounting of waterfalls, for in the act of spawning most of the males have sealed their death warrant, and only a proportion of the females will return to the sea.

The objective of the cock fish is to dig a nest in the gravel with his sharp snout, and fertilise the few thousand eggs of the hen with his milt. Then he covers them up, leaving nature to hatch the next generation in late March or early April.

152

But the river is full of enemies for the salmon parr, and in the two years it takes to become a smolt 95% will die, which is why we need to look after our rivers, and control illegal drift-netting, if we are to enjoy the sight of a fish which is also a £1.5m industry.

Duncryne Hill

Suddenly on 13 September autumn arrived in Gartocharn where I live. I recognised it by the soft gold of the morning, the thin gauze of mist softening the outline of the village, and the big sea of cloud stretching across the hollow where Loch Lomond should be.

More positively, there on the kitchen table was a pail containing 10lb. of ripe brambles gathered the evening before by my wife while I climbed the ridge above the house to enjoy a red sunset over loch and islands, the burnish extending right across Strathendrick to the hog backs of the Ochils and the Campsies.

I had a friend say hello up there too, a greenshank which gave me its shrill salute as it flew over.

I would have made a bet on a splendid morning following such an evening. But I didn't expect anything quite so atmospheric as the soft mist and brilliant colours outside my window. Cup of tea in hand I stepped outside to investigate a loud twittering coming from the oak tree at the gate.

My presence caused an eruption of shining goldfinches, greenfinches, and yellow hammers. But it didn't disturb the pied and grey wagtails running on the lawn, or the glossy blackbird listening for worms.

We are lucky in this village to have what I believe to be the finest viewpoint of any small hill in Scotland. Moreover it is the perfect old man's mountain. Duncryne is only 463ft. high, and its glory is in the northern view of Loch Lomond, its broad base spattered with wooded islands, then narrowing like a fiord to pierce the 3,000ft. wall of peaks on each side.

Duncryne is a crag-and-tail, a little volcanic neck shaped by the pushing of the glaciers of long ago. I go up it most mornings, and this is where I made for when I left the house, up through the oak and ashwood enjoying the sight of strings of pearls across my path, beads of moisture on the spiders' webs, some of them strung across the glowing red of rosehips. A nice feature of Duncryne is that you don't get the view until you are almost on top.

It was not as exciting as I had hoped, because the mist had risen at such speed that it had wiped out the Highland hills in greyness. Nor was there any clarity in east or west where normally you can sweep your eyes from the hills of Cowal across Perthshire to the Ochils.

So the only real colour was in the immediate scene, the green of the fields contrasting with the yellows of ripe barley and oats. Thankfully we have not yet rooted out the hedgerows from this part of the world.

From Duncryne top you can learn a lot about the Endrick. Now I could see what a fortnight of rain had done by raising the level of the loch to swamp the little islands at the mouth, and innundate the sandbar where the arctic tern raised its two chicks successfully just in time.

No doubt they are away en route to the Antarctic now, but the more aggressive of the arctic tern parents did me a good turn before it left. It had been wavering about, catching flies and splashing in for fish, when suddenly it let out a stream of curses and began dive-bombing a branch projecting out of the water.

I had just time to focus my glasses and pick out a bluish-grey hawk perched on the branch before it was dislodged and came flying my way, showing black face-mask and pointed wings. It was a merlin, the first I have seen on Loch Lomondside in thirty years of birding there.

Sortie to the Whangie

Over 100 years ago a rambling enthusiast by the name of Hugh MacDonald wrote weekly articles about his walks in the *Glasgow Citizen.*

In time they were immortalised in a thick book called "Rambles Around Glasgow and Days at the Coast." This is how he describes the Whangie, hidden on the shoulder of Aucheneden Hill and reached from the Queen's View car park on the Stockiemuir.

" . . . a vast section of the hill has by some means been wrenched asunder, leaving a lengthened and deepened chasm yawning along the line of separation.

"Entering the narrow ravine, we proceed, as it were into the bowels of the firm-fixed earth. The passage is tortuous and uneven, the projections of one side corresponding with singular exactness to the hollows of the other."

Anybody who has walked the path along the face of Aucheneden Hill as far as you can see, then rounded the shoulder beyond to find the Whangie rearing ahead, knows how accurate MacDonald's description is. The ravine is 346ft. long, its depth feels gloomy, heightening the savagery of the pinnacled crest jutting 40ft. and more against the sky.

Last Saturday evening about tea-time we walked that pleasant path which climbs briskly from the car park, turning along the edge of the high wood, to cross a style, then continues as a gentle traverse under the rock escarpment forming the edge of the hill. Note, you always keep to the right-hand path at any junction of paths. Leftward branches will take you too high.

Keep going. Your target is right round the shoulder of the hill, past a

154

little rocky feature called "The wee Whangie." Walking briskly you should be there in about forty-five minutes from the car park, seeing before you, pinnacles jutting askew, cleft from the parent rock.

Now for the delightful bit as you go into the gloom of the canyon to thread its sinuous depths. The walls are as close as 2½ feet at one place, emphasising the verticality of the pinnacles towering over your head in a ridge which is a miniature of the Cuillin of Skye.

The monkey in you will want to get up there, but on top it is airy on the cat-walk, very exposed, and not all the rock is sound. I've been having fun for most of my life up there, so I couldn't resist some of the well-known problems, and it was grand to be on top looking over a great prospect of Highland bens curved round Loch Lomond, from Cowal across Strathclyde to Tayside.

How did this "terrible fissure" come about on an innocent hillside where it is so unexpected? The old rambler talks about a natural "convulsion." An older explanation concerns the Deil himself. Old Nick was so pleased after a night with his favourite witches and warlocks that he wagged his tail too violently and the hillside parted.

The colder truth denies the Deil such fiery passion. Modern geologists favour an ice-age explanation, a moving glacier that plucked at the hillside and caused the volcanic rock to fracture like a broken cream-jug, hence the projections of one side seeming to fit into the hollows of the other.

So remember if you go looking for the Whangie not to turn back too soon. Don't climb to the top of the hill, but keep along the lower path after crossing the style. Last Saturday I noticed that although there were dozens on the first mile of the path, only one party reached the Whangie. The others were enjoying themselves. So were we.

It is my hope that this article will not start a rash of signposts, for part of the fun is finding the way, and getting a surprise.

Let's keep things as they are.

The Other Lomonds

When it's drizzly and grey in the west the sun can be shining in the east, and it took only a quick telephone call to Kinross to discover that I should be heading for Loch Leven for a day with Will on the Lomond hills.

Even before Stirling the world had opened up with the Ochils tawny behind the grey plinth of the Wallace Monument and a warm sun intensifying the yellow-gold of harvest colours along the winding blue ribbon of the Forth.

Willie was waiting at the rendezvous. "We'll start wi' Bishop's Hill and pay a visit to the auld witch Carlin Maggie, then ower by the

Covenanters' Glen to West Lomond. Does that dae ye?"

It did, especially in the company of such a knowledgeable local man who could direct my attention to things; the big standing stones of Orwell on the knoll where they have stood for 4,000 years, and the Puddin Wynd at Kinesswood with the cottage where Michael Bruce was born in 1746.

"He was the Loch Leven poet, you ken aboot him. He herded cows on the slopes where we're going. At four years of age he was reading bible stories. His calling was the kirk, but he never preached. He died of TB at twenty-one. But famous lines of his live on in Paraphrase 19:

*'To ploughshares men shall beat their swords
To pruning hooks their spears.' "*

Heathery Bishop's Hill rises steeply over the big shallow loch that covers most of the former county of Kinross. Black dots of boats were everywhere on its surface that day, angling for the red-fleshed trout for which its shallow waters are internationally famous.

Not far above our heads were other folk looking down on the view, glider pilots soaring and turning their silent bird-like machines in the air currents draughting up the rocky escarpment forming the edge of the hill.

A cheery place to meet the dark shape of Carlin Maggie standing angularly out from the rocks, 42ft. high and frozen in stone. It was her punishment for challenging the Devil's authority, but until recent times she kept her dignity by foiling every attempt to scale her.

Submit she did, however, to an acrobatic Dunfermline chiel by the name of George Shields. And maybe because of that she lost her head. She had her crown of a shrunken skull ten years ago when I last visited her, but now it's gone, nor could I find the decapitated head below her gaunt form as we scrambled on the rocks.

The next landmark ahead of us was the deep cleft of the Covenanters' Glen, places of secret religious meetings and more distantly associated with the preaching of John Knox.

As we advanced on it, we glanced down to the Castle Island on Loch Leven from which Mary Queen of Scots made her famous escape. History in every stone here. Didn't Prior Andrew Wyntoun of St Serf's Priory write the *Oryginale Cronykil of Scotland* down there on Loch Leven in 1420, telling the tale of Macbeth and the weird sisters, the witches?

West Lomond rises nobly above the deep cleft of the glen, dome-shaped above a grove of larch trees with moorland, lochs, and the wide Forth beyond.

The climb to 1,713ft. is steepish to the very top, so you have a fine moment when suddenly you are there with the spreading Howe of Fife and its wee villages making a foreground for the Highland Bens, summit on summit stretching as far as the Cairngorms.

You can walk on by a fine track to East Lomond if you feel inclined and enjoy the hang-gliding enthusiasts swinging about like dragon flies in curving sweeps from the summit. We preferred to drop down a big rock gully of screes which scars the north face and takes you down to a most curious landmark eroded from white sandstone to look like a giant mushroom.

It is known as the Bannetstane and will set you a neat problem of getting on to its crown. "Bannet" means a "bunnet," and it sits above the Maiden's Bower, on the lower slopes of the hill, only two miles west of Strathmiglo where a side road goes off to the hill.

Allow five to six hours for Bishop's Hill and West Lomond inclusive of return to the starting point by the low flanks of the hills—you'll enjoy it.

It's Much Better When it Rains

Good weather is dandy. Everybody likes it. But there are places in the Highlands that are more impressive during or immediately after heavy rain.

The gorge of Glen Nevis is one of these. You can't see it by sitting in the car. True there is the cascade that slides and leaps 1,000 ft. down the rock slabs close to the car park.

Give yourself two hours in the rain by climbing 400 ft. in a traverse of one mile through the finest ravine in Britain, and perhaps the whole of Europe. The path is good, steep in only one or two places, for what you are doing is threading the gorge along the southern rampart of our highest and rockiest Scottish ben.

Austere, yes; but not naked, for the walls hemming in the deep cut of the roaring river are hung with opportunist Caledonian pines, birches, rowans, etc., safe from the mouths of sheep or deer.

The path may look daunting from a distance, but the going is easy if you keep to the leftward branch at any junction. In my experience it is typical of many a Himalayan path, a traversing staircase of easy rock steps, except that the scenic changes come more swiftly here.

One moment you are enclosed by the mountain wall, the next you see out to the mountain spurs and a peak discharging a curtain of waterfall framed above the gorge.

Gradually the top of the gorge is drawing level and soon you can look down into its verticalities and see how the huge boulders have been strewn by the force of the thundering torrent hurtling through the canyon.

Then sudden surprise when you step round the corner and find yourself on gentle meadows, a grassy Shangri-la, but now you are directly under the waterfall of Steall—the one that looked like a curtain from below. Now it spouts out of its hanging valley looking much higher than its 350 feet.

Here indeed is a truly unique square mile of Scottish scenery, set above by some of the highest and shapeliest peaks in Scotland, the Nevis range on one side, the Mamores on the other, eighteen peaks over 3,000 feet whose traverse involves thirty-six miles and 20,000 feet of climbing.

At least two men have traversed them in one day—who says modern youth is soft? The best have never been harder.

Notice the wee cottage across the river below the waterfall, now a mountaineering hut, reached by a high-wire act on a single strand across the river running wide and deep here. Crossing on that wobbly strand is none too easy to the uninitiated, but if you should cross, don't go up the side of the Steall waterfall without taking great care for people have slipped and died there.

Better to take your time savouring the gorge and enjoy its weird formations and rock sculptures. Reflect too that less than twenty years ago the North of Scotland Hydro-Electric board published a plan to put a concrete dam across our finest gorge and reduce the height of the Steall waterfall to make a reservoir of the meadows for a handful of kilowatts.

The board believed that the scheme would leave the natural beauty of the glen undiminished and added for good measure that motorists would be able to drive up to the dam. But engineers are not the best judges of what is best in landscape conservation.

The public were loud in their protest. Glen Nevis was saved from plunder for a mere handful of kilowatts and today we regard it as one of our great treasures.

The same argument that saved Glen Nevis holds true of the Craigroyston shore of Loch Lomond. The cry should be "hands off" the miraculous eastern shore. Confine development to the west, at Loch Sloy which has already been hydro-electrocuted.

Cairnsmore of Fleet

I spent a recent sunny weekend on the Solway coast with the professor who lives in these parts, and of the various things we might have done my choice was the hill called Cairnsmore of Fleet because I had never been up there.

I've been around its flanks and have had good fun rock-climbing on the Clints of Drumore, but I'd left the summit for the right day, knowing it must be an exceptional viewpoint, standing as it does 2,331 ft. above Wigtown Bay and the estuary of the river Cree.

The professor was now going to show me his favourite way. "Just look at that path the way it winds up through the trees, a grassy thread that's an invitation. It makes you want to walk up it."

He was right. No erosion and degradation by the tramping of too many feet that wears away the grass and makes a drain.

Soon we had caught up with the white-shirted figure above us taking a rest on a boulder. He was a cheery seventy-five-year-old who announced his age and told us that his grandchildren were ahead of him. "I'll be ready for ma piece when I get tae the tap, but they've got it. Tell them no tae eat it a'."

We came upon them on the springy turf of the summit and there was no need to relay the message for the old fellow was in distant sight. He was well pleased when he joined us.

For a day of such little air movement and hot sun the visibility had remained remarkably crisp. South over the glitter of Wigtown Bay were the pale blue hills of the Isle of Man like one of the Hebrides. Northward rose the hard grey granite and rich browns of high Galloway, signposted by the Merrick, true Highland country, yet in the Lowlands.

From the Mull of Galloway beyond Luce Bay the eye could follow all the indentations of the Solway coast from Kirkcudbright to Kippford and Criffel, most of it a soft quilt of rolling agricultural greens.

We were following the rocky edge of the corrie which leads to the Knee of Cairnsmore when suddenly a great bird came over the rocky rim, followed by another.

Angled against the blue of the sky they soared as silhouettes, long wings stretched straight out, ragged upturned fingers at their ends feeling the air. We only had moments to look at them, before one up-ended in a power dive, wings tucked into its sides to fall like a heavy stone. In watching that acrobatic movement I lost the other. Nor did we see them again.

They could only have been the pride of Galloway, golden eagles which have bred there successfully for many years, and whose off-spring are thought to have colonised the Lake District across the Solway where they now bring joy to fell-walkers.

The problem for eagles in Galloway could be the forestry which swallows up the kind of open ground an eagle needs for hunting.

But Cairnsmore of Fleet is a National Nature Reserve now in a region good for moorland birds and other prey, which should ensure a future for the terrain of the eagles. The Forestry Commission have always been sympathetic to the problem.

Dangerous Stags

Come mid-October when the bracken is russet and the gold leaf is on the birch the rutting roars of the red deer stags begin as if announcing the end of their shooting season on 20 October.

Last week I heard my first for 1977, deep throated, more sonorous and echoing than a lion—the voice no doubt of a master stag that has come into the rut earlier than the others, one which will herd hinds like a sheep dog and hold them against other stags by reason of his impressive voice, large size, and big spread of antlers.

I heard the roaring in two different glens, but I saw only one stag in possession of hinds, and he was unchallenged. It will be a different story as he gets worn out with sexual activity. Then his hinds will be taken from him and covered again by more masterful stags.

Many people think that stags are dangerous to humans at this time. What is the truth of it?

Only one keeper known personally to me has been atttacked by a wild red deer stag, and he is Alan Fleming of Monar Lodge, Ross-shire. The stag had been hanging about the house drive and was alarming Alan's wife by roaring at her. Alan took a stick and walked along the drive where, sure enough, the stag went through its performance, prancing at him in a challenging way.

Alan raised the stick to threaten it. It charged head down, piercing a hole through two thicknesses of battledress and knocking him to the ground. Shouting and waving the stick he fended it off.

He went back to the house and returned with his rifle, but the aggressive beast had gone. Shortly after, close to the house, he found an old done stag lying dead, and he thinks this was his attacker.

Alan thought its aggression was a reaction to infirmity, similar to an example of rutting behaviour he saw in Glen Strathfarrar, where a stag was to be seen day after day brandishing its antlers and roaring. When the beast was shot it was found to have been totally blinded by fish hooks from a length of line and gut wound round its head.

Because of the aggressiveness of stags at rutting time, keepers do not regard it advisable to allow stags to become too tame. There is one authenticated case of a Ross-shire gamekeeper being killed by a stag.

John Maclennan was on his way to a funeral and crossed the path of a stag which was inside a fenced area. From evidence of his torn clothing he had fought hard for his life but was no match for this powerful and aggressive stag which had a record of attacking other men.

Being confiding to man has its problems. I knew a stag which used to rake a garbage dump until it eventually acquired a tin on its foot which it wore like a spat. Then when it wore through the sole of the tin it developed a limp from the metal cutting into it.

Bob Scott, the keeper, thought the animal must be suffering, so one day in the stalking season, when he saw it on a ridge above him in perfect position for a shot, he fired. The animal fell, and as it rolled over, legs in the air, it kicked off the shackling tin—too late unfortunately.

Winter Migrants Arrive

After the rain and the big winds of early October it was magical to get a still morning and sunshine warm enough to start skylarks singing above the thin squeaks of redwings erupting from the trees on each side of me.

To the north, mist buried the hills, the greyness serving to enrich the glow of warm colour on the lowland side of Loch Lomond.

There was lots of movement on trees and fields, grey squirrels plundering the hazel nuts, pheasants running over the stubble, redpolls flighting, jays rasping, and a loud communal shrilling from a feeding flock of long-tailed tits when a sparrow hawk passed, beating and gliding, a hundred yards away.

On the water were two golden-eye drakes, the first of the winter, smart in black and white beside about 200 dowdy coots. Close to the reeds I could pick out the movement of up-ending ducks, crimson flanks of shoveller, cinnamon of wigeon, green of mallard and teal.

No advance for me in their direction because of floods which have raised the loch spectacularly in the past fortnight. So I climbed gently to the edge of the wood and sat on a knoll overlooking the brown mat of the marsh and its two shallow lochans.

Very little was stirring except for flighting gold-finches and a warbling from robin and wren. I was watching two roe deer, already in dark winter coat, when I became aware of the chopper noise of a helicopter getting close between me and the lochans.

Until then I had convinced myself that the big arrival of geese we expect in early October had yet to come, when up they rose, an almost solid wave of screeching birds, fanning out and forming chevrons even as I looked.

That first sight of the first mass of swirling grey lags against the russet of Conic Hill was inspiring enough in itself without the added bonus of four geese winging their way directly towards me, two of them crying out that they were pink-feet, the other two showing stripes of black on their flanks advertising that they were Greenland white-fronts.

The movement of the clamouring birds seemed to have sounded a general alarm as flock after flock of duck came winging from the lochans, so that wherever you looked there were flights of long-necked birds going at different speeds. It was easy to tell which were teal because of the way they twist and turn like golden plover.

One bird I had hoped to see was missing—the cock hen harrier which has been here for a few weeks.

I had seen it a few days before in heavy rain when it was the only object moving above the drab marsh, and how vividly its contrasts of pale grey and black showed even in its bedraggled state, as it wavered only a few feet above the reeds, master of balance and buoyancy as it quartered for prey.

Then it favoured me by doing an unusual thing, dropping to the ground near me, so I was able to watch it at close range, pecking like a starling as it walked about on long yellow legs, a pale bird with an owl-like face.

Island of Seals

Eilean nan Ron is Gaelic for "Island of Seals," Atlantic skerries where the unfettered seas break round the southern tip of Colonsay, making it one of the most accessible Atlantic seal colonies I know.

Easy to reach but difficult to land on, when the south-westerlies whip the ocean, so you have to be patient and content yourself on the Oronsay shore, until it is safe to put out the boat.

I've had a few disappointments in the past. This time the weather allowed two visits on different days. The sailing distance is not great, and each time we came in among the table-top reefs, there was pandemonium as massive grey shapes of blubber hurled themselves from cliffs above our heads into the water to bob up all around us.

As we grounded and drew up the dinghy, barnacle geese in vivid black and grey rose into the air yelping over the green pancake of the island.

A step or two among the seaweed rocks and little sandy inlets we saw our first pups, creamy ones not long born who could hardly lift themselves on their arms but jerked their heads at us, mouthing threats and showing toothless gums.

These pups weigh 30lb. at birth but put on weight so fast that in less than three weeks they are adolescent, having trebled their weight and cast-off the puppy coat for a sleek grey-blue pelt.

It was a joy to move carefully among pups at every stage of development, the oldest had been born in the first days of October, most probably. These adolescents played in the tidal rock pools, diving away from our intruding faces but shooting to the surface, buoyant as corks because they were so blown-up with blubber.

In no time they were having a game with us, snuffling and growling at my woollen hat which I dangled over the water to them.

Under almost every rock there seemed to be a seal-pup or a nursing mother. Winning the confidence of the newly born is easy. All you need to do is squirm up beside it in the manner of Mum. It will rear up at you as you go close. Take no notice, but press yourself against it, and it will start looking for milk. I felt guilty when all I could offer was a moist forefinger.

Lying as they did on a bed of cold rocks these pups felt surprisingly warm, especially if you placed a hand between the hind flippers where you got a hot water-bag feeling.

We counted dozens of pups, and there was plenty of wailing and roaring from the big bulls, heavier jowled and much bigger than the cows, the heaviest of British mammals at perhaps a quarter of a ton.

Mating occurs within three weeks of a cow having its pup, and like red deer stags on the hill, each bull tries to possess as many of the opposite sex as possible. Challenges between weak and strong go on all the time.

We saw a number of these disputes as bull faced bull, chest to chest, mouthing threats to each other, and threatening each other with fore-flippers like feinting boxers.

But it is the teeth which do the damage. Bites are savage and we saw plenty of blood flowing as the huge animals bounced at each other against a background of wailing cows and crying babies.

Dawn Breakfast in Bed on Speyside

October is the month when the high hills take on their bronze rig and pull down a white helmet of first winter snow. All you need then for Picasso brilliance is a crisp night of frost and windless air to make every river pool and loch a mirror of startling reflections.

Thus it was on Speyside camping in a secret place in Rothiemurchus forest. Gas stove and breakfast things by our sleeping bags for a dawn breakfast in bed.

During the dark hours we had been hearing the skirling flight calls of wild geese and now as clear morning broke we were aware of the feeding calls of Scandinavian birds, squeaks of redwings and chucklings of fieldfares—winter visitors to Scotland from northern lands.

Great to be walking through the Caledonian pines and heading for the High Lairig Ghru.

From Coylum Bridge the route is easy to follow, clearly signposted to the junctions of two main streams spanned by the Cairngorm Club footbridge. Once across you are on a beautiful alpine meadow hemmed by silver birches. Ahead lies the deep V cut of the finest hill pass in Scotland.

In a mile you come to a junction of paths known as "Piccadilly." You take the right hand one climbing steeply uphill, the pines becoming dwarf-sized as the forest thins out.

This is an enchanting bit, and we had to pause awhile to take in the separation of two worlds; above us the last outpost of pines and beyond them heathery moraines backed by the granite spurs defending the notch of the pass. Below us, the skirts of the hills billowing away in crinkly waves of natural forest falling to the river Spey.

Two miles of peaty and soggy buffer zone between forest and bouldery wilds, and we were at the Sinclair Memorial Hut—a haven of shelter for which many Lairig Ghru trampers have been grateful. Today we merely passed on, savouring the narrows beyond where the soaring rock edges of the Lurcher's Crag change to walls of vivid pink screes on each side of the pass.

Then you are balancing on the boulders, across a tumble of rocks fallen from the cliffs above through which you pick your way—hard going, should you be wheeling a bike, as many path-storming cyclists do. The boulders extend from the 2,733ft. summit of the pass to beyond the strange rock-entrapped lochans known as the Pools of Dee, minute saucers of blue in a confusion of granite blocks.

Glorious to be here at lunch-time on a perfect October afternoon of rich sunlight, knowing we had time to dawdle, for Coylum Bridge was within easy three hours range. There was plenty to enjoy, the croaking of ptarmigan round our feet and the sight of more migrating geese, skein after skein using the cleft of the pass as a flyway from north to south.

Up there we were overtaken by a solitary walker travelling in the same direction as the geese, moving fast to meet up with friends coming from the opposite direction. They would have a snack together, exchange car keys, and drive home to Dundee by their different ways after a total of nineteen miles walking and 2,200ft. of ascent. For that they had estimated seven to eight hours—a reasonable time.

The joy of the walk from Spey to Dee is the changing scene as you descend from the arctic world of the summit of high plateau and rocky corries to the Caledonian pine woods which are a feature of north and south ends of the pass. No other hill pass is so rich in total reward, especially in October when the red deer stags are roaring.

For a family outing, make do with the walk from Coylum Bridge to the Pools of Dee. You will find it ambitious enough, and it leaves you with the option of turning back to a certain base not too far away.

A Road That May Lead to Golden Treasure

To find the place you take the A1107 which branches off the A1 just over a mile beyond Cockburnspath. Now you're beginning to get the feeling of being an explorer, climbing over ground rising to 500ft. But in three miles keep an eye open for the farm road to Dowlaw, for this is where you strike left and follow along to the dead end beyond the steadings where there is room to park by a row of cottages.

You want boots on your feet now for you are going on to precipitous ground, not visible yet for a bit. Easiest way is to go through the gate ahead, not turning right until you see the footpath which winds in a delightful grassy mile to the sudden dramatic plunge of the Wolf's Craig. Perched on top of it as if grown from the rocks is all that remains of the castle.

To mount the pinnacle cross a small gap protected in days of yore by a drawbridge giving access to the strangest fortification in Scotland, and one of the most mysterious, for no one knows who built the original structure. Nor has a great hoard of Spanish gold worth over £1m been found, though the search for it began more than 400 years ago and is still continuing.

The story of the gold is that it was brought from the Continent to finance a Catholic invasion of England from the Scottish side and hidden here. The next we hear of it is in 1594 when the help of the great mathematician John Napier of Merchiston was invoked to help Robert Logan of Restalrig find it on a profit-sharing basis.

Napier, renowned as a wizard, was expected to use his knowledge of astrology and the occult to locate the treasure, but the wizard bones and moon dials apparently failed.

Modern searchers pin their faith more on science, but so far all they have found are some coins from the reign of Elizabeth I and James VI.

You can see where the excavations are still in progress, but unless you make a dangerous climb down the cliff you can't see the deep cave which runs through the cliff under the castle.

Legend has it that there is a secret exit inside, leading up into the castle. But the boldest skin divers of the Eyemouth Sub-Aqua Club have failed to find anything inside that dark tunnel.

For my walk you don't stop at Fast Castle, but continue east along the coast, until you can drop down and look at the superb rock needle of the Souter rising from the shore more dramatically than the Inaccessible Pinnacle from Sgurr Dearg of the Cuillin of Skye.

More Hebridean delight lies ahead, but first you have to cross the ravine of the Dowlaw Burn which means a retreat inland to find an easy place, then you can return to the coast down the other side.

Ahead of you now is high coasting, fresh air all the way with the finest cliffs on the whole east coast of Scotland plunging 500ft. into the sea for the next three miles. From up there on clear days you can see the snow on the Grampians ninety miles distant. I made my turning point the neat little inlet called Pettico Wick, an easy step from St Abb's Head lighthouse.

Just one word of warning. Don't walk along the edge of the cliff. Select your spots to look over and make sure it is solid rock beneath your boots, not crumbly earth. In any case it is better to keep back a wee bit to look at the ancient forts and settlements which dot the ground just back from the plunging rock faces.

For the return journey from Dowlaw to Pettico Wick via Fast Castle allow four to five hours which gives time to look around. For the return journey easiest way is to strike inland from Oatlee Hill and pick up a track that goes all the way back to your car.

Mating of Atlantic Seals

Dreary weather dogged me on the Atlantic seal rocks of Eilean nan Ron, but I am now satisfied that this most massive of British mammals with such sharp underwater vision does not see too well when it is ashore at mating time.

This was revealed to me in a tight situation when I confronted a bull and a cow at a few feet, yet they failed to get my shape until I made a noise.

Crawling carefully and soundlessly—for seals have very sharp hearing—I had no clear notion of how close I was to my target, until suddenly they were before me, the bull, dark grey, massive with whiskery top lip; the cow in light fawn pelt with black splotches.

The bull had his back to me, but the cow was staring in my direction as I came into view. And she reacted by rising up on her hands, swaying her head, and looking intently as if trying to focus her bulging black eyes. Then she subsided as if satisfied, but before I could breathe easily, her head came up again, to the annoyance of the bull who snarled at her with open mouth.

They wailed and bickered at each other until the cow made a sudden turning-away movement to a higher position commanding the ground where I lay. And she stared at me so hard that the bull swung round as if to see what she was looking at.

For me it was a tense moment. "Suppose the bull seal takes me for another bull poaching on his territory and hurls itself at me?" Unwilling to admit this disturbing thought I reached for my camera and inadvertently scraped it on the rock beneath my chin.

The speed of the reaction was startling, for instead of a picture of seals all I got was an impression of two objects bouncing over the rocks like rubber balls. What energy they must have been using up in that hundred yard sprint of caterpillar movement, since the weight has to be lifted on the hands, the tail end brought up, and the stomach heaved, to slide forward seven feet and more of heavy body. And that output of energy is all the more remarkable when you consider that for the last few weeks they had starved and lived on their blubber.

Even the cow will have lost 200lb. between calving time and the renewal of the coat at the end of November. As for the hard-working big bulls, they are truly worn out and little more than shadows of themselves by the time they have done their duty.

We saw only one fight between two well-matched bulls, and the possessor of the harem lost. First bite went to the challenger, but the attacked bull riposted by seizing the aggressor's hind flippers and held on despite repeated bites on neck and back. Then they broke to face each other, arms out, teeth showing as they wailed. Both of them spurted blood.

The challenger leapt first, seized the hind flippers of the other and returned in bigger measure what it had received. Disengaged and mouthing at each other again, the territory-holding bull tried to retreat, but had to endure a few bites before he was allowed to go.

We watched him head for neutral ground, leaving blood on the rocks as he went. He would go back to sea, eat, grow fat with blubber, and the wounds would heal.

Glen Lyon

Eager as we were to get to Glen Lyon for a few hours, on the tops above 3,000ft., we simply had to stop at Killin for twenty minutes to pay homage to the spate waters of the River Dochart roaring down to Loch Tay.

Flashes of sun and the lingering brilliance of the autumn colours made a feast for the eye.

Spirits were high where they had been low. Now we were reaping the reward of rising early and leaving home in the rain. Just over on the other side of the Tarmachans in Glen Lyon lay the corries of Stuchd an Lochain where we were going. But it needed an iron will to keep going, instead of stopping to watch a red squirrel dancing across the road or look at the fieldfares and redwings which seemed to be everywhere on the red rowans and golden birches.

Our destination was Loch Giorra, and as we wound above a gorge of pink-barked Caledonian pines a capercaillie cock and two hens flew out of the trees when we stopped to open a gate. The head keeper lives up there, and since this is deer forest I could hardly pass without letting him know where we were going.

Stalking for stags ended on 20 October, but now it was the hind shooting season, and I had to make sure I was not going to spoil anything.

No problem for us, but bad luck for Bill, who was in hospital after a painful injury to his spine, resulting from a fall on the hill. It can happen even to the most experienced. "Sure-footed as a deer," is a common phrase to describe nimble climbers like Bill. But even deer can fall to death, as two of us witnessed one November when a herd of them traversed a very narrow heather ledge on a big cliff.

Watching, and wondering if they were going to make it on such difficult ground, we saw one lose its footing and turn over and over in the air as it hit ledge after ledge until it was out of sight. The herd watched it too and began to make their way back, which showed wisdom. We rock-climbed with unusual care that day.

On the hill we had to climb high to reach a position for spying into the corrie to see the bellowing stags neurotically parading or running angrily to drive off poachers on their hinds. One stag would charge at another, stop suddenly, jerk forward his neck, point his head up, antlers laid back, and send out a rumbling deep-throated roar. We saw no fighting. Threats were enough. Worn-out stags know when to give way.

To our delight, the sun shone on us at 3,000 feet, and on the wings of ptarmigan, white as doves in flight, but showing dark speckles when they landed confidingly close. Then there was the big antlered stag on the ridge, crossing no doubt from one side of the hill to the other. The wind was in my favour and it merely ambled across, giving out grumbling grunts as it went.

On top we were at the junction of two weather systems. Ugly clouds were blotting out grey Rannoch Moor and its lochans. Nevis had disappeared. Mist was swirling towards us as we took the north ridge which falls narrowly and steeply to the loch.

We beat the rainstorm and no more.

Capercaillie Aggression

Here is a wee capercaillie story from Glen Lyon.

The *capull-choille,* the horse of the woods, is the greatest grouse in the world, turkey-sized and notably aggressive in the breeding season.

The cock bird who was the villain of my story had taken to attacking humans instead of rival cocks. Alas, he died when he attacked a Land-rover, but before that time he had drawn blood from ornithologists who had come to see him. He was very much alive on the day when I visited the keeper to find out where the crusty character lived.

"I'll take you, but you'll be on your own for the last bit, for I'm not going near," laughed the keeper as he pointed to a distinctive knoll. "Go up there and he'll come to you." Armed with cine-camera to capture the action, up I went. And in a trice I was watching through the viewfinder a great bird climbing fast up the knoll, its legs moving in a mechanical glide over the ground like a life-size clockwork toy.

It stopped just as its great hooked beak and hanging ruff of feathers filled the frame, and I had just time to put up my boot as it leapt, colliding against it, and began biting at the rubber sole. Then, as if dignity had asserted itself, it threw itself back, stood tall, and virtually blew itself up as I watched.

The neck swelled, the tail became a huge fan, the red wattle round the eye enlarged, the feathers of the neck projected. Head up and wicked beak open, its display was an unmistakable threat to all-comers.

This was too good to miss. I resumed shooting—the film has been shown on BBC Television—when it leapt again, colliding with my heavy boot once more. Involuntarily I stepped back a yard and, as if taking a cue, he did the same. So I played a game of advance and retire with him, and it was great fun.

What a colourful sight he made, a grotesque greenish-blue bird with brown wings ornamented with a white spot, puffed up with anger. I did the decent thing, I began a decisive retreat, at which he bounced off the ground to land on top of a fallen pine trunk, pirouetted like a ballet dancer, then from his wide open beak delivered a tiny rattle of sound, laughable to hear, coming from one so huge and noble.

The capercaillie has been increasing steadily in my lifetime, and we are lucky to have them, for they became extinct in Scotland in 1785, and the population we have today is descended from birds brought over from Europe in the nineteenth century.

We are fortunate, because the capercaillie is in serious decline on the Continent, while in Scotland, there is still enough natural forest to support it. Native pine-woods with old trees are its stronghold.

Europeans will now pay £1,000 for ten guns to shoot capercaillie for one day in Scotland. In economic terms this is good, but no wood should be driven more than once in a season, or Scotland too will lose its capercaillie.

Gamekeepering Memories

True enough of life, there's now't so queer as folk.

There was this old keeper with the lively pink face and elfish smile who greeted me as an old friend and took me round the back of his remote house to show me his pet fox.

"That's Trixie, and you see she's a vixen, faster than any dog and quicker than a cat at catching mice. I reared her on the bottle as a cub after fixing her broken leg with a splint. Look at her playing with Simon the terrier, who's deadly on foxes, but now they're pals."

Then he told me the story of rooting out the cubs from the den that contained Trixie, and sparing her life, knowing that as long as she was in the den the mother could be lured back and shot before going underground. Then when it was all over the keeper hadn't the heart to kill the wee cub within, so here it was living the life of Riley.

"Would you like to see my museum?" was the next question, as he led the way into a collection of birds and animals worthy of Glasgow Art Galleries; an osprey with wings outstretched as in flight and, beneath it, golden eagle, hen harrier, peregrine, short-eared owl, buzzard, a collection of wading birds, and a row of whiskered wildcat faces on miniature tiger skins.

"I was a taxidermist for five years before going into keepering," explained the keeper. "It makes a grand hobby for a man whose business is birds and animals." He could see that I was specially interested in one exceptional wildcat skin. "Yes, that's the biggest I ever killed."

"That wildcat is 46in. long, and animals like that have enormous strength and ferocity. Unlike the fox, the wildcat doesn't hunt away from home. It hunts where it lives and it won't move to another place until the prey gives out. That's a help when it comes to trapping them. "I'll tell you a story," he said. "This day on the hill I was forced to take shelter by a big thunder shower. I got under some rocks forming a sort of cave, and as I was sitting there I noticed the pad marks of a cat, and got out my traps to have a look at them, but neither was really suitable for holding a wildcat.

"So down to the burn I went to try and guddle a trout and came out with a wee 4in. one. Then back to the cave I went, picked a place where the cat couldn't get at the fish too easily, and set both traps at places where it would be likely to put its feet.

"It was a trick I didn't expect to come off, but when I went back up there a day or two later there it was in the trap. Its keen scent must have led it to the fish."

The old keeper had the most mischievous grin I have ever seen on a grown man, and it was never more evident than when he told me the story of the time the laird held a party for three families in the glen and was astonished to find thirty-four children milling around him when he arrived with the picnic things.

"Where are all the children from in the name of God?" he demanded. "Oh," said the keeper, "the shepherd Will has thirteen, Don the other shepherd has ten, and there are eleven of us."

"Three familes with a brood of thirty-four," exclaimed the laird. "I hope the grouse will do as well."

Source of the Clyde

Away back in the distant days when I was a lad and railway excursion tickets were a few pence, you could take a train from Glasgow to Elvanfoot, advertised as a journey to the source of the Clyde.

Lacking geographical knowledge, it didn't occur to this unsophisticated passenger to doubt the railway posters, or suspect they might be advancing a spurious claim, for hadn't the great Neil Munro himself written about the trips?

True he had hinted at other possible sources, but fine story teller that he was, he made a wee tale of finding the source, corking it up, and imagining the destruction of Glasgow's proud commercial enterprise as big ships heeled over and laid in the ooze as the river trickled to a stop.

All good fun, and maybe Munro knew fine that the spring he corked up was the Annan, where it begins its life as the Elvan Water, and that to find the true source of the Clyde you have to go nine miles from Elvanfoot into another valley which makes a nonsense of the ancient rhyme:

So my walk today is to the true source of the Clyde, by driving down the M74 and branching off it just south of Crawford on the A702. Now you can relax, look around you on the quiet byway and branch off left in three miles for the Daer Reservoir.

Now you are in a charming side-glen climbing gently past wee farms and big forestry plantations. No problems until you come to a road junction. Fork right at this point and you loop through the woods to come out level with the big sheet of water which is the Daer Reservoir.

Keep driving on into the rounded tawny hills until the tarmac changes into rough gravel. Now you can don your boots, abandon the car, and take the continuing track to the lonely house of Daerhead just over two miles distant. You can see it below you on the left. Branch down to it and you pick up a footpath which keeps to the edge of the burn winding down from Earncraig Hill (2,000 ft.).

In just over one mile of easy climbing, involving the crossings of the thick Cleuch and Ganna Burns coming in on the left, and a third unnamed burn, you are in the hollow in the hills where the Clyde begins its life as a rivulet.

And a fine moment it is to be in a vast amphitheatre of hills 106 miles distant from where Clwyd—Welsh for strong river—reaches the sea at Dumbarton. Up there your only company is red grouse and sheep, a far cry from the hurtling juggernauts of the M74.

Rannoch Moor in Blizzard

Brilliant moonlight—stars and not a cloud; black ice warnings on the radio; wind from the north. Why not make an early rise, catch the West Highland train at Dumbarton, get off at Corrour, summit of the line, and enjoy the first real snow of winter on skis?

But overnight a thin skiff of snow had come to us. The wind blew it in our faces, and the dark world felt unfriendly until we boarded the warm train and dozed, while listening to wheels crunching as it climbed Glen Falloch. Crianlarich was a dour place; snow peaks half lost in grey mist; and cattle huddled miserably, backs to the gusts of spume.

Now for Rannoch Moor, where I delved for my camera at the sudden vision of the peaks of the Black Mount and Glencoe pink in the sunrise— a sight that made the early rise worthwhile, even though it was soon lost as the train creaked into another blizzard. Herds of red deer, whitened with shrouds of snow, were scarcely recognisable. We were in a world of frozen burns and big snowdrifts, but the diesel coped well.

Corrour is merely a "halt" in this wilderness, serving a shooting lodge. Beyond Loch Ossian there is nothing but the wilderness of Ben Alder stretching to Dalwhinnie.

Deer stalkers were out on the hill we would have chosen, so we opted for Ben Bhreac. It is not very often you can put your skis on at a railway station. We slid off, moving fast uphill to keep warm against the spindrift.

Snow causes territorial grouse to forget their differences and form huge packs. One such mob rising ahead of us looked black as starlings, rather a distorted vision as the whole surface of our world was ribboned with spume, blurring every outline, including the dim yellow disc of the sun.

Then a thrilling vision as everything suddenly became sharp and sparkling in unobscured sunlight—an arctic landscape on which crawled a goods train, but there was no sign of railway line, only the little specks of the station buildings towards which it was heading.

It was our only clearing in the next thousand feet as squall after squall battered us. Our intention had been to go right over the peak. Not a hope. Half blinded and half suffocated by the wind-driven snow we had to drop on our knees, turn our backs to it, and try to draw breath. We started back, but already our tracks had covered up. Frustrating to be up there unable to let yourself go on skis.

Then just when we needed it came another clearing and a burst of sun. We shot off on a line for the station buildings on a mixture of wind-crust and smooth powder, which was great fun. It was so pleasant down there compared with what we had been enduring that we continued on to Loch Ossian—all the more enjoyable for having the wind at our backs.

The only bird was a raven, feeding no doubt on the grallochs of the red deer hinds. We met the keeper returning to his Land Rover with three carcases—"easy shots in weather like this," he said.

Arran

The island of Arran has been making television news with pictures of a white deer on the northern hills, but that is not the reason I went there.

I had to give a lecture in Lamlash, and no timing could have been more perfect, for while Glasgow and Loch Lomond shivered in an arctic fog I was smiling in sunshine and blue skies.

Ah well, it's not always the most deserving that get the luck. Nor was I due it, since I resisted the invitation to visit Arran in winter because of its erratic boat service, and November posed a lot of problems for travellers. So the surprise of a sudden shift from eternal gales of rain to sharp frost and quiet air was all the more delightful for its unexpectedness.

Glorious, that first morning, to look out on hedgerows feathery with hoar frost and see behind the mirror curve of Brodick Bay the pink glow of a perfect sunrise on the snow-cap of Goatfell. Yes, a day for the high tops, and mine climbing hosts Grace and Verner Small were setting forth, but the call of duty bound me to the low ground.

No hardship on a day like that, when I had the car and could complete a sixty-mile circuit of the ring road and enjoy the best of east and west. In Corrie, looking up to the rock spike of Cioch na-Oighe, I felt a twinge of envy of my friends. Thin vapours like steam were rising from the "Punchbowl" and drifting up its dark sides to swirl on the granite rim and dissolve even as I looked.

That was an effect of hot and cold air. And I felt it in the car, leaving the sunny warmth of Sannox Bay for the climb to the top of the Boguillie and the twist down the icy road into Lochranza, which gets no sun in winter. But it gets the reflection of the sunlit slopes of its northern shore spilling into the loch and only a Picasso could have done justice to the yellow and orange tints making water colours as foreground for the dark hulk of the castle.

Round the corner in Catacol Bay I was in sunshine again, a place to sit myself down at the burn-mouth and enjoy the pellucid greens of the Kilbrennan Sound and the birds floating with their reflections on it, eiders and mergansers mainly, and engaged in a bit of billing and cooing.

The sound the drake eider makes is not unlike the soft contented note of the woodpigeon, but it is made communally, which gives it fine resonance. The drake mergansers were more eye-catching.

Two red-breasted drakes were actually displaying to their dowdy ducks, jerking forward sinuous necks and shaking their blue-green crests while at the same time snapping open long red bills, displaying their feelings in fact in red, white and blue.

Driving south down the coast I stopped often to look for divers and found them, long low shapes of great northern and the more stream-lined red-throated, both in quiet winter shades of grey-white.

The Ythan Estuary

The scene is the Ythan estuary at Newburgh to the north of Aberdeen, and we are listening to the bagpipe sounds of long-tailed ducks as they drift down river, stubby little pied birds which soon come flying upstream for another drift down, diving and flirting their tails as they go.

They are not the only arctic visitors, for on the sands are a running party of sparrow-like birds showing white wings when they take the air with musical tinkling calls—snowbuntings.

The snow-sparrows of Greenland whirl around us like a little blizzard keeping together, settle again, and sprint along ahead of us, leaving tiny footprints in the fine sand. What are they getting? Our eyes can detect nothing but we conclude there must be grass seeds invisible to us but obvious to such well-adapted cold-weather birds.

The River Ythan wriggles to the sea in a relatively short course, held in to the north by the Sands of Forvie, a sombre place in the greys of winter but made lively by the flocks of wading birds, innumerable oyster catchers and redshanks and turnstones, flighting curlews, scurrying dunlin, and fast-running sanderlings.

Among the skylarks and linnets we find corn buntings, and almost before we have registered surprise, a covey of partridges whizzes past. Over the other side, on the sands, we begin looking for the ruins of a village destroyed by blowing sand centuries ago. We find the remains of the chapel of Forvie among other stones, with rigs of cultivation—all that remains of it.

But the shifting sand uncovered as well as destroyed. When it blew away it revealed a record of 3,000 years of human history, in ring cairns, kitchen middens, stone implements, fragments of pottery, and stone circles, dating back to the Bronze and Early Iron Age.

We take the footpath which leads us to Logie Buchan Bridge to look at the red sunset making a crimson lake of the broadening Ythan where it swings down from the treeless fields. The tide was full and everywhere were throngs of birds.

On a lower key, waves of sound merged into each other, the cawing of thousands of rooks drifting across the red sky to their roost, their wavering chorus becoming submerged in a higher pitched sound, the skirling of a huge ribbon of pink-footed geese.

Why such a large density of birds in this place, you might ask? What is so special about it? The answer is in the exceptional density of water snails. The gritty sound under your feet is the sound of their shells being crushed. The density of these snails on the Ythan is 50,000 to the square metre, and sometimes double that, not to mention the water shrimp corophium. The estuary is also one of the main nurseries of the flounder—another source of food for the birds.

The Big Shepherd in a Bad Mood

"Aye" said the man, shaking his head with disapproval, "I don't know why they do it, upsetting everybody. Every Christmas they get lost in the hills, fall off, get buried by avalanches, and other folk have to risk their lives in helicopters or on foot looking for them. What makes them want to go up there anyway in weather like this?"

I knew fine he was getting at me by the twinkle in his eye behind the disapproval. "It's because they can't stand the television and the bonhomie," I said. "They don't want to stuff themselves and sit gowping at the screen like the other millions in the country. They want to know what it's like to be hungry, tired, frightened, insecure. To enjoy warmth you've got to know what it's like to be chilled and wet, maybe fighting for survival. Nobody enjoys home more than a man who's had a night out on a mountain, in blizzard conditions."

Little did I know it but I was about to put my theories into practice on

Buachaille Etive Mor on one of the three shortest days in the year. And it happened because my climbing pal Len had agreed to be Santa Claus at our village Christmas party on the understanding that next morning we would leave early for a climb in Glencoe.

So it was up in the dark to lift rope and ice axes and see daybreak dawn on a monochromatic world of soot and whitewash, the lochs grey and snowpeaks disappearing into engulfing clouds.

Wind buffetted the car as we crossed Rannoch Moor, and after the warmth of the car, fingers chilled quickly as we tied the laces of our boots and checked that electric torch and food were in the sacks with spare pullover, cagoule, and scarf.

"It looks grim," opined Len, looking up at the impressive peak which is one huge front of rock whose perfect point was lost in a grey cloud. Today the face was a white shroud, in snow deeper than we expected, as we found out in the hour or more it took us to reach the foot of the North Buttress, rising a thousand feet over our heads. This classic winter route can be moderately difficult or very hard depending on the cover and quality of the snow.

In sixty feet we knew this was not going to be an easy day and were beginning to regret that we had opted for the steep eastern flank in preference to the normal route. Every buried rock hold had to be scraped out, mostly one-handed axe work which is very tiring. Completely absorbed we forgot the passage of time, and hardly noticed that at half-way the weather had deteriorated to very strong wind and semi-blizzard.

Len and I pride ourselves on being fast movers on difficult ground, but the mid-section of the buttress was proving a teaser,complicated by swirling snowflakes and fierce stabs of wind dislodging bursts of spume in our faces.

One tiring section of 40ft. took nearly an hour, each of us leading in turn. My wristwatch said 3 p.m. as Len made the last very hard move.

It was the last major problem. An easing of angle told us we were up and would now have to decide whether to go on to the invisible summit a few hundred feet over our heads or try an escape westward by traversing right over notoriously steep ground.

The argument against the traverse was that it left no room for error. If all went well we would get into Laggangarbh corrie and an easy way down. If it didn't we could be in real trouble in the Raven's Gully area.

With more than forty years' experience of the mountain between us we felt we could find the way if we took off the rope. Our problem was to find a continuous rock shelf which we knew could take us across the top of two gullies which we would have to cross to reach the easy corrie. We must not strike down too soon. Darkness was almost upon us when we came to a great snow wall disappearing beyond the light of our torch. We knew that the corrie had a steep beginning.

It was certainly steep as we plunged down above the knee at every step, nor did it seem to be relenting in angle as it should be doing if it was the corrie. Also steep walls were closing in on us. We wondered if we should climb back.

"I must eat," said Len. The "piece" was in my pack unopened since leaving the house. In the excitement of the climb I had not noticed the lack of food in my stomach. Two bites out of the marmalade roll and Len found he had had enough.

We actually started to climb up, then with one accord decided on pushing down into the unknown gully.

The problem was to make that surface veneer hold, which meant distributing our weight so that if a foot slipped the other would hold. Each of us had slithers, but corrected them before sliding off. And we knew we were getting down as the snow began to thin out and the big wet flakes of the blizzard had turned to heavy rain.

Now we could see lights on the Glencoe Road, motor cars that didn't look far away. And in our torch beam we made out a big rock drop below us which we recognised as the 80ft rock step of Great Gully. A traverse rightward and we avoided it. Ten minutes later we were on the heather, the rocks behind us.

The time was only 6 p.m., yet we felt we had been on the mountain for an ice-age. Now, walking along the climbers' path from the foot of the gully to the Glencoe road we realised we were soaked to the skin, and we felt very happy. Yes, we had been tired climbing on some of the pitches on the climb. We had been frightened, and we certainly had felt insecurity.

But just down there was the car, and once down there and into dry clothes and gulping down hot soup from the flask, we knew the satisfaction that comes from hunger satisfied. The soup and sandwiches were better at that moment than the finest Christmas dinner. Maybe it is to do with being tested and not found wanting.

Thrilling Moment As We Saw The 'Earl'

Reading an old diary last week I came upon an entry headed "A day on the Campsies," and it described being caught out in a blizzard on the way to Earl's Seat, highest point in Glasgow's own "fells" at 1,897ft.

It was a sudden snowfall, the kind we had on Thursday, which caught us out in the featureless no man's land near the summit.

The whiteout was almost immediate, but it was the way the wind got up which was demoralising. We staggered on, unable to look up because of the sting of the snow on our faces.

Sinking deeply in the drifts we were getting bewildered. It was impossible to read a map. Then a miracle, we hit the wire fence which we knew should lie across our track, and turning along it we found the ordnance survey pillar. Not an inch of shelter.

The juvenile entry in my diary reads: "To wander over a waste like that eternally must be the worst kind of hell."

Last Sunday I had exactly the opposite kind of day on Earl's Seat, a morning in a million with icing sugar sparkling on the tops, the ground underfoot crisp with frost, and the fields and woods of Strathendrick warm with colour against the backdrop of blue Loch Lomond. After weeks of clouds and rain and glaur underfoot, uphill moving was a joy!

Full of vigour we moved fast up the Balglass Burn, three miles west of Fintry, into the big corrie whose rocky horseshoe is so reminiscent of the Cairngorms. Going from sunlight into its shadowy north face was like stepping into a fridge, and produced from us an invigorating burst of speed. Up the boulder field for a wee scramble into a rocky gully was fun.

Up past the black tooth of a wee pinnacle, a glittery snow rim fringed the roof of our gulley, and a thrilling moment it was to haul out of darkness into the full blaze of the sun and see ahead of us the point of the "Earl" one mile from the corrie edge.

First of all we scrambled up to the airy point of Allanrowie 1,568ft, to enjoy the exceptional clarity and identify snow peaks stretching from Cowal and the Arrochar Alps to the big Perthshire Bens. Easy to appreciate too the route the cattle drovers took, by Killearn and Balfron to Fintry from the end of Loch Lomond, or across Flanders Moss by the Fords of Frew. Both routes led to Falkirk.

The snow cover was just right for walking, only ankle deep and against it, mountain hares looked grey instead of white. They sat tight until we almost trod on them. Soon we were following the march fence described earlier and enjoying the sight of Ailsa Craig and the Arran hills. The climb from the car to the top had taken only two hours. Another world for very little effort, and we had it to ourselves, except for the barking of a raven and the "go-becking" of grouse.

The Otter That Wouldn't Get Lost

Here's a story which proves that otters are not only great travellers, but from an early age have an uncanny sense of direction.

The keeper who told me this story found a young one curled up in a barrel in a sheltered spot at the back of the house. There was not much life in it, until he put down a bowl of milk and bread, when it accepted him as a friend and to his surprise decided that the barrel was its home.

Then in no time it was nosing into the house, playing with the children, rolling about on the carpet, and snatching at anything liftable within reach.

But the keeper knew that otters have the bad reputation of getting jealous and turning savage so he decided to lose his new pet by taking it ten miles down a loch and slipping it over the side of a boat. Returning home a few hours later he found the otter had beaten him to it and was at the fireside, to the annoyance of his wife.

He tried giving the otter away, but knew nobody who wanted it, so he decided to try to lose it, using the car to try to bamboozle it; hoping that the otter would be completely disoriented by all the twists and turns between the house and where he set it down fifteen miles away. But again the otter beat him to it. The next bit is the sad bit. He shot it, very regretfully, but he thought it was for the best.

Alas, otters are not protected in Scotland any more than pine-martens.

Then there was the story told to me by Dick Balharry, of being given a blind bedraggled little animal about the size of a mouse, which never stopped squeaking. Dick knew what it was, a baby pine-marten, but the extraordinary thing was that it had been found in an empty golden eagle's eyrie which the marten must have been using as a den.

Dick thinks the infant had probably been left behind when the marten shifted its kits as a frightened parent sometimes does.

Now followed sleepless weeks for Dick, his wife, and two children, taking turns to feed the squeaker every four hours. Despite such frequent applications of milk from a tiny filler the fractious infant hardly seemed to grow, and was refusing to open its eyes it seemed. They were getting tired of it as a bore.

Then magic; the eyes opened, it changed into a sharp-eared, yellowish bibbed, busy-tailed brown acrobat, lightning quick, and with a sense of humour. Nocturnal by instinct it became most active as daylight ebbed, and it was great fun when it would leap from Dick's shoulder to mine, wriggle into my pullover and come down my sleeve, then back on to my shoulder and leap ten feet on to Dick.

Offered its freedom, it refused, and now it is too confiding to be released, or it would be shot for certain. It's time we revised these laws to give these rare and marvellous animals protection.

We need comprehensive legislation for otters now while we still have them. The pine marten needs the same protection, and even more vitally.

Birds at the Bank

A warm evening in late August where the river Endrick loses itself in Loch Lomond.

The red ball of the sun is dropping on the purple of the Luss hills. But our eyes are on the near sand-bars where a string of herons make a 100yd. line of gargoyles, each in a different feeding attitude, long legs, hunch backs, snake necks coiled or tense, spear bills ready to dart. Broad wings stretch, sticks of legs and big feet shake in the air as some lift off or drop down.

Wisps of snipe, bobbing sandpipers, twitching redshank and flighting duck are of less interest to us than the migrant waders, pausing to fatten up on long flights from northern nesting grounds, black-tailed godwits, four elegant aristocrats dwarfing a party of slim ruffs and reeves. We search for Temminch's stint, turn-stone and wood sandpiper reported by other observers.

No luck, but there is something up river which excites my friend John, a white dot where he forecast he would see it. And as we approach, it is joined by a black-headed gull and up it gets as if annoyed by the intrusion.

We see that it is smaller and whiter than the black head, a very small gull which lands by the river edge and begins to feed like a wader, constantly picking and chattering "Like young woodpeckers in a nest," says John.

The bird is the little gull, only the second I have seen on Loch Lomond in my lifetime. The first was an immature bird, easily recognised in this plumage by its vivid black zig-zags on the upper wings. The adult before us has no black on top, but shows dark underwings as it flies buoyantly in our direction.

I know of no other estuary in Britain so pictorial as the mouth of the Endrick, and this was a particularly splendid evening for colour, finishing with a flickering of sheet lightning at dusk from a storm that never reached us.

It was a wet morning a few days earlier which led to my meeting with John that evening on the Endrick, for I had made a discovery which I wanted him to confirm. In the rain I had watched a tern splash into the river, lift a slim silver fish, fly to a sandbank, and feed it to a small, crouching chick which sat waiting for more. At that stage my only curiosity was that the chick should be so late.

Then the fishing parent turned its attention to me, winging at my head as if trying to knock off my woollen hat, cursing me stridently.

And it was these curses which excited me, for if there is one bad language in which I am an expert it is that of arctic terns, for I lived with their constant sound for a whole summer in East Greenland at latitude 72 when I studied the breeding biology of these circumpolar travellers, from the egg-laying in July until the chicks were flying in August.

This particular parent was determined to prove its credentials to me, exhibiting crimson needle bill, very short legs and projecting tail streamers which distinguish it from the common tern.

Before I left I had proved there were two arctic tern parents and two chicks. John confirmed my record, and who better than the senior warden of the Loch Lomond Nature Reserve to see for himself the first breeding of arctic terns this century on our finest loch.

He will remember it, too, for one of the aggressive birds clobbered him on the head. The last record of arctic terns nesting on Inchmoan, near Luss, was 100 years ago.

179

Taste the History before the Climb

There are odd hills in Scotland that you make a special effort to reach, not because of their distinctive character, but for their exceptional situation. Such a one is Criffel, the dominating point of the Solway between New Abbey and Kirkbean on the river Nith below Dumfries where it opens to the Solway.

From Glasgow it is pretty distant. You have to be a glutton for driving to drive there and back in a day. Far better to spend the night at New Abbey and spend the whole day letting this quiet part of the world make an impression on you as it did to us. Great to stroll round Sweetheart Abbey after breakfast while waiting for the soft sunshine to lift the mist off the top of Criffel.

Plenty to enjoy, the softly glowing 90ft. tower of the Cistercian Abbey founded in 1275 by Lady Devorgilla in memory of her husband John Balliol who founded Balliol College, Oxford. The "Sweetheart" bit comes from the way they were buried together here, his heart laid on her bosom. The setting is splendid, a village street of wee white cottages backed by fields of cattle and sheep. In the strengthening sun the rich autumn colours glowed against the grey sky.

Criffel was clear, almost to the tawny top now, and off we drove south for two miles, turning off right for Ardwell Mains into a secret little oasis below the peak, a basin of sloping fields and woods containing Loch Kinder, a sizable water. The path up the hill is well marked, climbing delightfully through larches and following the burn for 800 feet to a forestry fence.

Now the footpath winds through the heather, easy going. We were on top at 1,866ft. in seventy-five minutes from starting, looking down on a vast pale water and ragged shore, Scotland on this side, England on the other.

But Moricome Bay and the straggling coast to Port Carlisle was gloomy, the clearance had not reached them, while on this side all was brightness, a maze of harvest fields on land and an even bigger maze of mud, marsh and quicksands over the Nith, with behind it the great cooling towers of Chapelcross nuclear power station half-lost in its own private murk.

The bigger of the two cairns on top of the hill commemorates the Black Douglas who was thrown from his horse and killed nearby. The monks of New Abbey pastured their sheep on Criffel.

You can make an easy descent to Kirkbean from here, the hamlet where the "Solway Pirate" was born in 1747, Paul Jones, the fighting seaman who embraced the cause of the Americans in the Civil War and who used his local knowledge to raid the Solway coast.

Father of the American Navy, he was elected to the United States Hall of Fame in 1925.

180

Don't leave for home without driving down to Kirkbean and on to the shrimp fishing village of Carsethorn on Solway, just a line of cottages on the point of a bay with skeletal poles of stake nets showing the salmon fishing interest of the folk who use the fast flowing Solway tides to entrap the fish.

I direct you there not just for the attraction of the place, which is considerable, but for the throngs of birds on the water and feeding below you on the shore, waders galore, dunlin, redshank, oyster catchers, godwits, golden plover, sanderlings, curlews galore, and bobbing on the waves great rafts of duck, more pintail and scaup than anywhere else I know. Look out too for barnacle geese, recently arrived from Spitzbergen.

Regretfully we left in the late afternoon as the birds were flighting for the tide. Motoring north by Kilmarnock we were home on Loch Lomondside in three hours.

Fiordland of Loch Goil

The last time I visited my friend Willie Shand he showed me a cairn he had just finished, unique of its kind for it has 280 stones making up its pyramid, each taken from a Scottish mountain of over 3000ft. with the status of a Munro.

To get them all took him fourteen years and now he is interested in doing any mountain of any height that is new to him. So when I suggested Cruach nam Miseag above Carrick Castle on the far shore of Loch Goil he was delighted.

And we were in luck with the weather, for the rain went off before we reached the top of the Rest and Be Thankful and by the time we swung down to the head of the finest sea loch in the southern Highlands our sharp peak stood clear, all 1,989 ft. of it.

Willie from Kinross doesn't come Clydewards very often, and his enthusiasm was heartening as we parked the car by the Cormonachan Glen to take the climb from the south-east side, following the steep edge of a burn of waterfalls.

Now we were getting a view of almost Norwegian character, with rocky peaks thrusting above timbered slopes, the slit of the Gare Loch running parallel with Loch Long, and the houses of Helensburgh edging the glint of the Clyde estuary.

The top is further back than you think. You think you're there, but discover you've to drop to a col and strike up steeply to the right of a fine big rock buttress. And we were just ready for the "piece" when we got there, munching steadily as we sorted out the Highland hills stretching from Ben Cruachan over a host of Willie's Munro friends—Ben Lui, Beinn an Lochain, Ben Ime, Ben Lomond and many another.

181

But Willie was more interested in the hills he hadn't climbed, the wee ones of Cowal, Ben Mhor and the lumpy tops extending to Bishop's Seat.

From the top we chose to strike northward, steeply down to a deep ravine where red deer stags were sheltering, a good place to take stock of Lochgoilhead, a thousand feet below. And from this bird's-eye viewpoint the ribbon development round its shores looked pretty solid—Victorian mansions with the look of affluence to the east, and mathematical rows of chalets and caravans creeping ever farther down on the west.

"A VERY FERTILE PLACE"

Ever since I saw the white croft houses gleaming on the rocky island of Eilean nan Ron I have wanted to land there and see how such an unlikely pancake of land at the mouth of the Kyle of Tongue could support a population. Last August I was not only successful, but the lobster fisherman who took me over claims to have been the last to leave, in 1938. So from him I learned the story of "the happy island".

Donald lives in Skerray now, only two miles across the water from where he was born. He still keeps sheep on the island, and at the time of my visit was taking off the lambs to sell at Forsinard. "It is a very fertile place. You could always get a good return from the croft. I don't think there's a better place in Scotland for growing cabbages. With the fishing we were practically self-supporting. With the cows we had plenty of milk and butter and crowdie. The only thing we bought in was flour. There was plenty of peat."

The story of the island-folk begins with the clearances, when the people were evicted from the straths and forced to find some sort of living on the coast. In those hard times of 1820, three young couples tried their luck on Eilean nan Ron. I was able to piece the story together from what the lobster fisherman, and from what another son of Eilean nan Ron, John George Mackay, wrote.

In his thin pamphlet, printed in 1962, Mr Mackay said; "I was born on the island and spent my childhood and adolescent years there, and now, with old age creeping over me, and having to spend most of my days alone, I often think of those happy times.

"Now that the island is desolate and its surviving natives getting fewer and fewer, I feared that soon there would be no one left to recall the old days. The thought grieved me. Why, I said to myself, why allow the memory of the island to die? But then how was it going to be kept alive?"

John Mackay told the story simply and well. I spoke to one of his relatives, who filled in some gaps, and from Donald Mackay, the lobster fisherman, I pieced together the tale of the vanished people.

First, I had to see the island, and as we bobbed across in a boat strewn with crabs caught that morning, and pincering below our legs, Donald told me of his boyhood, when there were eighteen scholars in the school and eleven families on the island. "I had to leave to finish my education at Golspie Academy. There was nothing on the island except fishing and crofting. The girls wouldn't stay. Then one family after another left for

America and Canada, some went to Australia.

"We were happy, but look at the landing! Everything coming from the sea had to be carried up these steep rocks. There was no machinery. There was not even a horse." The landing was certainly impressive, a flight of steep steps built up the rocks above a concreted jetty on the edge of a horse-shoe bay. "I'll pick you up about six", said Donald as he pulled away and headed back to Skerray to clip some sheep.

Taking possession of a small island is always marvellous. This one, where people had lived for 130 years, starting from scratch, forced the mind back to the first three couples, who would have to build houses for themselves, break in fields, lay a store of food and fuel in for the winter, fish the rocky coast when possible, enter caves to kill Atlantic seals for their blubber, and begin rearing their families.

Donald Mackay's parents, and their parents, were born on Eilean nan Ron. And no doubt they had the best kind of adventure, pitting their wits against nature, surviving, and building up an independent community. It was all their own work, with the women attending the crofts, mending nets, spinning wool from the sheep for clothing, while the men fished for cod and haddock for winter storage in a special cave whose currents of air had a magic property of keeping the fish soft so that it still tasted fresh months after it was caught.

Life was communal. When a new house was needed for a young couple, the menfolk blasted the rocks from the quarry cave and hauled wood, slate, lime and sand from the harbour. But as the population grew bigger they needed a deep-sea boat to fish farther afield, and it was provided by the Duke of Sutherland who got his money back in yearly instalments. A sister boat was added, and as the days of sail passed, the islanders chartered a steam drifter to fish herring the whole year round from the Minch to Lowestoft.

With the men away most of the time, the women had to work harder, and even manned their own boat between the island and the mainland. Religion played a very important part in their lives. All days began and ended with prayers. The Sabbath was sacred. The only travel was to church across the water and if this was impossible, a morning and evening service was held in the school, with an islander acting as minister. The language, of course, was Gaelic.

Wandering around the ruins of the village and the green fields sandwiched by heather on both sides, I had a sense of being in a happy place, not too lonely with crofts just across the water. And for inspiration there was the silver of the Kyle of Tongue backed by the knobbly peaks of Ben Loyal and Ben Hope. Climb a little and you had the Orkneys. From the nearest point on the mainland you could walk to Tongue village in an hour, and school children had to do it when the dreaded "Inspector" was visiting.

The whole island is roughly one mile long by half a mile broad, yet everywhere you are cut off from the sea by rocks. Two pairs of bonxies dived at my head as I strolled across the marshy southern end to look at the kittiwakes on the rock stacks, which are mainly devoid of birds other than shags and fulmars because of a lack of ledges.

The north end of the island is much more thrilling, with bigger cliffs of conglomerate, sheering the north-western tip off from the main island. The detached portion is called Eilean Iosal, roofed with smooth emerald turf and much dissected by reefs. It was an impressive wall of rock, pierced by a natural tunnel through which the sea plunged, which attracted me down to investigate. The scrambling was on sandstone con-glomerate, compressed to a pink-crush of grey stones like large plum puddings. Getting into the tunnel meant climbing over the chunks fallen from the large roof, and creeping along inside was rather eerie, with the water crashing in the semi-darkness as you edged along the inclined slabs, not daring to think of the possibility of slipping in.

Back to daylight on the far side was another mass of fallen blocks, offering a 50ft pyramid from which to attack the upper cliff. It looked unlikely because of its steepness, but it proved to be straightforward if airily exposed. It was a little climbing adventure I would not have missed.

We had time to look at the northern peat banks now, before crossing the ridge that leads to the houses. A few skeletal remains of gable-ends are the result of houses being dismantled for their materials when the island was abandoned in 1938. Two of them had names written on room walls with sprayguns, done most probably by a succession of hippies who took over the island in the summer of 1972, one or two of whom stayed through the winter. Unfortunately when they left in March 1973 they left behind a cat which is still living wild, killing the stormy petrels which breed among the stones.

Another strange episode in the island's history was when it was used for three months in 1950 by immigrant volunteers and scientists experimenting to find a cure for the common cold. No one is allowed to stay overnight on the island now, except by permission of the Sutherland estate. Possibly a logical use for Eilean nan Ron would be as a bird migration station, for it has been proved to be good for autumn passage.

The ornithologist who discovered this was a man who is commemor-ated on the island on a door lintel where an inscription reads: "In Memory of Ian R. Downhill, Lost on This Island, September 1963". Ian was a fellow member of the Scottish ornithologists' club who disappeared, and was presumed drowned, while out in his rubber boat. Ironically there was never a case of an adult drowning or being lost at sea during the whole fishing history of the island. Downhill's bird notes from Eilean nan Ron, which he calls "Island Roan" were published in *Scottish Birds*, Vol 2, No. 6, 1963, and result from a six-week stay the previous year from 3 August to 13 September.

There is no record in Downhill's notes of the bonxie breeding, which means the birds I saw have colonised since 1963. The peregrine had also bred successfully. Downhill's observations of sooty shearwaters and great shearwaters were the first for Sutherland, and among an interesting variety of visiting waders he recorded spotted redshank. Strangely enough I saw no seals, yet it is well attested that they breed in caves, and that the islanders killed them for their skins and blubber.

From Donald I heard some more about the decline of the island. He had been born at the peak of its prosperity at the beginning of the century, at a time when newly-wed couples had to leave because of over-population. Then came the 1914 war. Eighteen men left and seventeen returned to find the seas had been cleared of fish by trawlers. Let John George Mackay speak:

"Education was advancing, and having been all over the world during the war years, the younger generation had been given an insight into what was going on elsewhere, and that sealed the doom of the island. It was the same all around the north and west coast of Sutherland. The younger people were leaving to make a living elsewhere. Fishing and crofting as their forefathers knew it was reduced to a shadow of what it used to be."

Houses were dismantled and families sailed away to make new lives for themselves, so that by 1938 only twelve people remained, eight of them old. They hesitated about going, but on the stormy night of 6 December they sailed away for the last time, having to delay their departure until the hens went to roost at dark and they could be caught. In imagination I can see the light of the lantern on the slippery steps of the rocks, the boat heaving on the dark sea, and the transfer of hens and odd bits of hand luggage before the old women were helped aboard and settled for the stormy crossing of the Kyle Rannoch to Skerray.

The islander I like best to remember on Eilean nan Ron is Betty Macdonald, the first-born of one of the original three young couples. She lived to be ninety-five, and never once left the island. Her world was 700 acres, mostly peat and heather, but she must have had a rare sense of "belonging" in a community that was one big family.

JURA IN THE SUN

In the brilliance of the full moon it was no hardship rising at 2 a.m. and driving off for Jura to meet up with my sister Molly and her husband Sandy, who had rented a holiday cottage at Craighouse. "We'll meet you off the early ferry at Feolin. And tell Rhona to bring a hot-water-bottle for herself—the nights are cold."

Sure enough, there was a white glitter of frost on the grass verges as we climbed over the Rest-and-Be-Thankful and wound round Loch Fyne to a sleeping Inveraray. The glory of the sunrise hit us at Tarbert, and I grabbed my camera at the sight of the glass-calm loch and its silhouetted fishing boats.

The early rise was worth it for that moment alone. All we had to do now was drive seven miles down the West Loch to Kennacraig, where the squat car ferry stood waiting to leave at six. As the time was not yet 5 a.m., we parked the car, went aboard, located a comfortable corner couch and stretched out. I didn't even hear the ship leave port, but woke up as we arrived at Port Askaig.

The time was only 8 a.m. We were half an hour ahead of schedule, and a minibus stood at the jetty on the Jura shore. "If you want a lift, step in—we can't miss any car that's coming to meet you." Glad cries of pleasure when we met our hosts only a mile or two from the house. Soon we were sitting down to a ham and egg breakfast and hearing about the marvellous peace and tranquillity of Jura in the sun.

Looking out of the window, I was reflecting that my first arrival on Jura nearly twenty years ago was as sudden as this one, in that I was there before I knew it. I had been invited by a Jura man to sail in a cabin cruiser from Largs, so our route had been through the Crinan Canal, reached by the Kyles of Bute, so it was in darkness on the second evening we were beating down the Sound of Jura.

Dan McKellar was the navigator, examining the charts and reading off our position from the flashing lights marking rocks and shore. The night was black, and we seemed to have been bumping down the choppy sound for a very long time. Dan was confident. "Any man who can't find his own house in Jura even in the dark is no sailor," said he. And his steering was so faultless that when he switched on the searchlight on our deck its beam picked out the white square of his house.

Sorry to say, my old climbing friend Dan is dead now, and it was maybe because of that I hadn't been back to Jura. It had been a great week there, and my chief memory of it was of social visiting and much laughter and Gaelic song.

Now I felt ready to come back and to renew old memories of the landscape. We set off first for the southern tip. I certainly didn't expect to be remembered on Jura, but the very first native I met stood aside from the Highland cattle he was herding to shake hands and say it was a long time since I was there, adding, "I still have the photo you sent me of the horses drinking at the burn!"

I asked him about the crofting. "I've thirty cattle and some sheep, but I don't do much cultivation now. Indeed, nobody is doing any. We're all getting old. My brother died last year, and we lost another crofter recently, so you could say there are only five crofters left on Jura. Apart from some potatoes for the house and very little oats, we're growing nothing else."

Archie lives in Keils, the only hamlet which preserves its old world character in the form of a township group with a few thatched houses. "You'll be coming up," he said. "You know when I was young there were fifty living in Keils. Today there are only four."

Walking to the new distillery block behind Craighouse pier, I learned that the new bungalows along the road had been built for incoming workers. Since the total labour force is only ten, plus manager and Exciseman, it had made little difference to employment among locals, though this was supposed to be part of its purpose in 1963 when the distillery was built. The initiative for it came from two of the four Jura landowners in company with Scottish and Newcastle Breweries, Ltd.

Molly and Sandy couldn't understand why I had taken so long to come back to Jura. And I must admit the island seemed to be reproaching me by its brilliance that morning of shining sea as we took to the wild shore and followed the ups and downs of the craggy coast, enjoying the flowers on the greensward and the elegant fluttering of the terns as they fished the green waters, where eiders and shelduck floated with flotillas of youngsters astern.

No dull stretch here, with rocks for scrambling and remnants of natural woodland clinging to burn-mouths and steep places; birches, oaks, alders, rowan, ash and hazel lingering on despite the depredations of red deer which we kept disturbing, mainly stags in velvet.

Then we came to the Forestry Commission plantations at Sannaig, well grown Sitka spruce. The Commission had acquired 2,000 acres in 1951, but at the time of my visit only a man and a boy were employed. Houses were built and a gang of eight men were eventually recruited, but it seems the Jura men were not keen on the work. Nevertheless, some 1,500 acres had been planted, here and on the Lagg-Tarbert coast. The Commission tells me that the remaining 500 acres will be planted over the next few years by forest workers based on Islay.

Nearing the attractive bays below Jura House there was a sudden squealing of alarm from lapwings, redshanks, curlews and crows as a huge tawny bird swept down at an angle, a sinister "bomber" being attacked by "fighters" as it was buzzed by the angry mob. In this low country the eagle looked even more massive than in a mountain setting as it beat across the green sward, the sun gleaming on its out-thrust golden head, the long, broad wings giving an impression of sinister power as we watched it swing away, still under attack. "Imagine the cheek of these wee birds!" said Molly, flabbergasted.

Just ahead of us now was a rocky pancake of island called Fraoch Eilean with the ruins of a castle on it. The great Somerled built Claig Castle to guard the Sound of Islay. King of Argyll around the year 1130, he built a fleet of ships to fight the Norsemen, and the naval battle was fought off Islay's west coast in 1156. His victory drove the Norse galleys from Kintyre and the Southern Hebrides. Thereafter he ruled all the islands south of Ardnamurchan Point from Islay.

Just a little farther on and we moved from history to pre-history at the superbly sited standing stone of Ardfin. This twelve-foot-high stone goes back 3,000 years before Somerled, to the Bronze Age. Of the men who carried it here we know little. Strangely, it is in Jura that traces of the very first men in Scotland have been found—flint arrowheads uncovered in the sand dating back over 9,000 years. Perhaps the proliferation of caves, large and small, made Jura a natural island for colonisation by the first shore-dwelling people looking for a place to settle.

The caves lie mostly in the north and west. Behind them stretches the largest extent of the most poverty-stricken bedrock in the Highlands, rising in peat desert and quartzite screes to over 2,500 ft. in the Paps, and falling east to a narrow coastal strip of relatively fertile schists indented with natural harbours. This is where the present half-dozen hamlets of the Jura folk are sited, within easy reach of twenty-four miles of coast road running from Feolin on the Sound of Islay to Ardlussa, the last settlement. The entire western desert is uninhabited.

We went exploring north up there next day. The sun was warm again, yet visibility extended from distant Ben Cruachan to the Arran peaks. Following the road to Lagg, I tried to imagine Jura when its total economy was in small black cattle, and drovers would leave to walk them to Falkirk or nearer markets. From Lagg they would load the cattle into boats and land them across the water in Keills, Knapdale. Thousands from Islay and Jura crossed that way every year, and Lagg must have been a lively place then.

Nothing stirred about the pier that dreaming day. But at Tarbert there was something I hadn't seen before, a big herd of red deer paddling in the salt water on a curve of silver sands. Binocular inspection showed they were nibbling at the seaweed and not drinking the salt water as I thought at first. More red deer were dotted among the cattle on the slopes above. We had seen deer on other cultivated grazings on the way up; the name

Dyr Oe—deer island seemed as true today as when the Norsemen bestowed the name upon it.

No doubt the first cave men and the Vikings found a source of food in hunting the deer. But the subsequent Gaelic population who raised cattle and tended the fields held them in check, for in Martin Martin's time, as reported in his classic *Western Islands of Scotland* (1695) he mentions the figure of 300 red deer grazing on the hills and "not to be hunted without the steward's licence."

Today the deer figures for Jura can be estimated as around 5,000, reflecting the devaluation of first cattle and then people and then sheep in that order. The peak of the Gaelic population was in 1841, when it stood at 1,320, before rising rents forced them aboard emigrant ships or to seek a new life on the mainland. And with their going the red deer were waiting in the wings to take over from the sheep, whose hungry mouths had eaten the fertility out of the best ground.

Beyond Tarbert, along the road came jogging towards us a Highland pony with a slim figure on its bare back. Barefooted herself, the girl looked the picture of contentment as she told us she was riding seventeen miles to the ferry to cross to Islay to get new shoes on the horse. Her name was Katie Nelson and she had come from Ardlussa.

On the stretch between Ardlussa and Tarbert I had the feeling of being in Sutherland, among lochs fringed with bog cotton, and summits grey with quartzite whose slopes were peat-blanket. What I did not expect to find were skirling Arctic skuas cavorting in tern-like flight above a nesting flat. Beneath our feet were flycatching plants, butterworts in blue flower, and red hairs of sundew baited with sticky moisture.

After this barrenness, Ardlussa seemed a fertile oasis of trees and singing birds, with a salmon river emptying into a fine bay. This was the place for a picnic, but first we had a paddle to cool off in the hot sun, then on the greensward scented with thyme we lay back and just enjoyed being there.

Originally we had intended to go up on a deteriorating track for nine miles to the lonely croft of Barnhill, where author George Orwell looked into the future as though with second sight and wrote *1984,* a transposition of 1948 when he did his writing. Amazing that such a forward-looking vision of modern society should have been written in such a backward place, and frightening that it should be coming true today.

Orwell, in 1946, was critical of the four landowners of Jura and of the sporting economy to which he saw everything being sacrificed, including the crofters. Yet times have moved on here, too, and the facts of today are that few except the old *want* the crofting life. The able-bodied of today are looking for a modern standard of life which can be obtained only by a weekly wage packet. The truth of this can be tested anywhere in the Highlands and Islands, even in former strongholds of crofting like the Outer Hebrides.

During his West Highland Survey, at the time Orwell made his criticism, Frank Fraser Darling found that the Jura crofts were better able to give a living than the smaller crofts in most of the Highlands. He saw the need, however, to cut down deer numbers if crofting was to enlarge further. But in summary he saw Jura as hopeless except as deer forest because of the large area of its 146 square miles which is acid ground.

However, there is nothing like talking to folk who are actually trying to win a living from the land, and next day on Knockrome I got the chance when I met a fresh-faced lady of vigour walking up the track. She told me her croft was twenty-three acres arable and 300 acres hill, but that you couldn't get much of a living from it, not after you had paid the freight charges to get the beasts to market.

Knockrome is the most superbly sited crofting township on Jura, sitting high above the sweep of Small Isles Bay with a view to Craighouse and the Paps rising gracefully above. And just above the houses by a short climb, another vista, over the perfect horseshoe of Lowlandman's Bay to the north coast.

It is customary to think of Islay as Queen of the Hebrides for its fertility, fine farms and general prosperity, and Jura across the sound with its peat and rock desert and scanty population as the joker. This is a modern view. Martin Martin thought differently. This is what he wrote 280 years ago:

> "The isle is perhaps the wholesomest plot of ground either in the Isles or Continent of Scotland, as appears by the long life of the natives and their state of health, to which the height of the hills is believed to contribute in large measure, by the fresh breeze of wind that comes from them to purify the air; whereas Islay and Gigha, on each side of this isle, are much lower, and are not so wholesome by far, being liable to several diseases that are not here. The inhabitants observe that the air of this place is perfectly pure, from the middle of March until the end or middle of September.
>
> Several of the natives have lived to a great age. I was told that one of them, called Gillouir MacCrain, lived to have kept one hundred and eighty Christmases in his own house. He died about fifty years ago, and there are several of his acquaintances living to this day, from whom I had this account."

Alas, Jura has had a sad year for deaths amongst its grand old folk, no fewer than eighteen, which is a very big loss in a community now numbering well below 200. The children were playing outside the fine new school as we passed, and I had a word with the head teacher.

"This is only my second year here," she told me. "I came from England to Jura, but I love it here; the children are so nice and it is such a

191

beautiful place, away from the rat-race."

We would have liked to accept her invitation to visit the school, but time was running out since we were due off on the ferry that evening.

Molly and Sandy still had a week, during which the sun shone almost non-stop, and they walked and bathed in delectable coves where they had the sands to themselves without another human being in sight. And as they enthused to me afterwards about the island, I thought I could see the sun-tanned face of my old friend Dan McKellar, his gold tooth showing in an "I told you so" smile; Jura was always the perfect place in the world for him. Often enough Dan talked to me about giving up his work in Glasgow as a manager and retiring to his cottage perched above Small Isles Bay. Tragically, he died in an accident, but maybe his Tir nan Og is not so unlike Jura.

ISLAND OF LOOMS

It's many a year now since I've taken a flight from Glasgow to the Outer Hebrides. I was surprised to find that the plane was a Viscount, yet the time was slower than in the days of the wee planes, for I had to change at Inverness and await the arrival of the London flight and transfer to it. Total time from Glasgow to Stornoway, 3½ hours—such is progress. In the old days it took half the time.

Still, I'm not complaining, for the journey back was the most exciting I've ever had in Scotland, especially the part from Inverness to Glasgow, flying parallel and just a bit east of the Great Glen that splits the Highlands from North Sea to Atlantic. It was fascinating to see all the passes to the west that cut off from it; the silver slit of Loch Garry backed by the peak of Ladhar Bheinn, the peaks of Glen Moriston and Glen Affric. Then below me, passing at amazing speed, the parallel fault lines which match the line of the Great Glen; Laggan-Ericht-Laidon, Rannoch Moor, the Tyndrum and Loch Tay basins pin-pointed by their peaks.

Hard to take it all in, Westward I could see the island hills and gleaming bits of sea, but the colours were monochromatic, until the plane began losing height, and over the Trossachs the prickly hills and wooded lochs were as brilliant as in a colour transparency. It was like looking down on some wonderful and constantly changing relief map. I could see the southern shore of Loch Lomond and my own village, then sliding down over the green Kilpatricks and banking over the Clydebank cranes, I looked down-river to the Arran hills. It hardly had time to register before the plane was racing over the runway and we were descending into evening sunlight at Glasgow Airport.

Part of the pleasure of that trip was because I knew the country so intimately. It is not the flying that is enjoyable, or the speed of it—I'd rather go slowly overland any day—it is the new way of seeing that is thrilling, if you have the good luck to get the weather and a window seat. One day I hope to take a helicopter trip up the Great Glen, preferably on a clear spring day when Ben Nevis is sparkling white and all its attendant summits clear, because I want to see at a glance how the Ice Age glaciers of the past shaped the landscape we know today.

The reason for my hurried trip to Lewis was to tell the story of its famous tweed industry through a series of radio interviews with people involved, which meant I had to start in Harris for it was there it all began.

193

the first thing was to hire a car and speed off over the peat blanket and follow the green crofts of Luerbost and Balallan to Loch Seaforth, where the climb into the hill barrier of Harris begins.

There's wild country where the road crosses the Clisham, highest of the fine peaks stretching west to the silver sands of Husinish. Between gleams of sun, clouds were scudding along the splintered crags, with Glen Laxdale far below. I swung the car down to Ardhasig and followed the coast into Tarbert, perched on its rocky shore between the two sea lochs which almost pinch off South Harris from North Harris.

I've always liked the wee town that sits in that narrow neck between the West Loch and the East Loch. The hard rock that rises all round it tells its own story of sterile land incapable of supporting any but a small and vigorous population. Perhaps it could have been a fishing empire, which was the dream of Lord Leverhulme, but long before his time its people had become renowned as weavers of a unique kind of cloth— Harris Tweed.

The story of Harris Tweed which today is a monopoly of Lewis began here at Drinesheader, and after a short run south of Tarbert down the rocky east coast, I was shaking hands with Mrs Alex. MacDonald, a smiling lady glowing with health, whose white hair belied her liveliness. She was delighted to tell me the story of the cloth.

"Yes, it was the women of Harris who won the reputation for Harris Tweed when the whole process was done by hand over a hundred years ago. Lady Dunmore, who owned the Harris Estate at that time, did a lot to encourage the local people. She talked about it and showed it off in London, and a great demand sprang up for it among the sporting gentry.

"It was the soft colours of the patterns and the warmth of the cloth even when it was wet that attracted them. Also its nice heather smell, and the fact that the cloth kept its shape and was so hard-wearing.

"I've kept on the old hand-ways of making the cloth because there is a demand for very special cloth—people are prepared to pay for a specially good thing. I use the plants from the hill and the shore to make the dyes; the lichens on the rocks, water lily leaves from the ponds, dandelions, bracken, yellow iris, even soot from the chimney. You can look at these fleeces which I dye in batches to get my colours for the pattern. Then it has to be carded, scraped back and fore between the wire teeth of these flat boards. You take one in each hand and the movement tangles up the wool and you take it off in soft rolls for spinning on the wheel.

"This wheel has been across The Minch dozens of times," she said with a smile. "I've given so many demonstrations of spinning and weaving, at the Royal Highland Show, in Edinburgh at Festival time, and in London. The spinning is the slow job, which keeps you busy in the winter evenings. You tease out the soft rolls you have carded and feed it and twist it on the wheel to make the yarn for the warp and the weft. Then you can begin weaving on the handloom. I get orders from all over the world. I could sell more than I can make."

Nothing succeeds like success. Such was the demand for Harris-made tweed at the end of last century that a mill was erected in Tarbert in 1900 to take the sweat out of hand carding, using water power and machinery to prepare the wool for the spinning wheel and enable the crofters to meet the rising demand for their cloth.

By that time, however, the folk just across the border in Lewis were taking up weaving, and by 1903 a mill had been set up in Stornoway as in Tarbert, and still the demand for the cloth outstripped the supply. Within the next seven years ownership of looms in Lewis had risen six-fold and they were using a different kind of loom, one with a flying shuttle which had to be pedalled. Moreover, the Stornoway mill had carried the machine process a stage further. It not only carded the wool but spun it as well. Such competition was to the disadvantage of the people of Harris, especially when pedalling the new looms was work for men demanding muscle and strong legs. In time Lewis was to be the home of Harris Tweed-making.

So I would have to return over the Harris border now and resume my quest where the byroads lead by the Callanish Stones and Carloway Broch to the busy township of Shawbost. My target was Kenneth MacLeod's mill, strategically centred among some of Lewis's busiest crofters and weavers. Arriving unannounced, I expected to have to fix an appointment to be shown round and have the relationship between the mill and the home-weaver explained.

Not a bit of it. One of the busy directors left what he was doing to take me on a conducted tour, following the dyed fleeces through the whole process, from the mixing and blending of the different coloured wools to the lifting up of the multicoloured piles for machine carding on toothed rollers, then on to spindles to give the yarn twist and strength on the wheel. Talk was impossible through the clatter of these machines.

In a quieter part of the mill, men were selecting the different coloured threads and winding them in order on wooden frames according to the pattern design. They have to tie it at intervals for the threads are eighty yards long and run the whole length of the tweed. This is bagged and placed beside the yarn for the web which will shuttle across it to make the cloth. "That warp and web, with the pattern of the tweed, is what is sent out to the crofter, and I'll take you to see one of our weavers who works just a mile up the road."

Even fifty yards from the shed we could hear the clatter of the loom as we got out of the car a few minutes later. The silence was welcome when Malcolm Campbell looked up, saw us and stopped pedalling.

Alas, he looked at me as if I was daft when I asked him if he enjoyed the work. "Look," he said, drawing up his trouser legs to show me his varicose veins. "That's what you get working on the loom. I hate it. It's strenuous, monotonous, noisy work. You have to take a few wee breaks

195

from it. You can't keep at it all day. I was doing some croft work before you arrived. That's the best bit of being a self-employed weaver, you can please yourself.

"Weaving is a means to having a good life. By that I mean the kind of life I want to live. It gives me independence, and the wherewithal to have modern comforts. I enjoy working the croft, but I have a good house which I built with my own hands, as do most of the folk here. We value what we have here on Lewis, especially when we read of what is happening outside. We prefer the old moral values. I would hate to leave this island. We've had bad times, recessions, but there's no unemployed weavers now, though numbers have dropped from over a thousand to less than six hundred. The present demand could put the numbers up."

Mr MacLeod agreed with that. "Yes, man-made fibres and changes in fashion caused a serious slump a few years ago. There was talk of streamlining the industry, switching over to power looms and abandoning the cottage industry by going on to double-width cloth woven in wee factories sited in different parts of the island. It would have meant the crofters becoming employed persons and working factory hours. I'm glad the crofters rejected it, preferring to remain independent.

"I believe our exclusiveness is our strength. It's true our clumsy-looking method of work makes for expensive cloth. We have to import most of the wool, prepare it for the weaver, send it out to him, bring it back to remove the grease and make the tweed soft and close. Then we inspect it to make sure it is worthy of the coveted Orb mark.

"It all works out right in the end though, for we have a cloth which is unique in the world—and people are prepared to pay for it. We've moved with the times, the cloth comes in a variety of weights and the range of patterns is limitless. Two-thirds of what we produce on this island is sent abroad in bales from Stornoway Harbour."

It was to the harbour I went next, and what a hive of activity it was that Thursday afternoon. The fish auction was in full swing and boats were arriving continually, all of them local, a scene of colour with Atlantic seals swimming round snapping up fish and Lewis Castle grey among the trees overlooking the lagoon of the big harbour.

Enjoying it all, I got talking to a young man repairing a net. As he told me how good the fishing was with high prices for prawns, I discovered he hailed from Bridge of Weir and at the age of sixteen had come to Stornoway and taken to the sea.

"It's a good life. I've been at it five years now and I wouldn't like to leave Lewis." Talking some more, I asked him what chances he had of having his own boat one day, of being a skipper. He smiled, "That's my boat, the *Girl Isobel*. She's just under fifty-nine feet. I bought her second-hand on a bank loan. I couldn't get a grant because she was too ancient. I studied for my ticket up at the Castle, but I'm not allowed to sail anything over fifty tons. I've a long way to go yet."

196

I complimented him on his enterprise and took a note of his name, Scott McLean, so that I could send him a photograph of himself along with a member of his crew, twenty-one year-old William John MacDonald, a time-served plumber. Like me, William is not a particularly good sailor, and how he gets on as a fisherman will determine whether or not he will stick it.

Stornoway has a modern fleet of about forty boats, most of them obtained with help from the Highlands and Islands Development Board under their very successful fisheries scheme. Now a new boat has been added, a very expensive deep water trawler, to exploit the ocean 200 miles out where the future of the industry may lie in catching the blue whiting.

Lewis was certainly looking its best on the morning of the flight home, when I had a last spin north-east up the coast from Stornoway to the limit of the road on the sands beyond New Tolsta. How fresh and sparkling everything looked that morning! Crofts popping up everywhere, haystacks dotting the green fields fringing the sea backed by the rock escarpment of Tolsta Head. I would have liked fine to have had the time to walk on beyond the limit of the road, on the footpath which runs for ten miles and comes out at the Port of Ness.

But there was that plane to catch, and next day on Loch Lomondside I just stayed at home in order to digest the experience and enjoy a sunny day of warmth on the shore.

ISLES OF INSPIRATION

I have a confession to make. Until recently I had never visited the Old Man of Hoy, though I must admit that I felt we were very old friends, for in the spectacular film of its ascent by three different routes I was the stand-by commentator for BBC Television from the Glasgow studio.

Now here I was in Orkney, on the pier at Stromness, in the rain, waiting for the morning boat that leaves at 8.30 a.m. every weekday, returning at 4.30 p.m. Of Hoy just across the water, nothing could be seen, and I would have put off the visit until another day if the met. Office at Kirkwall hadn't told me there was no hope of a clear-up for some time.

So off we went to Linksness pier on Hoy under the highest hills of Orkney, guessed at rather than seen that morning. We took the hill road west until it became a path bending south past the Sandy Loch where great skuas wheeled overhead and fulmar petrels had nest sites on wee rock outcrops just round the corner.

Once off the road and on a true hill-pass, spirits rose. My wife averred that the rain was refreshing. It was also going off, and there was even an illusion of sunshine as we came in sight of green Rackwick and the sandy curve of its bay set between pillars of pink cliff, the houses perched here and there giving it a feeling of life.

Alas, Rackwick is a ghost village of ruins and memories of times past, as talented local artist, Ian MacInnes of Stromness explained when he invited us into his holiday cottage for coffee. "The school, which is now a hostel for outdoor folk, closed over forty years ago. It's the old story, the young folk left to better themselves, and the old folks remaining died one by one. At last there were only two wee boys in the village. They used to play with my youngster. One morning they drowned playing with a raft in the burn. It was the end, but the Highlands and Islands Development Board is helping Jack Rendell to restore 'The Glen' and make a go of crofting the place, so maybe the idea will spread. It's such a beautiful place."

Certainly Ian finds inspiration in the setting as does the composer Peter Maxwell-Davies who needs complete peace to write his highly acclaimed music. Perched high above the bay and reached only by a steep footpath, his simple cottage has the finest outlook in all Orkney. I climbed past it on my way to the Old Man of Hoy, interrupting him only for a moment to say hello, for there was a lot on his mind and he had much to do.

The easiest way to the famous pinnacle is from the school over the flank of Moor Fea among the skuas and the greater blackbacked gulls. Although not marked on the map there is a good footpath, as well as a notice warning climbers that they go at their own risk for there is no rescue service on Hoy. We were in luck when suddenly in front of us the Old Man stuck his head out of the mist, lower parts invisible until we got to the edge of the cliff and we saw his great skeleton.

The story of its first ascent was brilliantly told by the late Tom Patey in the December 1966 issue of *The Scots Magazine*. Patey wrote "As you climb higher there is a unique sense of physical detachment and height ceases to have any morbid significance. We were higher than St. Paul's Cathedral, and by the time we reached the top we would be level with the new Post Office tower, Londons' highest building." Tom had declared after the feat that there wouldn't be a next time. But of course there was, or I would not have been in the television studio watching the antics of Dougal Haston, Joe Brown, Peter Crew, MacNaught Davis, Tom Patey and the other stars.

How has the Old Man fared since he was first conquered thirteen years ago? The answer is that it is now a commonplace climb and done by over a score of parties every summer. I spoke to a quartette of English youngsters who had just done it. I asked if they had found it hard. "Not too hard," they opined. "But it took us quite a time, even although the ironmongery was in place."

While we stood up on the airy headland, looking down on the fulmars on their ledges, the mist swirled clear of St John's head and a gleam of sun warmed the great Orkney cliff a rich red. Plunging in great overhangs and verticalities for 1,100ft. It too has been climbed, but it took five days, the climbers using mechanical aids and sleeping out on the face. To honour the lifeboatmen of Hoy who died in a wild storm they have named their climb "The Longhope Route."

The cliffs and moors of Hoy could hardly have been in more contrast to the scenery of the island we had just come from, North Ronaldsay, most northerly of all the Orkneys looking to the Fair Isle and the Shetland Mainland. Our plan was that we should go there on the once-weekly boat.

Fate conspired against us. First, the car broke down on the road to Skara Brae and had to be towed back to Stromness, which meant us taking the bus to Kirkwall and finding digs for the night to be aboard *The Islander* by 7 a.m. next morning. We were in grand time for the boat but were very puzzled when we got to the deserted quay and found no sign of folk or ship.

Then we noticed a man in working clothes coming towards us. "I'm looking for *The Islander*," I said, hoping he could help. He pointed out to sea. "She left nearly an hour ago. Were you booked?" I nodded. "It's not the first time it's happened," he grimaced. "The sailing time was changed late yesterday." I said that somebody would be sure to be inconvenienced.

"You didn't give them a telephone number?" We couldn't, because we didn't have one.

What now? The harbour official said he would drive us to the airport to be there at 8 a.m. in the hope of getting a Loganair inter-island plane. Placed on stand-by we were in luck, we each got a seat though on different planes. Waiting to go I had been watching a short-eared owl quartering the grass just beyond the terminal building.

An added bit of luck was that each of us had a pilot seat position for a superb flight, first stop Eday, flying low over the sea to skim Shapinsay and another stretch of sea for Eday. We could hardly have been more intimate with the land, with terns and skuas just below us on the peat moss, and a fine feeling of speed with the hill changing from brown to green as we touched down bumping along on the grass.

Off again following the bays of well-named Sanday and ahead of us was the flat line of North Ronaldsay, blue in the distance but suddenly rich green and yellow with flowers as we pitched down and dismounted into fragrant air. I am all for airstrips without tarmac, and the informality of collecting your own luggage and walking off.

The story of why I had sought out this particular island begins in a Perthshire post-bus. I had contacted David Dove of the Scottish Postal Board for information about the mail-bus routes serving the glens, and as a result he had asked me if I would act as one of the judges of an essay writing competition open to school children. The essay had to be in the form of a letter, and the subject was "Places to Visit."

There was no doubt about the winner in the Scottish senior section. The £50 prize went to Mary Elizabeth Muir for the description of her home in North Ronaldsay, and the attractions of Mainland Orkney where she attends Kirkwall Grammar School, as do other children of this outlying island once they reach the age of twelve.

We were looking forward to meeting Mary and her family and getting a wee conducted tour of the little island which she had described as being "three miles long and one and a half miles wide." Her father was down to meet the plane and soon whisked us to the house of Garso at the north end a good four hours before I could have reached it by boat.

How nice to arrive in a home from home and be made instant members of a family, sharing the normal way of life on the croft. Mary's mother takes everything in her stride, including an Open University degree. Father not only works a croft but runs the school bus and the island taxi service. It was lucky for us to have the two boys and two girls at home before the summer holidays ended and took them to Kirkwall.

First though, a walk with prize winner Mary to the north point of her island, and an exhilarating daunder to the bouldery shore through green fields and amongst shingly lochans alive with flying birds, golden plover and peewits by the score, Arctic terns by the hundred, rock doves in the fields and shelduck on the water.

We walked along the famous wall which entirely surrounds the island and is something of a mystery. High and thick its length has been stated as fifteen miles following the windings of the shore. It is maintained by the crofters to keep out the unique breed of sheep which feed on seaweed and are renowned for the quality of their mutton.

I thought them vaguely reminiscent of the goat-like St. Kilda sheep, in their agility and dun colour. Ewes are brought to grass inside the wall at lambing time. The earmarks denoting the owners are identical to the type used in the Faroes and Iceland. Mary says that the sheep are under the auspices of the sheep court, elected by men of the island, and that is one of the oldest courts in the world. As to the age of the perimeter wall girding the island, a recent book on the Orkneys states that it was built last century.

As we watched the sheep eat the seaweed, picking up mouthfuls of juicy ribbon-like morsels, a flock of migrant knots landed beside some turnstones, only a small indication of how good this island is for bird migration, akin to Fair Isle.

In the old days there was a fishing station at Noust and there are still plenty signs of kelp burning from so long ago. I was to hear about this later. Meantime we were interested in the seals basking along the shore, wailing to each other but unwilling to forsake the warmth of the sun for the cold water.

Just beyond was the Burrian Broch whose outer face has been incorporated into the wall and the entrance blocked up. Excavations around here have yielded a hut settlement and finds of bone combs and needles, spinning whorls, scrapers and flints. Mary describes in her letter the most exciting thing which has been found, the shoulder blade of an ox, with Pictish symbols and a Christian cross incised on it. This Burrian Cross and Pictish symbols are now used in Orkney Silvercraft jewellery.

Virtually the whole of North Ronaldsay is farmed to rear beef, with the emphasis on silage, hay, pasture, a little barley, turnips and some vegetables. Most crofts are small, but mechanisation is widespread.

Willie Thomson, of Neven near the Muirs' house, spoke to me of the changes he had seen in his seventy-seven years, remembering when the population was three times what it is now and cash in your pocket was relatively unimportant. You lived on what you could grow and the fish you could catch. "I remember watching boats going to the Fair Isle fishing grounds, sail after sail. I was told not to count them going out, it was bad luck, but to wait for them coming back. There were sixty pupils in the school when I was a boy. Now it's only five, four girls and one boy.

"Stronsay was a great fishing station in my day. The boats were 40 to 60ft. with a lugsail, and we went away for a week at a time. There was a crew of five. It was after the 1914-18 War the island started to go down. Of course there had always been a lot of emigration to Canada and Edinburgh. In Leith there are as many North Ronaldsay men as in North

Ronaldsay itself.

"I'd rather be here than in any city. Look at Kirkwall, people hurry past, never giving you a look. The hard pavements are sore on your feet. The world is full of crime today. You would nearly need a lock on your pockets. Here on North Ronaldsay I never knew anybody who locked a door. There is no such thing as crime, thanks be to Providence."

Willie, retired now and in not too good health, has a hobby which passes the time, painting schooners and sailing ships in full rig on the glass floats which fishermen use on their nets—real works of art produced on a curved surface. He also paints conventional pictures of them.

He remembers with pleasure the days when he was a crofter-fisherman, when the island was well populated and everyone worked at the same task, the kelp gathering, the ploughing with horse and oxen, hay-making, harvesting, sharing a communal life. "I think we were happier," he opines. "Now it's all machines and money and hardly anybody keeps a milking cow. In the old days there was a lot of fun, and the quality of your work was noticed. You always wanted to be the best at a job. Without the variety of crops the island is not so bonnie as it was. It was lovely in the harvest time with the different colours."

Yet it is unlikely that North Ronaldsay will ever be a Rackwick in terms of decay. The trend is that farms will get bigger, crofts will be enlarged as population declines, and fewer people will make a better but duller living. Things are fairly healthy at present. Of the 120 or so people who live on North Ronaldsay about forty per cent are old age pensioners, but there are over a dozen under five years old and about fourteen families between forty and sixty, plus four couples between twenty and forty. In terms of children, a dozen go to Kirkwall Academy, as well as the five in the village primary school. This does not include lighthouse keepers, the resident doctor and the school-teacher who is from England.

I'd like Mary Elizabeth Muir to have the last word. She ends:

> "When I think of home in summer, I think of the smell of clover, wildflowers and warm hay. In winter I think of the glittering constellations of Orion, the Great Bear, the pale iridescent streamers of the Northern Lights. The moon glimmering on the dark waters of the loch where the wintering swans are sleeping. The sound of the sea, in all its moods, is never far from my ears . . ."

THE SHETLAND WAY

Here indeed was wonderful luck—a spring-like morning of soft sunshine and we were booked in a slow-flying Loganair Islander to take off from Sumburgh at the southern tip of the Shetlands and fly the whole length of the hundred islands whose ultimate points, Muckle Flugga and the Out Stack, are in the same latitude as South Greenland.

What a surprise it was to see the mammoth size of the £10 million airport compared to the tiny strip I last saw twelve years ago! Planes and helicopters of all sizes were buzzing about in a constant landing and taking off, for Sumburgh is the aerial hub of Britain's North Sea Oil industry and shortly it will have its own special terminal to deal with this activity serving the rigs.

The airfield occupies what seems a tiny neck of land between the "tail fins" of Shetland on which perches Sumburgh Head Lighthouse, and the approach on a big passenger aircraft is exciting as the plane almost grazes the cliff face. Taking off in the slow-flying Islander, I could appreciate it even more, seen in relation to the thin spine of mainland stretching ahead, and out on the southern horizon the dark shape of Fair Isle to the south.

A subtlety of colours passed below us: the browns of moors, hard greys of seacliffs, the white of bursting waves echoed by a dusting of snow on the whaleback summits, the green cirques of cultivation dotted with the squares of clustering croft houses, and below them wee, natural harbours with white boats drawn up.

A tilt of the wing over Sandwick and we were skimming its neighbouring isle, Mousa, for a look at its broch, the best preserved of all these mysterious structures built as defence points in pre-Norse times against unknown enemies. Wigeon duck rose with a flash of white wings and Shetland sheep raced over hillsides divided with stone walls and peppered with the ruins of a vanished people. On we flew for Bressay Sound to curl over the only town in the Shetlands, Lerwick, built on a steep-faced peninsula above a great natural harbour much extended since I was last here. What had been green shore to the north is now a great oil service base, with a constant coming and going of oil-rig ships, while on the hillside above it was a vast armoury of pipes and other equipment.

The most striking thing about the town itself was the number of new housing schemes, the result of the big expansion of population due to its new industrial importance. Former shops in Commercial Street are now offices, and the congestion of traffic has caused the shops to move north where there is space for parking. Signs of wealth are all about. In figures, harbour revenues which were £400,000 in pre-oil days, amount now to round £1.5 million. Are the people happier for it? This is what I wanted to discover.

Curving over rural Bressay, served by car ferry every hour from Lerwick, we headed north into the land and seascape of the voes, the big inlets which segment the coast. Opposite the broad inlet of Dury Voe I looked down on Whalsay, well named the "Bonny Isle." It looked green and prosperous—as I knew it was, for its fields and harbours support about a thousand people. Fishing is the mainstay here, and at Symbister School men can study for a skippers' ticket if they feel inclined. Just beyond to the east was the cluster of rocks called the Out Skerries, rocks which support another enterprising fishing community. By contrast I could see to the west the crowding timber squares of the Toft work-camp which houses many of the Sullom Voe workers.

The flight line now was up the east coast of Yell, peatiest of the Shetlands, with a population of over 1,000 living on an island seventeen miles long by seven miles broad, largest of the North Isles. Our flight line gave us a fine view of the crofting townships, and colourfully attractive they looked, lit by shafts of sun and rainbows in a sprinkle of showers.

Only one more island to go now—Unst, and it was a thrill to look down on the Loch of Cliff, the most northerly sheet of fresh water in Scotland, three miles in length and with evidence around its shores that trees grew here around 500 B.C. Only a narrow neck separates this slit of loch from the sea inlet of the Burra Firth, and flying low over it for three miles we were waiting for the moment of turning its headland. Suddenly it was there, Muckle Flugga Lighthouse, perched on a grey ridge of rock, and beyond it the pancake of the Out Stack—*Ultima Thule*—edge of the world indeed.

The pilot swung round in a geat arc to let us savour this meeting place of oceans—the Atlantic, North Sea and the Arctic ahead, and behind us the cliffs of Herma Ness rearing up 600 ft. Countless birds flew out in alarm, mostly fulmars and shags and gulls, and a few gannets. We felt like birds ourselves as our wings tilted steeply into the cliff to follow the line of a gully and climb sensationally to 1,000 feet over the perched cupolas of the Royal Air Force early warning station which is part of the NATO defence system.

The population of Unst is about the same as that of Yell, and the way the clouds were behaving it was impossible to separate one island from the other as we flew straight towards the vast yellow blob which was the out-of-focus sun magnified hugely by a curtain of rain. Racing over a peat-dark land spattered with innumerable lochs, each a winking eye of reflected light, was a strange other-worldly experience akin perhaps to looking down on another planet.

Down by Yell Sound I recognised the beach where, earlier, I had been slithering about on boulders black with oil and looking with apprehension at another slick out on the water. With me was Bobby Tulloch, who had advertised for helpers to search for dead and dying birds along ten miles of coast contaminated by the spillage from Sullom Voe.

Bobby works for the Royal Society for the Protection of Birds as their Shetland representative, and we have been friends for many a year now. He was furious at what had happened. "Tell people about this mess," he said to me. "Explain to them that there is no known way of clearing it up. It has wiped out the duck and diver population of Yell Sound. Look at this great northern diver, one of over a hundred dead we've found, the biggest kill of these rare birds in history. Twenty otters who use this bit of shore have had a miserable death. The tysties and eiders who live here have been almost wiped out, so have long-tailed ducks and scoters. I could tell you of the 3,000 birds we've picked up as black as if they had been dipped in treacle.

"Look at these sheep. See the oil matting their wool? they come to the beach to eat seaweed, and when they get the oil inside their stomachs they die. The death rate is bound to be high. The Shetlanders are furious at the inadequacy of the preparations to deal with this accident. Now we'll find out the true cost of North Sea oil, for this was only a small spill of 1,100 tons. What will a big one be like?

Sullom Voe lies across Yell Sound, and in a few moments' air-time we were there, and I was having my first view of the largest oil terminal in Europe, with storage tanks to receive the black gold by pipeline from fields over 100 miles out under the North Sea. The first tanker took its first cargo out on 30 November last year, and it was the twelfth which spilled its oil.

Prepared in mind as I was for something gigantic, I was staggered at the sheer size of the development on a thousand-acre site which, although operational is far from complete. I now appreciated the statistic that just one oil tank would supply enough petrol to take a family car to the moon and back twenty-five times. Sullom Voe is a "common user" plant, with thirty companies having an interest in the processing and export of oil and liquid gas from the North Sea fields. To build it has been an army-type operation involving massive excavations and big shipping movements in difficult seas to bring the materials to keep thousands of men employed.

In twenty-three days on Shetland I was to talk to plenty of oil workers and hear the views of many clear-thinking Shetlanders on the impact of oil on their way of life. Meantime, I was concentrating on the topography, with out there to the west the snowy hogback of Ronas Hill at 1,475 ft., the highest in the Shetlands, and beyond it, out on the horizon, the triple crown of Foula, remotest inhabited island in Britain and still holding on to its tiny population.

Now for Scalloway and all the narrow slits of voes between White-ness and the islands of Trondra and Burra. Across Clift Sound at

Dunrossness the scenery became exciting, with St Ninian's Isle and the Loch of Spiggie backed by the great cliffs of Fitful head—some of the loveliest country in all Shetland.

The airfield was just round the corner, but between us and it was Jarlshof, one of the most important archaeological sites ever discovered, containing as it does, on a single three-acre site at the sea edge, a whole chronology in stone, covering a period of 1,500 years from people who lived a Stone Age way of subsistence to the builders of the brochs and the colonisation of the Vikings. It was their invention of the Long Ship, a real breakthrough in technology, which enabled the Norsemen to win their way from Norway to Orkney, Shetland, the Hebrides, Faroe, Iceland, Greenland and eventually America. Here at Jarlshof are the foundations of the most complete Norse farming site found in Britain, though a recent find of similar foundation in Unst may prove its equal.

In Scalloway, I found myself at the house of Shetland author James R. Nicolson, author of four definitive books on the islands, his latest being *Traditional Life in Shetland*, which is well researched and beautifully written. He was busy on a fifth when I called, sheaves of paper round his armchair and a big ledger of one of the famous trading companies on his knee from which he was gleaning information.

Strong, broad and in his prime, the eyes below the curly black hair had a humorous twinkle as he settled down in his living-room while two of his four children played with their toys. The son of a crofter-fisherman, and a graduate of Aberdeen University, he holds a combined M.A., B.Sc degree. He handed me a thin red book saying, "That's one of my books which very few people have ever seen. It didn't make me or my publisher any money. It was my first, and I wrote it when I was working as a geologist in Sierra Leone in West Africa. I like it because it's about that country, which I enjoyed and I just had to write it.

"The Shetlanders are great readers, and seem to be very aware of their historical roots. A lot of people feel afraid of what oil has done to Shetland, because crofters and former fishermen commute fair distances to Sullom Voe. Mothers who stayed at home now go out and earn relatively big money making beds or working in canteens. Local schools have filled up with children from outside. New roads and ferries make it possible to get quickly from Unst to Lerwick.

"Before I took to full-time writing I had started work in the oil industry with a firm of consulting engineers in Shetland. There is no doubt at all in my mind that we needed an additional industry here if we were to keep our population. It's true that the fishing, knitwear trade and crofting were doing well and that Shetland didn't really need the oil industry when it came. But we were finely balanced, vulnerable. Look what's happened to the fishing. Iceland and Faroe have extended their limits, so the foreign boats come here and are cleaning up our waters. Catches are down drastically.

"The oil industry gave a sudden opportunity for Shetland brains to come back to Shetland, and the islanders have come flooding home. Never mind the 6000 and more incomers at the camps. The Shetland population is now up from 17,000 to over 21,000, the highest for forty years, and that can only be a good thing for the future of these islands.

"There's vigour and vitality—inflation too—but the important thing is that there's money coming into the Shetland kitty from that oil, which will be used to build up the old industries and create new opportunities when the oil has gone. There are bad side effects—a rise in crime, more death on the roads (usually due to drink). Youngsters have got too much money. But look at Lerwick's Up Helly Aa, when 800 guisers with blazing torches march the streets. The whole thing is perfectly disciplined with never an accident. Thousands are out in the street to watch. Dances go on right through the night until the following morning, and there is never any damage or hooliganism. That's the kind of folk we have in Shetland."

Well, I had the pleasure of fulfilling a lifetime's ambition by being present at the 1979 Fire Festival, and the reality of it all went far beyond my hopes on that great night when the guiser Jarl, another Jim Nicolson, sailed his dragon ship through a waving double row of flaming torches held aloft by 794 guisers.

What made it all the more impressive was the sense of occasion—waiting for it in the darkness of a windy, bitter night and seeing shadowy forms passing to the mustering place to draw their heavy paraffin-impregnated torches and be marshalled into position with military precision. There they awaited the splendidly attired guiser Jarl's squad and the galley to pass up their ranks.

Down in the crowd we lined the route, waiting for the explosive bang of a lifeboat maroon, the signal for torches to burst into red flame like struck matches. Then the whole splended sight was revealed: the vivid colours of the exotic dragon ship, the Jarl mounted aloft, and his crew marching alongside, their breastplates and horned helmets gleaming in the fire glow, the brass band playing and the roar of *The Up Helly Aa Song* sounding from the counter-marchers like a mighty fragment of an opera, with the galley in a maze of torches.

In mere words one cannot capture the emotional dimension of the blend of sound and colour and spectacle behind the whole experience: the guisers in their weird masks and comical outfits contrasting with the Jarl's squad in their garb of cloaks, horned helmets, tunics; armoured breastplates and gartered legs. Now I knew why Jarls of other years used to tell me of having tears in their eyes at the climax of the ceremony.

That night Jim Nicolson was Egil Skallagrimsson, an Icelandic hero of the 9th century. There he was, his feathered helmet against the flames above his galley. And as he stood tall, more and more torches were forming the circle round the galley. Then sounded an explosion like a

207

cannon shot—the maroon signal for the singing of *The Galley Song,* and out it thundered.

As the night air echoed with the splendid song, the guiser Jarl's squad circled the galley raising their battle-axes to cheer the galley-builders and the torchmakers with a specially loud shout to honour the most important person in the event, the principal actor, Jarl Jim Nicolson, who climbed down amongst them from his ship as a rousing fanfare was played.

And as the last note died away, wave after wave of blazing torches were hurled at the dragon ship to send it leaping into flame with sparks flying and a great crackling. The beautiful ship that had taken months of spare-time work to built and ornament was beginning to sag in less than five minutes, and the open mouth of the dragon seemed to nod sagely before it fell to be consumed in the flames.

As it fiercely burned, the last song, was sung, *The Norseman's Home:*

> *The Norseman's home in days gone by*
> *Was on the rolling sea,*
> *And there his pennon did defy*
> *The foe of Normandy.*
> *Then let us ne'er forget the race,*
> *Who bravely fought and died,*
> *Who never filled a craven's grave,*
> *But ruled the foaming tide.*
>
> *The noble spirits bold and free,*
> *Too narrow was their land,*
> *They roved the wide expansive sea,*
> *And quelled the Norman band.*
> *Then let us all in harmony*
> *Give honour to the brave*
> *The noble hardy, northern men*
> *Who ruled the stormy wave.*

The words hearken back to a far remembered time before the annexation of Shetland by Scotland and the gradual decline in status from freeman to oppressed tenant following 1471. It was this colonisation which caused the ancient Norn language of Norway to die out to become in time the rich Shetland dialect we know today.

Perhaps this explains the determination of the Shetlanders to go it alone with the oil companies and extract from them a profit from every barrel and a fair rent from every structure built on their ground, not for the sake of cash alone but to finance survival of the old way of life when the oil men pack up and go.